Also by Jeremi Suri

Henry Kissinger and the American Century
Power and Protest
The Global Revolutions of 1968
American Foreign Relations Since 1898

Liberty's Surest Guardian

Rebuilding Nations After War
from the Founders to Obama

Jeremi Suri

Free Press
New York   London   Toronto   Sydney   New Delhi

Free Press
A Division of Simon & Schuster, Inc.
1230 Avenue of the Americas
New York, NY 10020

First Free Press trade paperback edition July 2012

FREE PRESS and colophon are trademarks of Simon & Schuster, Inc.

For information about special discounts for bulk purchases,
please contact Simon & Schuster Special Sales at
1-866-506-1949 or business@simonandschuster.com.

The Simon & Schuster Speakers Bureau can bring authors to your live event.
For more information or to book an event, contact the Simon & Schuster Speakers Bureau
at 1-866-248-3049 or visit our website at www.simonspeakers.com.

Designed by Carla Jayne Jones

Manufactured in the United States of America

10 9 8 7 6 5 4 3 2 1

Library of Congress Cataloging-in-Publication Data

Suri, Jeremi.
  Liberty's surest guardian : Rebuilding nations after war from the founders to Obama /
Jeremi Suri.
    p. cm.
  1. United States. President (2009– : Obama) 2. Nation-building—United States—
History. I. Title.
  JZ6300.S87 2011
  973—dc22
                                                            2010051296
  ISBN 978-1-4391-1913-6
  ISBN 978-1-4391-4170-0 (ebook)

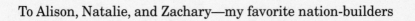

To Alison, Natalie, and Zachary—my favorite nation-builders

Contents

Introduction

To the efficacy and permanency of your Union, a government for the whole *is indispensable.* . . . . *Liberty itself will find in such a government, with powers properly distributed and adjusted, its surest guardian.*

George Washington, 1796[1]

Our values are not simply words written into parchment—they are a creed *that calls us together, and that has carried us through the darkest of storms* as one nation, as one people.

Barack Obama, 2009[2]

When George Washington wrote of an American "Union" with "a government for the whole," his vision was radical, perhaps foolhardy. Such a thing had never existed among a diverse people, across a vast continent, with no established royal or military authority. The Union of politically empowered citizens that Washington described was an aspiration more than a reality. It was a dream after two difficult decades of revolution, war, and reconstruction.

Washington's vision was prophetic. He was ahead of his times. His contemporaries, especially in Europe, expected tyranny, anarchy, or the return of foreign empire in North America after the British defeat. Eighteenth-century thinkers had few models of a good government "with powers properly distributed and adjusted." They had even fewer models of a strong government that became a "guardian" rather than an oppressor of liberty.[3]

1

George Washington's eighteenth-century radicalism evolved into the twenty-first century's conventional wisdom. The success of the American experiment in building a prosperous and democratic Union discredited other options. When Washington wrote his words people advocated many kinds of government: monarchy, theocracy, confederation, empire, city-state, and even small republic. Representative government for a large, diverse, and united population living in a dispersed but discrete territory—that became the contemporary standard for the modern "nation-state." It was almost nonexistent during Washington's lifetime. In its early American formation, the political institutions that we now take for granted were an eccentric experiment—an "exception" to the common arrangements of the era.[4]

Two hundred years after Washington, American exceptionalism became the normal expectation for citizens. The United States proved that large, diverse, and united societies—"nations"—could achieve more than their fragmented counterparts. The United States also showed that the first president's claims about the virtues of a representative government were well founded. A powerful government of the people did more for the people, and it was generally more stable than its predecessors. The American model stood out for its unity and its representativeness. Although many Americans—including women, African Americans, and others—did not initially have full rights of citizenship, the society they inhabited encouraged more popular participation in politics than any late-eighteenth- or nineteenth-century counterpart. Politics was part of the nation's common culture. The state birthed from rallies, debates, and conflicts claimed legitimacy from its roots in the street, not the gentleman's club.[5]

By the twentieth century virtually all governments organized themselves as nation-states. Dominant state institutions claimed legitimacy because they spoke for the people—not divine authority or a borderless ethnicity—in a particular place. Modern political power was nation-state power. National populations claimed particular rights and privileges because they were constituted in a single state.

The ties between nation and state became symbiotic and near universal.[6]

Political power centered on territory, institutions of control, and repertoires of consent—all symbolized by the flags and passports distributed to mark simultaneous identity and authority. The unbound merchant traveler of an earlier age became the Chinese citizen regulated by the Chinese government, or the German citizen protected by both the German and European Union governments. When entering the borders of another nation-state, one must show one's passport to prove that one is a bona fide part of the larger nation-state system, with clearly defined loyalty and responsibility. If you do not have a nation and a state, then you have neither a homeland nor a right to travel safely beyond. If you do not have a nation and a state, you do not count in the modern world.[7]

The antiterrorist measures implemented across the globe since 11 September 2001 to control the free movement of peoples, weapons, and products have reinforced this nation-state system. Borders are rigidly policed by states. People are closely categorized by nationality. "National security" takes precedence over all other claims. Nongovernmental organizations (like Amnesty International) and intergovernmental institutions (like the United Nations) continue to exert important influence, but they are tightly tied to nation-states for their resources, recruitment, and leverage over policy. International advocates of human rights, environmental protection, and religious freedom are most effective when they work within and between nation-states, not as alternatives to nation-states. The same is true for multinational corporations. Although they operate globally, they remain regulated by nation-state laws and organizations composed of nation-states, especially the World Trade Organization. The world of the early twenty-first century is a world dominated by political "Unions" that resemble Washington's farsighted conceptualization. He would be surprised only at their uniformity and their near universal spread.[8]

The United States did not create this system alone, but it contributed to its development and expansion. Washington's calls for "Union" in a new country began the wider diffusion of the nation-state as the foundation for political power in the modern world. Other forms of political authority declined as the American-inspired version rose. The United States influenced this process by model, by rhetoric, and often by direct policy. Since the eighteenth century, Americans have sought to create a world that would be "safe" for their form of government—a world that would adopt harmonious political institutions, despite continued cultural diversity.[9]

That is, of course, the deeper meaning of pluralism: "unity in diversity." It was the foundation for Woodrow Wilson's famous—perhaps infamous—call for a "League of Nations." Franklin Roosevelt followed with plans for a "United Nations." His successors have furthered this process through the creation of the North Atlantic Treaty Organization, the European Union, the World Trade Organization, and other international bodies that define power around nation-states—not races, religions, or other markers of identity. American pluralism is the pluralism of nation-states. Modern globalization is the globalization of nation-states too.[10]

There are very few substitutes for this system in the twenty-first century. If you want respect as an international player, you must be a nation-state. Compare the circumstances of Egyptians, who have a recognized nation-state, and the Kurds, who do not. United peoples represented by strong institutions in a given territory can claim voice in global negotiations. Those who are not united, not represented, and not identified with a particular place get little attention. Political sovereignty in the modern world is based on national identity and effective state governance. Other forms of authority get little recognition. Politics has become less diverse since the eighteenth century.[11]

President Barack Obama's description of contemporary American foreign policy reinforces this point. When he echoed George Washington, extolling the United States "as one nation, as one people," his words were neither original nor revolutionary. They were common to American political statements. Obama was describing the obvious, articulating the standard clichés, appealing to American triumphal self-regard. His words were ritualistic, repeated by nearly every president. United action in a strong nation-state had become the touchstone for protecting security and liberty, especially after attacks by vicious nonstate actors. Building stable nation-states in regions filled with "tribal" hatreds and "failed" states—both of which sponsored terrorist activities—had become the most accepted approach to ensuring peace and prosperity. This is what Obama meant when he spoke of an American "creed that calls us together, and that has carried us through the darkest of storms."[12]

Applying the wisdom of accumulated American experience, Obama and most of his listeners believed that the suffering citizens of Afghanistan, Iraq, and other countries would live better if represented by institutions that governed local groups "as one nation, as one people." Effective nation-states in those countries would establish security, they would help their citizens, and they would keep extremists out. They would also serve American and other international interests in stability, access, and profit. Afghan and Iraqi nation-states were the solution to terrorism, as they had been the American solution to other threats in prior decades. From the founding to the first years of the twenty-first century, the history of American nation-building repeated itself.

Obama pledged that the United States would continue to support nation-building abroad, despite all the other demands on resources at home:

Our union was founded in resistance to oppression. We do not seek to occupy other nations. We will not claim another nation's resources or target other peoples because their faith or ethnicity is different from ours. What we have fought for—what we continue to fight for—is a better future for our children and grandchildren. And

5

we believe that their lives will be better if other peoples' children and grandchildren can live in freedom and access opportunity.[13]

Nothing could be more American than to pursue global peace through the spread of American-style institutions. Nothing could be more American than to expect ready support for this process from a mix of local populations, international allies, and, of course, the United States government. Between the presidencies of Washington and Obama, nation-building became the dominant template for political change among Americans. Matched with the growing power of the United States, this template gained unparalleled global force. That is the story told in this book—how American nation-building became global nation-building.

One can chart this history in abstract and theoretical terms. One can also focus on isolated cases in great detail. Both are worthy approaches. This book does neither. Instead, the forthcoming chapters examine what we might identify as the six most enduring American nation-building projects: the founding of the United States, Reconstruction after the Civil War, and subsequent interventions in the Philippines, Germany, Vietnam, and Afghanistan. These are the cases that defined American politics, and the politics of other societies, for successive generations. These were ambitious undertakings, involving extended commitments of resources and long-term sacrifices. Each effort was controversial in its origins and its consequences. Each nation-building project set the terms for subsequent endeavors. The hopeful, frustrating, and inconclusive experiences of each generation created the memories, the precedents, and the patterns that shaped policy in other places.

The United States pursued nation-building projects in many additional countries, especially in Latin America. Other powerful societies—including the British, the French, the Germans, the Soviets, and the Japanese—had their own programs for political construction in the twentieth century. This book covers only a small collection of cases, but it argues that they mattered enormously. They strongly connect our present to our past. This is a history that explains why Americans pursue nation-building today in the ways that we do, and how we are likely to act in the future. We can better calibrate our expectations about nation-building going forward, if we look carefully back upon two centuries of experience. The results in Afghanistan and other countries will build on the legacies of prior efforts in the American South, the Philippines, Germany, and Vietnam.

For each of these historical cases, nation-building was domestic and foreign, local and global. The distinctions we draw between "at home" and "abroad" in our daily discussions are not helpful. Whether engaged in North Carolina in 1869 or northern Afghanistan in 2009, the question has always been: how can Americans help to nurture more stable, modern, and sustainable institutions?

Americans have intervened by force of arms to destroy "criminals" who prohibit nation-state development. Americans have also invested—often insufficiently—in peoples and programs designed to replace anarchy, empire, and tyranny with nation-states. These efforts defined Abraham Lincoln's Northern Republican program in the former Confederacy, just as they characterized a later Republican's anti-terrorist program in former Taliban territory. Despite all the changes in technology, the United States has employed similar military, political, and social instruments close to and far from home. Despite all the differences in circumstance, the United States has relied on some of the same ideas from one century to another.

The experiences of nation-building reinforced one another. Abraham Lincoln looked back to George Washington and the American founding to articulate Union aims in the Civil War. William McKinley, William Howard Taft, and others drew on their experiences with Reconstruction after the Civil War to conceptualize nation-building in the Philippines. The men near Franklin Roosevelt and Harry Truman who made policy in postwar Germany began their careers in and around the Philippines. The German experience defined American efforts in Vietnam. And Vietnam, of course, haunts contemporary Afghanistan. Americans fight the last war. They also nation-build as they did in their last mission. This dynamic reinforces the recurrence of common themes.

If nation-building is the American grand strategy, what differs from one case to another are the tactics. As in any endeavor, day-to-day decisions determine outcomes. That is the key point of each chapter in this book: to examine how human choices shaped the practice of nation-building for successive generations. With broad agreement on aims, how did different figures put principle into practice? How did the implementation of nation-building policies change the hopes, expectations, and experiences of citizens touched by each project?

The goal is not to show how simple ideas came undone when applied to a complex world. That is nothing new. The aim of this analysis is more ambitious. The most difficult part of policy is making change. Time pressures, resource constraints, cultural diversity, bureaucratic red tape, and the fear of the unknown reinforce resistance to reform. This is true within both rich and poor societies. For this reason, many leaders give up. They satisfy themselves with efforts to work on the margins, to preserve rather than to progress. This is often called pragmatism, but it really is not. It is the politics of least resistance and the tolerance of the lowest common denominator. Never understimate how risk-aversion prolongs failed policies, including wars and other conflicts. To sue for peace and invest in reconstruction—that is often the most uncertain and unsettling endeavor. That is the history examined in this book.

Americans have made more wars than many others, but they have also tried more often than anyone else to build nations after battle. That is why I call Americans "a nation-building people." That is why Americans are continually trying to change societies. That is why American policies are so unique, so interesting, and sometimes so baffling. How has the United States initiated change at home and abroad during intensive moments of effort? How has the United States undermined change at the same time? How have Americans adapted to the unintended consequences of their reforms? Understanding these dynamics of change and stagnation, as well as reform and adjustment, has a lot to offer contemporary observers.

The story of nation-building is the story of political and institutional reform. How has it worked? How can we do it better? Even the most local policy problem could benefit from this more global analysis. Even the newest test will draw on this inherited history. Looking back at ourselves and our actions, we can see the origins of our current world, and the glimmer of what comes next.

This book will close with some thoughts about the lessons we can draw for navigating our unpredictable future. These lessons will focus on five historical themes that run through each chapter: *partnerships, process, problem-solving, purpose,* and *people.* I call these themes the 5 Ps. Americans are a nation-building people, defined by the partnerships we have formed in a two-century-long process of problem-solving with a clearly defined, if rarely fulfilled, purpose. The 5 Ps are the axes around which American politics spin. They are the basic material for what began as the early American nation-building creed.

Chapter One

The American Nation-Building Creed

The same advantage which a republic has over a democracy, in control-
ling the effects of faction, is enjoyed by a large over a small republic—is
enjoyed by the Union *over the States composing it.*

James Madison[1]

No legislative act, therefore, contrary to the Constitution, can be valid.
To deny this, would be to affirm, that the deputy is greater than his prin-
cipal; that the servant is above his master; that the representatives of the
people are superior to the people themselves.

Alexander Hamilton[2]

merican society has never lacked ambition. During the last
two centuries the global reach of the United States has spread
like rushing water, moving with ever-greater speed across the
landscape, around barriers, and into the nooks and crannies of what
were once distant locales. This dynamic dispersion of U.S. influence
shows no sign of stopping in the twenty-first century. In recent years
the nation's soldiers, treasure, and social media have expanded into
Afghanistan, Pakistan, Yemen, Somalia, and other places Shakespeare
described as "monstrous," "desolate," and largely inhospitable to foreign occupiers.[3]

Shakespeare never visited the exotic lands of his plays, but Americans have prodigiously trod in what the playwright called the "mud-
ded" terrains. The growing presence of the United States in these

regions transformed the applications of the country's power beyond the dreams of the Founding Fathers. James Madison, Alexander Hamilton, and their many contemporaries could never have imagined that their new nation would one day dominate all the oceans of the globe, with permanent military bases in more than fifty countries. Compared to its most powerful predecessors in Europe and Asia since the Middle Ages, the United States became a much larger and heavier global presence. "Soft" cultural power was both a product and a producer of America's unprecedented "hard" economic and military might.[4]

The Ever-Lasting Revolution

Despite the nation's extraordinary growth, the early assumptions of American power remained fundamentally unchanged over more than two centuries. Basic ideas about politics transferred with consistency from generation to generation, and from territory to territory. The image of the American Revolution, and the founding of a new nation and a new government at the time, framed all future discussions in the United States about how to live with other societies. The Revolution was an experience, a myth, and also a paradigm for defining political mission.[5]

Nothing could exemplify this point more than the American reaction to the horrible terrorist attacks of 11 September 2001. Amidst the smoking remains of New York's World Trade Center, President George W. Bush memorably announced that "America today is on bended knee in prayer" for its people and its principles. In a two-minute pep talk to tired rescue workers he used the word "nation" four times, along with a flag that he proudly waved, to affirm American unity and power in the intrepid defense of individual liberty. Appearing before Congress less than a week later, the president spoke in revolutionary terms: "this country will define our times, not be defined by them. As long as the United States of America is determined and strong, this will not be an age of terror. This will be an age of liberty here and across the world."[6]

In the most powerful pamphlet written to defend the war against Great Britain in late 1776, Thomas Paine had proclaimed the same militant American purpose in defending individual liberty against frightening enemies: "These are the times that try men's souls. The summer soldier and the sunshine patriot will, in this crisis, shrink from the service of their country; but he that stands by it now, deserves the love and thanks of man and woman. Tyranny, like hell, is not easily conquered; yet we have this consolation with us, that the harder the conflict, the more glorious the triumph. . . . Heaven knows how to put a proper price upon its goods; and it would be strange indeed if so celestial an article as freedom should not be highly rated."[7]

From Thomas Paine to George W. Bush, Americans have reaffirmed their sense of purpose as defined in their Revolution. When threatened, Americans have mobilized around the global expansion of freedom—protecting their rights by ensuring that foreign peoples accept them. Americans have consistently emphasized their common identity as a single people, and they have militantly fought to destroy evil enemies who would deny their rights and their unity. Most significant, Americans have done all of these things by working to build new nations with constitutional governments, like their own. That is the history of the late eighteenth century that the United States has replayed from the Constitutional Convention through Southern Reconstruction after the Civil War, and all the conflicts of the twentieth and twenty-first centuries. Crises consistently produce war and constitution-writing in American history. Scholars have, in fact, contributed to this process as they have told the story of the Revolution during each of these moments to remind citizens of their inherited purpose, born of political ambition.[8]

For some observers, the constant reinforcement of American ideals is a source of strength; it makes the United States a global force for progressive change. Robert Kagan writes: "Americans believed the world would be a better and safer place if republican institutions flourished and if tyranny and monarchy disappeared. Americans believed a world reformed along liberal and republican lines would be a safer world for their liberal republic, and that a freer and multiplying commerce would make them a more prosperous nation. They were arguably right on both counts."[9]

President Bush obviously agreed. His Second Inaugural Address captured the most radical American revolutionary urges in the face of foreign threats: "From the day of our Founding, we have proclaimed that every man and woman on this earth has rights, and dignity, and matchless value, because they bear the image of the Maker of Heaven and earth." "Advancing these ideals is the mission that created our Nation," Bush reminded listeners. "[I]t is the policy of the United States to seek and support the growth of democratic movements and institutions in every nation and culture, with the ultimate goal of ending tyranny in our world."[10]

Bush's ambition to shine the light of American democracy on the entire world struck some observers as a dark nightmare. The problem for most critics was not the revolutionary principles articulated by the president, but their applicability to hostile circumstances in Iraq, Afghanistan, and other distant societies. Could the United States really overcome the Shakespearean difficulties of managing "desolate" lands? Was the image of the American Revolution really an accurate map for international change? Shouldn't Americans more wisely focus on fulfilling the ideals of the Revolution in their own society?

Skeptical voices have a long lineage in American history, with as much claim on the nation's past as the revolutionary zealotry exhibited by President Bush and so many of his predecessors. Advocates of a more limited American global mission—John Jay, Robert La Follette, George McGovern, Patrick Buchanan, and others—gained popular appeal in each generation as ambitious foreign adventures, predictably, failed to live up to their promise. Since the eighteenth century, strong assertions of American revolutionary principles have accompanied every war and smaller foreign intervention. Angry dissent against the application of those principles to the conflict at hand has also accompanied every war, with the notable exception of the Second World War. Americans continually replay not only the rhetoric of their Revolution, but also the early debates about the meaning and the application of the Revolution to contemporary society.

The clear pattern is that in moments of crisis the images, claims, and ambitions of the Revolution win out over more cautious voices. This is true in the history of the United States, almost without exception. "At times of heightened threat perception," Melvyn Leffler explains, "the assertion of values mounts and subsumes careful calculation of interests. Values and ideals are asserted to help evoke public support for the mobilization of power; power, then, tempts the government to overreach far beyond what careful calculations of interest might dictate." The goals of the United States in spreading a particular model of government are remarkably resilient, especially in the face of a fast-changing world. The willingness to use force for revolutionary purposes remains pervasive in the American experience.[11]

Making the "American Nation"

Despite its wide, repeated, and controversial applications, the enduring sense of American mission is firmly rooted in unique historical circumstances. The constitutional innovations of James Madison and Alexander Hamilton reflect these roots and their continuing influence in the United States and abroad. Madison, Hamilton, and their many literate counterparts in late-eighteenth-century British North America invented a new kind of government, fusing complex ideas about republics, democracies, and empires. Their creation drew its legitimacy not from tradition, from religion, or from the existing administrative units in the thirteen colonies. The Constitution challenged all of these inherited anchors of authority.[12]

North American Empires, 1763

Madison, Hamilton, and their fellow framers built not only a new edifice of government, but also a new foundation for that edifice. In this sense, they were at least as radical as the Thomas Paines who provoked the Revolution in the first place. The Constitution for the United States, jointly written, widely debated, and ultimately ratified in 1789, asserted that the power of American government rested on the definition of a new people—an "American nation." Free men, living in diverse geographic, economic, and religious circumstances across an already vast territorial expanse, provided the wellspring for shared rule. No king would enforce authority, as was traditionally the case. No religious deity would promise eternal salvation from collective sacrifice. The citizens, defined as a single community, would constitute the sovereign basis for political authority that would supersede all other bodies, institutions, and claims. The government would come from a common people. This was a very surprising idea, especially since no one really knew who these common people were.[13]

Popular sovereignty made the American Revolution a permanent part of nationhood and governance. It framed much more than a philosophy or a constitution. The creative work of designing democratic institutions continued because the figures assembled in eighteenth-century Philadelphia, and subsequent meetings around the country, developed a new language to transform the appearance, the feel, and ultimately the function of politics. Madison, Hamilton, and others designed a new reality from scattered materials—"Americans"—that did not yet exist as a coherent whole. The act of making the institutions for government created the people, just as the people made the government.[14]

This is what Hamilton meant, in the debates surrounding the ratification of the Constitution, when he called for the citizens of the states to approve this foundational document both to build a national government and to affirm the primacy of their collective will. You could not have a national government or a collective will without the other. The Constitution empowered the "people themselves," just as the "people themselves" made the Constitution. The relationship between nation and state—Americans and their government—was symbiotic in the late eighteenth century. It has remained so ever since.[15]

Most residents of North America were, of course, excluded from Madison's and Hamilton's definitions of the people and the nation. The institutions created by the Constitution remained extremely limited in their early influence within society. Perhaps most significant, the Constitution affirmed the continuation of slavery, with guaranteed protection from the national government, despite the widespread recognition of its evil and the worldwide efforts to eliminate it. The popular consensus behind the new American national government was neither as popular nor as consensual as the rhetoric, then and now, has claimed.[16]

These are important points, but they often receive too much emphasis in a twenty-first-century context that embraces, at least rhetorically, strong presumptions about inclusiveness. The creation of the American nation and government in the late eighteenth century unleashed an outpouring of participation on both sides of the Atlantic Ocean that forever changed the fabric of modern politics. "The Revolution," one historian writes, "resembled the breaking of a dam, releasing thousands upon thousands of pent-up pressures . . . suddenly it was as if the whole traditional structure, enfeebled and brittle to begin with, broke apart, and people and their energies were set loose in an unprecedented outburst."[17]

The energies of citizens found collective voice in the constitutional institutions created to manage them. As "Americans," literate individuals were now part of a national debate about a common government. "Public opinion"—measured in tone and attitude, rather than surveys or elections—shaped a national identity, government policies, and much more. The United States emerged as a new kind of broad and yet ordered democracy in action. "The Revolution," Gordon Wood writes, "rapidly expanded this 'public' and democratized its opinion.

Every conceivable form of printed matter—books, pamphlets, hand-bills, posters, broadsides, and especially newspapers—multiplied and were now written and read by many more ordinary people than ever before in history. . . . By the early nineteenth century this newly enlarged and democratized public opinion had become the 'vital principle' underlying American government, society, and culture."[18]

People felt they mattered as they had not before. Government now had to serve the people. Farmers and merchants, not kings and aristocrats, made the government. For these revolutionary circumstances to endure and prosper, nation and government had to remain closely tied together. The alternative was a reversion to separation and despotism. The alternative was a return of European empire on the ashes of the revolutionary experiment. American-style nation-building looked to many participants like the only viable alternative—then and now.

For the new nation to survive, the world had to be made safe for it *not* through war or imposition, but instead through a gradual nurturing of similar experiments far and wide. Thomas Jefferson, for example, hoped that the contagion of liberty would spread both to Indian "savages" and to French aristocrats. His *Notes on the State of Virginia* are filled with references to the "manners" and "moral sense of right and wrong" among Indians. Jefferson believed that a more organized government could transform Indian "aborigines" into modern citizens, enjoying what he envisioned as a peaceful and prosperous way of life—including Indians and whites side by side. Jefferson similarly wrote to James Madison, from France, of the goodness that could come from destroying European "degeneracy" and building new nations: "I hold it that a little rebellion now and then is a good thing, and as necessary in the political world as storms in the physical. . . . An observation of this truth should render honest republican governors so mild in their punishments of rebellions, as not to discourage them too much. It is a medicine necessary for the sound health of government."[19]

The spread of the American Revolution was the best security for the American Revolution in a hostile world. If Americans looked only within, they quite reasonably feared that powerful foreign actors would exploit and ultimately destroy them. They were probably correct in this judgment. The country's alleged ocean "isolation" was far narrower than many historians have admitted. British military forces occupied fortifications on the northern and some western borders of the new nation, while Spanish and French soldiers maintained a strong presence on the southern rim of the North American continent. European military, economic, and cultural influences surrounded the United States well into the nineteenth century.[20]

The American Revolution made a foreign policy of cautious nation-building, or what later advocates would call "democratic development," imperative. Early strategists did not plan for American international leadership in years, or even decades, but they firmly believed that the United States had to promote long-term changes beyond the nation's borders. Even George Washington's famous warning that his countrymen should avoid the temptation to "entangle our peace and prosperity in the toils of European ambition" closed with support for "diffusing and diversifying by gentle means the streams of commerce." Washington captured the inherent internationalism of the American Revolution, committed to separation from "permanent alliances with any portion of the foreign world," but also the expansion of global influence through trade, "impartial" relations, and political example. Although the United States had to live with global diversity, it sought to shape that diversity in cautious but significant ways.[21]

The Sacred Union of Nation and State

Nation-building through democratic development allowed the United States to increase its territory, its population, its wealth, and, ultimately, its worldwide reach. This process of continuing expansion, with all its positive and negative implications for different groups, rested on the strong shoulders of an enduring American identity. Despite the many challenges to a common collectivity, especially during the Civil War, more and more residents of North America began to call themselves "Americans." This certainly did not imply consensus on major political issues of the day—including tariffs, banking, or slavery, of course—but it did mean that when threatened by external or internal adversaries, people consistently demanded that a national government serve their rightful interests as Americans. Urban merchants, rural farmers, frontier settlers, and others invoked a common identity to justify broad government action on their behalf to regulate commerce, remove Indians, and create "free" and "slave" states in new territories. Active government, in turn, affirmed the power and legitimacy of the expanding American nation.[22]

This historical trajectory of the American nation and state was not preordained. If anything, it ran against the history of European and Asian territories that guided the expectations of foreign observers. The people of those continents had not embraced a common identity or a common government, at least since the fifteenth century, even when powerful military figures tried to impose such a phenomenon. Colonial rivalries in North America appeared to promise the export of a similar experience to the New World. In the absence of American nation and state formation after the late eighteenth century, informed thinkers expected the region to suffer much more violence, suffering, and despair. North American history could have easily resembled the fracturing and foreign imposition of Central Asia, Southeast Asia, and North Africa—occurring at precisely the same moment.[23]

Madison was among many who feared that exact outcome in North America. During the first years after the Revolution, he described the "evil" of narrow self-interests in the former British colonies, and the emerging prospect of "public calamities" because of "trespasses of the states on the rights of each other." Madison warned in 1787 that although the "foreign powers have not yet been rigorous" in pursuing their aims in North America, their "moderation cannot be mistaken for a permanent partiality to our faults." Prosperity, security, and independence in North America required a new form of political order.[24]

Madison's most enduring ideas about constitutions and nation-building emerged in this context. "The great desideratum in Government," he wrote "is such a modification of the Sovereignty as will render it sufficiently neutral between the different interests and factions, to control one part of the Society from invading the rights of another, and at the same time sufficiently controlled itself, from setting up an interest adverse to that of the whole Society. In absolute Monarchies, the prince is sufficiently neutral towards his subjects, but frequently sacrifices their happiness to his ambition or his avarice. In small Republics, the sovereign will is sufficiently controlled from such a Sacrifice of the entire Society, but is not sufficiently neutral towards the parts composing it." The United States, according to Madison, needed to build a government that was strong and unified, but also restrained and pluralist.[25]

The debates about the Constitution were debates about a new model of nation and state that would serve this purpose. Madison, Hamilton, and their colleagues across the states devised a form of government that was neither monarchical nor wholly democratic. Through new representative institutions this government would create a necessary alternative to the despotisms, anarchies, and wars of "normal" eighteenth-century politics around the globe. Instead of enforced uniformity or chaotic individualism, the United States would build a basis for unprecedented "concert in matters where common interest requires it." Europeans at the time experimented with a similar idea, but their inherited differences in self-definition prohibited the same "Union" on the other side of the Atlantic that Madison and others imagined for the new Americans.[26]

"Union" in the American context meant much more than cooperation, or shared territory, or even common law. For Madison and his followers across two centuries it came to embody a single people in a single government. American nation-building was the construction of a single Union from the free, diverse, and disparate elements of the land. It had a religious quality associated with a calling to something above "normal" politics. It was to be a godly community of souls, united in spirit if not daily behavior, to produce mutual peace and prosperity. On the backs of a new American identity and a new government, the Union promised, in George Washington's words, to "control the usual current of the passions" and "prevent our Nation from running the course which has hitherto marked the Destiny of Nations." Echoing Madison and Hamilton, Washington reminded Americans that: "To the efficacy and permanency of your Union, a government for the whole is indispensable."

> [I]t is of infinite moment that you should properly estimate the immense value of your national union to your collective and individual happiness; that you should cherish a cordial, habitual, and immovable attachment to it; accustoming yourselves to think and speak of it as of the *palladium of your political safety and prosperity*; watching for its preservation with jealous anxiety; discountenancing whatever may suggest even a suspicion that it can in any event be abandoned; and indignantly frowning upon the first dawning of every attempt to alienate any portion of our country from the rest, or to enfeeble the *sacred ties* which now link together the various parts.[27]

The Union was a reality based in faith. It was a touchstone for ordering the present and the future. Defense and promotion of the Union formed a creed that would define not only the interests of Americans, but also their behavior at home and abroad. This is what Washington meant when he described the Union as a "palladium" of security and wealth. It was an architecture that the first president called on Americans to reinforce and replicate for their permanence and growth. The alternative was the chaos and despotism of the Old

World. The Union faith made the unique fusion of the new American nation and state something more than the sum of its constituent elements. The Union became, in Washington's words, a set of "sacred ties which now link together the various parts."[28]

George Washington's Farewell Address (1796) envisioned an evolving international society of states, where the American nation-building model would remain separate but broadly influential. The painting shows Alexander Hamilton helping Washington draft his address. This photo has been cropped from its original version.
Allyn Cox, Architect of the Capitol

The first real test for the Union, after the ratification of the Constitution, was westward settlement. As citizens moved into the frontier lands largely unsettled by whites but populated by diverse Indians,

the promise of united representative government confronted serious challenges. Different states and land companies made conflicting claims to the same territories. Settlers demanded protections as
American citizens, but they also requested freedoms for land seizure,
resource extraction, and even forced population movement that exceeded the rights of their fellow citizens in more established areas
of government. Conflicts arose over whether slave or nonslave labor
should accompany territorial expansion.[29]

Americans did not resolve these issues until the Civil War and
subsequent decades, but they began a unique nation-building process
in the late eighteenth century. Instead of separate imperial extensions
of the most powerful American states, the Western territories became
part of a single continental government. Instead of creating subordi-
nate political institutions, the Western territories emerged as American states modeled on and equal to their Eastern counterparts. One
historian points to the "nearly universal support" among citizens then
and later "for the constitutional *ideal* that had guided the American
territorial system since its founding. Territories would not be held
in perpetual dependency but could look forward to statehood and
membership in the Union."[30]

This principle of popular inclusion and political sovereignty applied consistently for new territories until Americans reached the end
of their land frontier, until they came upon their ocean terminus.
Through the Northwest Ordinance of 1787, and its many elaborations
in territories west of the Mississippi River, the United States built a
Union of integrated, representative, self-governing institutions. White
settlers carried the American nation-building creed into new lands and
they constructed compatible representative governments and market
economies around it. They wrote constitutions, they elected governors
and legislatures, and they established separation between church and
state. Settlers in new states defined citizenship by belonging to both
a specific state polity and a larger constitutional Union. The specific
state polity guaranteed local culture and interests; the larger constitu-

25

tional Union protected basic security, rights, and property. Although Indians, African Americans, many women, and other groups were excluded from full membership in this system, its emphasis on political empowerment and equality for white settlers in the new American territories was unprecedented when compared to most foreign empires at the time, and thereafter. The creation of the continental Union was a powerful extension of American nation-building.[31]

A More Perfect Union

Despite the momentum of westward expansion, the Union remained comparatively small and weak in its early decades. That was not the point. What the Union offered was the fusion of republicanism and empire—the active political participation of the citizenry and the creation of centralized power over a large and growing territory. This was a formidable combination, even at its birth. Republics filled with yeoman farmers were generally too small for the challenges and opportunities of the North American continent. Vast empires, on the model of Europe, China, and the Ottoman world, were too large for the literate and free citizens who wanted to control their own destiny.

Madison defined the new synthesis of republicanism and empire in a Union that turned territorial expanse into a republican strength by preventing any faction or set of factions from dominating government power. A plurality of American opinions would ensure freedom from imperial tyranny. At the same time, republicanism would tame empire by ensuring attention to the will of the people. The American nation would hold the central government accountable, and therefore ensure that it served the citizens and not vice versa. This unionist vision promised cooperation rather than conflict among the small states and territories that composed the United States. Union also provided assurance of a collective capability for national defense, what later Americans would call, more expansively, "national security."[32]

The United States Surrounded by Empires, 1800

BRITISH CANADA

Mass.

Vermont

N.H.

Windsor

Exeter
Boston

Albany

Mass.

New
York

Hartford

Providence

Conn.

Rhode
Island

Pennsylvania

Trenton

Lancaster

New
Jersey

Indiana
Territory

Northwest
Territory

Maryland

Dover

Chillicothe

Annapolis

Delaware

Vincennes

Virginia

Richmond

Frankfort

Louisiana
Ceded by
Spain to France
in 1800

Kentucky

North
Carolina

Raleigh

Knoxville

Tennessee

South
Carolina

Columbia

ATLANTIC

OCEAN

South of
Ohio River
Territory

Louisville

Mississippi
Territory

Georgia

Natchez

West Florida

East
Florida

0   100   200 miles

0   100   200 kilometers

N

**The United States
Surrounded by
Empires, 1800**

United States

Territory,
state claimed

Territory,
largely populated
by Indians

British

Spanish

The "Unionist Paradigm" was the unique and enduring American contribution to modern politics. It was what the symbiosis of a new American people and a new national government became in practice. A common identity, although still exclusive, allowed for the mobilization of people and resources for collective purpose. Presidential elections where Americans across territories voted for the same office—unprecedented on this scale in the eighteenth century—embodied this common identity. Despite frequent incompetence and corruption, national institutions with perceived legitimacy brought stable rule. They allowed for creative adjustment to new threats and opportunities. They ensured political continuity amidst social and economic change.[33]

Leadership transitions are always the most difficult test for political stability. The electoral defeat of the Federalists in 1800, and their peaceful replacement by the Jeffersonian Republicans, affirmed the resilience of America's nascent national institutions. Through the end of the eighteenth century, what started as an eccentric and largely imagined Union became a powerful "magnet" that attracted, encouraged, and sometimes enforced consensus across region, religion, race, and gender. "From the springs of ardor and enthusiasm issued a powerful myth about America that," one scholar explains, transformed "ordinary labor into extraordinary acts of nation building." Recent historians have shown that even slaves, denied all public political voice, embraced elements of the Union before the Civil War in an effort to end their inhumane bondage. The Union was a high-minded aspiration that remade parts of a low and dirty reality.[34]

If there is a "genius" behind American successes, it is both the aspiration and the experience of nation-building as a single Union. For the United States this has always come back to the twin birth of nation and state, and their inextricable connection through succeeding decades and centuries. The expansion of the American Union has been a continual process of simultaneous national identity formation and national government building across an ever-wider terrain. Everywhere Americans have gone since the Revolution they have tried to make nations with accompanying representative governments. Everywhere Americans have gone they have imagined "founding moments" for national identity formation and modern state construction, even where nation and state seem alien to local populations. Along with guns and dollars, Americans have deployed their exceptional history in universalistic ways. Every war since the Revolution has been a "war to end all wars," a crusade to end "tyranny in our world," a struggle to protect and promote a more perfect Union.[35]

Society of States

Reliving their past, Americans imagine a global future that reflects their own national history. Instead of the empires, confederations, and various substate structures that have dominated the history of international relations, the American vision presumes discrete geographic units of power, deriving their legitimacy from popular consent, embodied in representative governing institutions. Each state, according to the American experience, should have a single coherent people; each people should have a single, united, and effective state. Americans imagine the governments of foreign societies resembling their own, with statewide institutions led by elected figures, protections for individual rights and private property, and strong constitutions.

The latter are crucially important because they serve, like the U.S. Constitution, to embody a deep expression of public opinion that transcends faction, fear, and short-term self-interest. Constitutions organize foreign nations and states in the image of a single American-style union. They also provide a Madisonian check on tyrannical dictators and unruly masses. Drawing on their own experiences, Americans perceive states as legitimate when they appear to unite a people around a consensual identity and a stable government that represents something more sustained than the temporary trade-offs of different groups, or the enforced authority of a powerful figure. This is the modern image of the sovereign nation-state.

This is also the wellspring for American assumptions about a peaceful "society of states." Americans have traditionally distrusted powerful international bodies designed to control the interests of diverse communities. Distant global regulators can easily become global imperialists, playing a role similar to that of European colonial officials, denying national and local autonomy. Americans have condemned a laissez-faire world of anarchical states too. Competition without control breeds frequent wars and destruction, as the very violent history of the eighteenth century readily displayed to observers at the time.

The American vision of a society of states posits an alternative to global regulation and global anarchy. It presumes that societies organized internally as constitutional nation-states will naturally preserve their independence and seek cooperation with like-minded countries. The society of states anchors peace to the ideological and institutional compatibility of governments. Compatibility breeds familiarity, and it serves the national interests of diverse peoples, according to this vision.[36]

Early American ideas about a society of states were not unique. Writing in the East Prussian city of Königsberg (now Kaliningrad) at the end of the eighteenth century, Immanuel Kant described how creating a world of modern nation-states could ensure a "perpetual peace." "The republican constitution," Kant explained, "gives a favorable prospect for the desired consequence, i.e., perpetual peace. The reason is this: if the consent of the citizens is required in order to decide that war should be declared (and in this constitution it cannot but be the case), nothing is more natural than that they would be very cautious in commencing such a poor game, decreeing for themselves all the calamities of war." Kant spoke of a "league of peace" among "free states," committed to cooperation based on the mutual trust derived from their representative and stable institutions. Conceived near the end of his life, Kant's scheme was a testament to how reasoning citizens—like the American revolutionaries—could reorder the world by remaking their national governments.[37]

Thomas Jefferson echoed Kant in his Second Inaugural Address, written as the warring British and French empires attacked American ships at sea: "We are firmly convinced, and we act on that conviction, that with nations, as with individuals, our interests soundly calculated, will ever be found inseparable from our moral duties." "[H]istory," Jefferson continued, "bears witness to the fact, that a just nation is taken on its word, when recourse is had to armaments and wars to bridle others." For Jefferson, as for many Americans in coming centuries, a peaceful society of states required morally acceptable nations and governments.[38]

Encouraging American-style states abroad preoccupied Jefferson and his successors. U.S. foreign policy largely rejected the traditional realpolitik focus on military and economic power, separate from moral judgments about local politics. This is where the American vision of a society of states, and the hold of Kant's "perpetual peace," are exceptional. More than any of their counterparts, Americans have consistently defined the world in terms of good and evil actors, deserving of inclusion or ostracism from the society of states. More than any of their counterparts, Americans have consistently deployed their power, often in extreme forms, to eliminate perceived threats to the society of states. All of these actions have, of course, served U.S. interests, but they have constituted something much more profound. American foreign policy positions have displayed an urge to Kantian perfection, a desire to convert selfish international actors into a free and ordered community.

Advocates of realpolitik, especially George Kennan and Henry Kissinger, have condemned this American moralism as a quixotic vision—a futile chasing of false windmills for global democracy and constitutionalism. International politics, Kennan and Kissinger argue, is too violent and unequal for such American-centered presumptions. This is a powerful, but unfair, criticism. The American pursuit of a society of states serves the deepest interests of a people forged in revolution. The spread of American-style nation-states, and the destruction of their challengers, matches the realistic interests of citizens in the United States. Alternative forms of foreign government limit American influence, access, and long-term trust. American-inspired forms of government promise, at least in American eyes, to benefit everyone—those living in foreign societies, as well as those residing in the United States. Contrary to Kennan and Kissinger, nation-building is a form of what we might call "realistic idealism."[39]

Almost without exception, the United States has defined political ideologies that challenge its vision of the modern nation-state—Jacobinism, socialism, communism, fascism, and Islamic fundamentalism—as existential threats. Instead of negotiating, Americans have refused to recognize antithetical regimes. Americans have worked, where possible, to overthrow governments they abhor. Appealing to the interests of "peoples," rather than inherited sources of local authority, means that established borders around territories do not necessarily place legitimate restrictions on American influence, especially if those borders enclose nation-less and state-less violence. Invoking the peaceful promise of governments made from the people, the United States has often encouraged revolutionary changes in faraway places.

The central paradox, missed by many observers, is that ardent commitment to a society of states has justified internal interference in those countries that posed "criminal" threats to the greater society. Within years of the American Revolution, citizens spoke of "police" actions to protect order and prosperity from gangs of wrongdoers along the Western frontier, on the Canadian border, and even in the pirated waters of North Africa. The American policing force would grow and its writ to protect the society of states would expand by the mid-twentieth century to include most of the globe. This was precisely Kennan and Kissinger's nightmare as they criticized the American international commitment to moral compatibility, rather than narrow self-interest. Asserting leadership over a society of states was, in many ways, more ambitious than running an empire.[40]

American efforts to build institutions for cooperation among the states in "good standing" were the other side of a compatibility agenda. As Kant suggested, a perpetual peace required freedom and common practice among politically prepared actors, not false unity or shallow assumptions about laissez-faire. Americans played a crucial role in designing the League of Nations, the United Nations, and the World Trade Organization, among others, for precisely this reason. These organizations were intended to build peaceful and prosperous relations among free and independent states. They have pursued this goal by seeding an American-inspired fusion of nation and state—through aid, knowledge transfer, trade, and security assistance—across the globe. They have written constitutions and constructed representative institutions that encourage stable rulers, cohesive peoples, and open societies. What Akira Iriye identifies as the growth of "global community" since the nineteenth century has really been the promotion of a more explicit society of states, with organized mechanisms for cooperation on American terms. The United States does not rule or govern, as much as it leads from the power of its model.[41]

The society of states is really a "society," rather than an empire, because the powerful actors recognize certain basic rules more often than not—including the defense of territorial security, the fair treatment of visitors, and the protection of foreign property. These are all elements dating back to Kant's vision of "perpetual peace." Most international actors prefer peace to war, they acknowledge their interdependence, and they encourage external trade and other interactions, mediated by both national and international institutions. Power and wealth are unevenly distributed in the society of states (as they are within all societies), but states have widely recognized claims on some of both, as they did not in empires that traditionally denied statehood in the first place. At its root, the society of states extends Madison's pioneering union of nation and state in North America to an even more extensive and diverse global landscape.[42]

James Madison was one of the most original and enduring political thinkers of his time. He helped create an American government and an American people where neither had existed before. More than any other figure, he authored the American nation-building creed.
Portrait of James Madison, 1816, John Vanderlyn, White House Historical Association

Madison and Hamilton created an American nation by constructing a government that derived from that nation. Similarly, Woodrow Wilson and Franklin Roosevelt helped create a society of states by designing international institutions that derived from that society of states. The building blocks of local political order became more legible in the construction of the global political order. Systems theorists call this "self-similarity across scale." For Americans it is a way of reconciling independence and unity with new organizing mechanisms. American internationalism has promoted the fusion of nationalism and statehood across a historically nation-less and state-less globe.[43]

The Cultural Contradictions of American Nation-Building

The American vision of nation, state, and the society of states is sophisticated and shallow at the same time. The same could be said for American policies since the Revolution. No other country has devoted more resources to building a world that would support its way of life—including open markets, individual rights, and private property protections. No other country has created more problems for itself and others, especially in the twentieth century, by interfering in foreign societies and pursuing impractical changes—including the rapid "modernization" of traditional communities, the heavy investment in centralized economic "development," and, most of all, the imposition of constitutional democracy. The history of American nation-building is filled with these contradictory achievements and failures. The history of American nation-building is nearly impossible to categorize, as much as many might try.[44]

The sophisticated achievements of U.S. policy in the post–Civil War South, the Philippines, Germany, and Japan come, in part, from the ability of Americans to recognize the intersection of complex phenomena: national identity, democratic government, domestic interests, and international organization. All of these phenomena mattered deeply for the making of policy in these regions. All of these phenomena influenced the deployments of knowledge, wealth, and force that contributed to the construction of new political organizations in these societies, as well as within the United States. Nation-building at its best was as much about changing "us" to work with "them" as it was the reverse. Southern Reconstruction and the post–World

War II occupations of Germany and Japan, in particular, transformed the inner workings of American society—from the new amendments to the Constitution after the Civil War to the National Security Act of 1947. The American nation reshaped itself to help reshape others abroad.[45]

The elegance of the American system is its potential for productive flexibility. With an inherited vision of the union of nation and state on American terms, and a consistent belief that this vision can transfer across cultures, U.S. citizens have entered foreign societies with clear goals. They have aimed to build American-style nations, and they have known what that means. These nation-builders have, however, rarely possessed even the most rudimentary knowledge about how to achieve such lofty goals. Policy has emerged from adaptation to circumstances—trial and error, with frequent misdirection and adjustment. Americans have, in fact, experienced many productive failures, and policy has—at its best—responded to unforeseen challenges, shortcomings, and misperceptions. When most successful, Americans have possessed the resources and resolve to make the necessary adjustments in their nation-building efforts. They have also defined their nation-building goals in the long term, accepting locally inspired variations.

This point about a long time horizon is crucial. Change in societies is slow and it is not smooth. Entrenched interests and accepted habits of behavior resist reforms that they find threatening. They also reverse slow advances during periods of doubt and uncertainty. Large and complex societies, like big corporations and universities, are rarely flexible or experimental. This observation, of course, explains why democratic theorists before James Madison believed that representative governments had to be small republics, rather than large territorial states. The repressive force of tradition in the eighteenth- and nineteenth-century British Empire was a warning to Madison and others about the difficulties of remaking societies, even those with powerful profit-seekers.[46]

Nation-building is strategic. It requires targeted investments, sophisticated attention to legitimate sources of resistance, and, most of all, patience. There are no quick results. Nation-building occurs in decades, not years. Progress is uneven, and it comes with visible breakthroughs after extended periods of apparent stagnation, and even reversal. This was, of course, the case for the United States in its own history. The ratification of the Constitution was a breakthrough after years of disunion and conflict. Southern Reconstruction, at least in its early years, was also a breakthrough after a bloody Civil War that brought the country to the brink of dissolution. In an international context, the Marshall Plan in Western Europe and the "Reverse Course" in Japan were similar breakthroughs after years of postwar starvation and disarray. Breakthroughs occurred and they endured in all of these cases because of patient, long-term, and ever-adjusting commitments. Nation-builders must make sustainable and dynamic investments. At their best, Americans have invested in these terms. At their best, American leaders—in government, business, and academia—have encouraged this strategy.

Unfortunately, wise leadership and smart investing are not pervasive in American history. They are, in fact, somewhat rare. Too often, Americans have exhibited overconfidence and impatience in their commitments to nation-building. They have believed that the sincerity of their commitments will substitute for the sacrifice and sustained attention necessary for success. Americans have also embraced a simplistic view of their own past, one that raised false expectations about the pace of change. The hardest accomplishments have appeared easy for citizens who are proud of their own achievements and ignorant of the alternative aspirations, traditions, and habits in other societies. American successes have often undermined the patient and sophisticated attitudes that made success possible in the first place.

We might call this phenomenon a "cultural contradiction of American nation-building." The experience of success at home, and sometimes abroad, undermines the discipline necessary for continued success. Reflecting on the process of national and state transformation from the prosperous perch of twenty-first-century America, citizens discount the adaptations and redirections that made the present emerge from the past. They seek similar results without similar patience and commitment. The experience of American wealth and power encourages a belief in the simple, straight-line development of nation-states. Frustration follows when the course of history proves crooked, complex, and even a little chaotic.

Where American policy has contributed to calamities—in Cuba, Nicaragua, Haiti, Vietnam, Pakistan, and other countries—it has reflected the worst of the inherited impulse to create a new people and a new government at breakneck speed. Searching for a compatible popular will and a constitutional anchor for authority, Americans have peered into foreign societies, but they have not contemplated what they see carefully enough. The United States often acts in ways that distort its deeper aims. American optimism and impatience frequently undermine the respectful relationships across societies that are necessary for effective policy.

The problem is not that Americans have lacked local expertise or information. The United States has cultivated rich and diverse regional knowledge, especially in the twentieth century. No other country funded more private and public "area studies" programs during the Cold War. Nor is it accurate to say that certain cultures are destined to an illiberal fate. Democratic aspirations show broad popular appeal across regions and religions. Effective and representative government is, in fact, a sufficiently malleable concept to find potential echoes in very diverse locales.[47]

Regional expertise and democratic aspirations are not, unfortunately, guarantors of success. The problem is frequently with American policy, and its tendency toward a simple but stubborn deficiency: the allure of easy answers. Despite popular rhetoric to the contrary, nation-building is a complex process that never follows strict principles and formulas. Americans have forgotten this part of their own past when they apply their history abroad. Madison, Hamilton, and their successors were creative—and successful—because they invented a new way to achieve their goal of a united nation-state. They invested, they experimented, and they collaborated—in very unsystematic ways. Their nation-building project was indeed a shining City on a Hill, but it required an imaginative search for streams and paths up the mountain. Nation-building for the United States is a continual learning process. The Constitution is not an end point; it is a constant beginning for debate, interpretation, and application. Reverence for a "timeless" Constitution often creates a culture of democratic worship that restricts democratic practice.[48]

Americans have lived the history of nation-building forward at home, but they have often applied it backward abroad. They have defined government in foreign societies as a fixed starting point, with clear rules, cookie-cutter procedures, and imported "best practices," rather than experiments, adjustments, and adaptations among diverse actors—foreign and local. Americans have often been far more rigid in what they expect from "others" than from themselves. They have tried to find a common people through hastily arranged elections and popular strong leaders, rather than working with the population over a number of years to make real elections and leaders possible. From early-twentieth-century Cuba and Haiti to Vietnam and Iraq decades later, American efforts at government reform have decreed democracy from above instead of building it from below.[49]

The recurring American dependence on dictatorial strongmen to rule foreign countries is the clearest evidence of shallow efforts at nation-building. Entering societies to remove threats to good government, real and perceived, Americans have failed when they have demanded the most significant change in the least amount of time. Removing the vestiges of Spanish colonialism in Cuba, "civilizing" Haiti, "modernizing" Vietnam, and "democratizing" Iraq—these sincere programs deployed military power and social science knowledge in an effort to move history at hyper-speed. When the local roads to change could not carry the machinery of rapid transformation, Americans searched for shortcuts—a form of cultural laziness by Americans who refuse to invest in long-term negotiations and relationship-building across societies. The shortcuts in nation-building meant control instead of movement, centralization instead of experimentation, and, ultimately, order instead of change. America's strongmen were born from efforts at nation-building, but they distorted the process wherever Washington empowered them to run it. Impatient efforts at nation-building gave birth to "temporary" dictators, who hoarded power and turned on their sponsors.

At their worst, America's strongmen in places like Saudi Arabia and Pakistan have sustained the extremists—al Qaeda and the Taliban, in particular—determined to destroy everything the United States has helped to build. Some observers call this "blowback," where efforts to fund the bastards who hate our immediate adversaries empower those same bastards to fight us in the future. The most expedient enemies of our enemies are *not* our friends; they are only our future enemies.[50]

This argument is compelling, but it is not sufficient. American support for brutal dictators is most harmful because it cuts the people out of politics. It reads history backward in its assumption that you can build a people and a nation after you enforce order and security through the barrel of a gun. That is a recipe for authoritarianism, not nation-building. The people of a society, broadly and diversely defined, must be an integral part of state construction for the resulting institutions to stand on stable ground. Otherwise, national sustenance remains dependent on ever more violence and external support. Too often Americans have forgotten this truism when they favor a formidable national figure who promises to replace indecision, uncertainty, and debate with the firm guiding hand of a decisive state. Indecision, uncertainty, and debate are frustrating for impatient Americans acting abroad, but they are much more fundamental to creating a peaceful people and an effective government than any enforced political order. Real nation-building is messy and unruly; Americans fail when they try to make it neat and tidy.

Drawn to stability and security amidst disorder, Americans have inadvertently aided local leaders who are nation-destroyers rather than nation-builders. We have mistaken our enemies for our friends, and we have neglected our highest priorities. That is the real reason American-supported strongmen in Pakistan, Saudi Arabia, and other authoritarian countries have nurtured the likes of al Qaeda and the Taliban. These extreme groups help the dictators to redirect public opinion, expand their regional influence, and, paradoxically, justify requests for more support from the United States. The Pakistani government, for example, funds the Taliban through its intelligence services and collects billions of dollars in American aid to fight the Taliban at the same time. This is good business for the strongmen in Islamabad, but it is bad for anyone who cares about building a functioning and peaceful Pakistani nation-state. For expedience, the United States has allowed itself to become dependent on the leaders who most detract from its deepest aims. The terrorists are products of America's ill-begotten allies, and they draw Washington closer to the dictators who make the trouble, rather than the people who sustain prosperous societies.[51]

Nation-building can work only when the people own it. America's complicated domestic history reinforces that insight. Acting abroad, citizens often forget that fact. They define power as a constant dictated from above, rather than a changing phenomenon modified from below. This is a somewhat natural reaction to the immediacy of threats and the dizzying complexity of foreign societies. Although stable authority emerged from a nation-building process in the United States, embodied by our never-ending constitutional debates, policy-makers have neglected this experience when advising other governments. Too often, Americans have made authority the starting, and therefore restricting, point for beginning reforms abroad. It is not so much that foreign societies are backward, but that Americans have been backward in their policy priorities and the applications of their own history. The problem is not the aspiration to nation-building, but the desire to achieve a quick, rigid, and final solution to the pressing problems of disorder.

Fixing "Failed States"

The 11 September 2001 terrorist attacks in the United States exemplified the international dangers created by local disorders. The collapse of effective political authority in much of the Middle East allowed al Qaeda and other terrorist networks to form alternative loyalties. The creation of a new Islamist state in Afghanistan, dominated by the Taliban, provided sanctuary for those planning to destroy the heathen "West" in the name of Islam. Without the combined collapse and reconstruction in Central Asia of identity and governance—nation and state—the terrorists would not have been able to organize their vicious plot.[52]

This was, in fact, nothing new. Only the scale had changed. Since the eighteenth century, keen observers in the United States, Europe, and Asia have recognized that the stakes in nation and state formation are very large. New unions of mobilized national identity and effective governance have transformed regions, continents, and the globe. This is the story of the United States, France, Japan, Germany, and China since their respective revolutions in 1776, 1789, 1868, 1870, and 1949. None of these states became a traditional empire. Each of them formed a modern union of people and government in a new nation-state that challenged established powers around it. The key question was how the new nation-state would interact with other states. Those that chose war and conquest—France, Japan, and Germany—brought continental and global ruin. Those that pursued peace and cooperation, in addition to war and conquest, often contributed more to themselves and to their foreign counterparts. The fate of the modern world has been made and unmade by the fate of nation-states in formation.[53]

Both al Qaeda and the Taliban were the consequence of failed nation-building efforts. Al Qaeda emerged in states that lost their nation—states where the rulers could not command the allegiance of the ruled. The Taliban captured a nation of mobilized Islamist opinion (they began as the "students" of an abandoned, war-torn society), but they did not build a functioning state that could live peacefully with its neighbors. For all the apparent nonstate qualities of the men who hijacked four American airplanes on 11 September 2001, the terrorists and their supporters were from the society of states. They represented its dark and dangerous elements, mobilizing the power situated in diverse nations and states to destroy those nations and states. They proved that if successful nation-state formation promised a bright Madisonian world of democratic peace and prosperity, the failures of this process threatened nothing short of Thomas Hobbes's warring state of nature. Modern states grew large and powerful, and the modern stakes in their success grew even larger and more pressing. This is probably the most useful way to think about what globalization means in the twenty-first century.[54]

The United States cannot fix "failed states," just as it cannot manage global change. Washington has enough trouble keeping up with problems at home. It can, however, enable failed states to fix themselves, seeding new forms of representative government. It can also help empower diverse groups of people in foreign societies to seek political inclusion and policy collaboration. Most of all, the United States has a history of political creativity and adaptation that it can bring to other societies looking for models, inspirations, and alternative paths. States fail because they neglect the problems and demands within their borders. States can succeed and become functioning nations with the deployment of creative ideas and targeted resources from a country with America's wealth of experience and ambition.

The United States has the capital, broadly defined, to help the people of failing states seize their own history.

This claim means different things in different contexts. The American nation-building creed contains no universal formula for implementation at home and abroad. In some places—perhaps post-conflict societies like Bosnia, Cambodia, and East Timor—American nation-building involves direct economic and technological aid. In other places—perhaps democratizing societies like Egypt, Ukraine, Georgia, Kenya, and even China—American nation-building includes support for liberalizing institutions, investments in entrepreneurship, and advice on law and elections. In war-torn societies—Iraq, Afghanistan, Yemen, and many others—American nation-building requires the forceful containment of violence, the encouragement of cooperation among rival groups, and, most important, the nurturing of inclusive institutions that give the peoples of the country a common stake in the same future. All three approaches require adaptation, experimentation, and patience. All three approaches make the United States a major, but not the dominant, actor. All three approaches bring a useful American history of nation-building to the challenges of the contemporary world. Americans have a past that matters enormously for the present. In a global society of states, the U.S. nation-building creed is an indispensable promise.

Where Do We Go from Here?

To go forward we must look back. That is what nations and states do. That is what the United States has done best when it has been most successful. History is the laboratory for nation-building. It is the repository of wisdom, judgment, and especially imagination for creating global peace and prosperity amidst international war and suffering. The nation-state is not a static form of political organization; it draws its continual dynamism and relevance from a rich repertoire of inherited experiences. The challenge comes in understanding the past more fully for adaptation and application to the present. In the whirl of contemporary global changes, nurturing successful nation-states—old and new—is as important as ever.

The history of American nation-building efforts is both familiar and unknown. Diverse historical moments—from the American Revolution and Southern Reconstruction through the occupations of the Philippines, Germany, Vietnam, Iraq, Afghanistan, and other societies—have received separate attention from scholars. Writers have examined these cases in detail and mostly in isolation. Few studies have analyzed the patterns of nation-building across decades, the wisdom acquired (or neglected) from the mixed outcomes, and, most important, the enduring legacies from the global spread of this political form. Although American citizens have played a central role in nation-building, their activities have received attention mostly in isolation from other actors, or in isolation from the broader range of experiences across time. Despite the long global role of the United States as a major nation-builder, and the continued relevance of that history, serious studies of the topic are nearly impossible to find.

No one has done for the global history of American nation-building what countless writers have done for the global history of American business expansion or cultural penetration of foreign societies. These topics are related to nation-building, but they are not the same. They miss the complex intersections of ideology, politics, and social change that have exerted such formative influence on life within the United States and abroad. They miss one of the central patterns in American domestic and foreign policy. The existing histories do not explain the crucial connections between the building of the American nation and U.S. efforts in Afghanistan in the twenty-first century. Madison and Hamilton share more with Bush and Obama than one would expect from standard accounts.[55]

How has American nation-building changed the world? How has the experience of nation-building changed the United States? What have we learned as citizens, as policymakers, as people looking to the future? These are the questions one can answer only after analyzing the American nation-building creed, and its hold on the American understanding of collective identity, good government, and the society of states. The rest of this book will examine the uses and misuses of the American nation-building creed from its formative decades at home to its most expansive expressions abroad. The debates between Madison, Hamilton, Jefferson, and Washington have echoed across centuries and continents.

Chapter 2

Reconstruction After Civil War

By these recent successes the re-inauguration of the national authority—reconstruction—which has had a large share of thought from the first, is pressed much more closely upon our attention. It is fraught with great difficulty. Unlike a case of a war between independent nations, there is no authorized organ for us to treat with. No one man has authority to give up the rebellion for any other man. We simply must begin with, and mould from, disorganized and discordant elements. Nor is it a small additional embarrassment that we, the loyal people, differ among ourselves as to the mode, manner, and means of reconstruction.

Abraham Lincoln's Last Public Address, 11 April 1865[1]

It is not, however, within the scope of this paper to point out the precise steps to be taken, and the means to be employed. The people are less concerned about these than the grand end to be attained. They demand such a reconstruction as shall put an end to the present anarchical state of things in the late rebellious States, where frightful murders and wholesale massacres are perpetrated in the very presence of Federal soldiers. This horrible business they require shall cease. They want a reconstruction such as will protect loyal men, black and white, in their persons and property; such a one as will cause Northern industry, Northern capital, and Northern civilization to flow into the South, and make a man from New England as much at home in Carolina as elsewhere in the Republic. No Chinese wall can now be tolerated. The South must be opened to the light of law and liberty, and this session of Congress is relied upon to accomplish this important work.

Frederick Douglass, December 1866[2]

The nineteenth century was a century of nation-building on four continents. It witnessed the emergence of united, independent Latin American, Japanese, Italian, and German nations that would transform international politics and domestic society—and precipitate two world wars. Before 1800 few people thought of themselves as part of a coherent "Argentine," "Japanese," or "German" identity; after 1870 these national identities mobilized people across large centrally organized territories. New unions of diverse "peoples" superseded traditional local allegiances. The nation-state quickly became the common architecture for modern politics.

The United States was a leader in this process. No other government did more to remake the lives of citizens in a region, despite stubborn local traditions to the contrary. No other government devoted as much force, money, and policy innovation to the rapid formation of a new society. No other government redistributed property, power, and political voice with such rapidity and reach. Foreign observers studied the American Civil War as the first modern war; they saw Southern Reconstruction as the most ambitious, and perhaps foolhardy, effort at modern nation-building. This was a "Second American Revolution" that simultaneously devastated, liberated, and reordered a large territory on a scale unimaginable in the Junker heartland of Germany, the small southern towns of Italy, or the rural backwaters of Japan. Reconstruction imposed the Northern model of government and economy, developed in the shadow of Alexander Hamilton and James Madison, on the recalcitrant South. Fusing two nations into a single union, Reconstruction was the most intensive and aggressive nation-building endeavor of the nineteenth century.[3]

Abraham Lincoln and Frederick Douglass recognized that nation-building in the South would not be easy. It proved even more challenging than the bloody military campaigns of the Civil War, and it never produced anything close to total victory. As in every effort at nation-building, the ambitions for change far exceeded the available resources. In the aftermath of a costly and bloody four-year war, public commitment to financing and forcing transformation would soon flag, even among the most progressive citizens. Postwar periods almost inevitably encourage a simultaneous rise in popular expectations and a diminishment in public resolve. Postwar periods are always filled with hope and disappointment.

President Abraham Lincoln's Union program imposed the American nation-building creed on the former Confederacy, transforming the slaveholding region into part of a representative free labor society. Reconstruction marked the slow and incomplete, but still unprecedented, beginning of nation-building in the American South.
Abraham Lincoln, 1865, Alexander Gardner, Library of Congress

Hope was indeed a powerful commodity after the Civil War. Thousands of freed slaves, poor whites, and even some Southern elites embraced Lincoln's and Douglass's vision of remaking the Confederacy to look more like the Union. They ran for public office, joined new Union and freedmen leagues, built churches, opened schools, and created businesses. They worked courageously to take politics into their own hands, especially during the years between 1865 and 1877, when they could rely on some protection from Union armies occupying the Southern states. They also benefited from the inspiration and support of the Radical Republicans who dominated Congress for the first decade after Appomattox.

The former slaves and citizens of the Confederacy who looked forward to a better postwar life—with more access to freedom, wealth, and mobility—acted with strong determination to make a new nation. Historian Steven Hahn puts it very well when he writes that there "could be no mistaking the possibilities that the new constitutions opened up for the majority of freedpeople living in the plantation belt. Simply by enfranchising African-American men and prescribing that all county offices be subject to election, they created an unprecedented basis for local democracy."[4]

The greatest impediment to democratic transformation in the South, as in almost all other cases of nation-building, was the stubborn resistance of local spoilers. From the moment Reconstruction began, reformers confronted opposition from increasingly organized, vocal, and violent groups. Those who were most invested in slavery, plantation society, and Southern culture—those who had the most to lose from political and social reforms—undermined efforts at change. They used passive and active forms of sabotage: noncompliance with laws, intentional misinterpretation of laws, intimidation, and, most extreme, public lynching. Politics in the postwar South was filled with conflict that frequently turned bloody, especially for the most vulnerable citizens.

Violent assertions of "home rule" by groups of former Confederate sympathizers were common. These spoilers also stoked exaggerated fears about outside interveners. They appealed to the hates and resentments of their fellow citizens, and they resorted to terroristic attacks against advocates of reform. This is part of the history of American Reconstruction that continues to receive insufficient attention: the pervasiveness of terror and the formation of a violent insurgency in the post–Civil War South.[5]

The years after 1865 were *the* foundational nation-building case of the nineteenth century. The ambitious efforts to remake the post-slavery South on the model of the American North, and the frequent resistance to this program, epitomized the modern process of political transformation across societies. The United States would indeed form a new united nation-state on the ashes of the Confederacy, but it would also create lingering conflicts, resentments, and controversies. The process was incomplete and disillusioning for many of its strongest initial advocates. It was, nonetheless, radical in its implications for politics and society—North and South.

American nation-building after the Civil War extended the assumptions, habits, and patterns of the country's founding moment. In its successes and failures, Reconstruction transformed the meaning of these inherited ideas, institutions, and behaviors. The process was messy, unplanned, and often contradictory. The post-1865 United States was old and new at the same time. In this way, American nation-building after the Civil War created a framework for future American activities—at home and abroad—that combined Madison and Hamilton with Lincoln and Douglass.

Frederick Douglass, a former slave, demanded the full application of the American nation-building creed in the Confederacy. He sought racial equality through protections for freedom and assurances of representation in Southern institutions remade by the Civil War. *Photograph, Frederick Douglass, 1879, National Archives, Frank W. Legg Photographic Collection of Portraits of Nineteenth-Century Notables*

Reconstruction also created a model for ambitious nation-builders in Europe, Asia, and Latin America. Carl Schurz, the German-born radical who traveled to the United States after 1848 and became one of the most eloquent supporters of Northern efforts to transform the South, observed that even European conservatives wanted to learn from the recent American experience. Schurz recounted how German chancellor Otto von Bismarck, a former political adversary, spent two late nights asking probing questions about the meaning of the Civil War and Reconstruction. What kind of nation would the new United States become? How would it influence Europe? Bismarck was not sure, but he knew that the innovations, struggles, and violence of American nation-building would echo across the Atlantic.[6]

The Confederacy as Failed State

Bismarck was, in fact, one of many observers to recognize the profound obstacles to Northern nation-building efforts. In 1865 the Confederacy was a failed state, or more accurately, a collection of failed states. Political authority had collapsed during the last months of the Civil War, and Union troops were sparsely distributed across a devastated countryside. Basic food was scarce in many sections of the agrarian South, urban stores were barren, and freed slaves, former Confederate troops, and destitute families roamed the landscape—often competing with one another for shelter and sustenance. Confederate currency, the basis for family savings and economy throughout the South before 1865, had become worthless. No one would accept the paper of a destroyed government in exchange for goods and services. One embittered Southerner remembered: "Everything was scarce in those days except Confederate money. . . . After the war everything was in confusion."[7]

Rumors of insurrection among freed blacks pervaded discussions in the South. Many former slaveholders expected that their long-suffering laborers would now exact violent revenge. Observers also recognized that white citizens who had lost their wealth and status were organizing for violent attacks on the newly freed slaves and the Union sympathizers in the South. The losers of the Civil War condemned both groups as traitors who had murdered their society from within. In rumor and in fact, violence was "normal" in the South. The war between the states had become a war of all against all. The former governor of North Carolina, David L. Swain, confirmed this observation. "We are," he said after the Confederate surrender, "at the beginning of the war."[8]

This was a perfect recipe for spiraling attacks and destruction. One Tennessean vividly remembered: "It was the reign of terror—war at every man's door, neighbor against neighbor. . . . Neither property nor life was safe by day or night." Vigilante justice, blood feuds, and brute torture became commonplace as war-shattered citizens struggled to survive and make sense of their circumstances. The end of the war deepened the disorientation and insecurity of daily life. It offered little relief—often just the opposite—from the troubles of the past four years.[9]

The South had lost more than a war. It had lost its basic moorings, its inherited anchors of order, wealth, and authority. The Confederate male aristocracy was murdered, maimed, and emasculated by defeat on the battlefield. The most able-bodied Southern men who survived the battles were physically and emotionally crippled, often beyond repair. A region that had thrived on cotton production and genteel culture became a society of destroyed bodies and ghostly personalities. The proud Confederacy of Southern men was now a despairing "republic of suffering"—more open, but far less hopeful.[10]

The destruction of the Civil War devastated once-prosperous
Southern communities. This photo depicts the crumbling
and abandoned buildings of Charleston, South Carolina.
*View of Meeting Street, looking south toward the Circular
Church, the Mills House, and St. Michael's Church,
April 1865, George N. Barnard, Library of Congress*

African Americans could not save the Southern aristocracy, as they
had in other periods of economic difficulty. Emancipation, enforced
by the North, ended all slave labor in a matter of months. Almost
overnight, Southerners lost the wageless muscle that had long fueled
plantation life. The farms were emptied of the men, women, and
children who did the farming. The "big houses" of the gentlemen
and ladies were emptied of the servants, cooks, and cleaners who kept

order. At home and in the fields, Southern communities struggled with a postwar world where the traditional human sources of survival disappeared. Even the most hardened Confederate recognized that the slaves would never return. Southerners could not restore the "lost" life they had taken for granted. Slave dependence produced profound social trauma after emancipation.

In the months following the Confederate surrender, the South did not live in "peace." Violent struggles over scarce resources pervaded the landscape. As enemies to survival appeared everywhere, the logic of the jungle took hold in many areas. Those who had lost on the battlefield often carried the fight to civilian society. In North Carolina, soon after the last Civil War battles, two Confederate loyalists kidnapped a Union sympathizer, tied him to a tree, and beat him to death with chains in public. This was an all-too-common scene for years to come.[11]

Violence was not only one-sided. The victors in the Civil War, and their supporters, also exacted revenge. Attacks on former Confederates were public and popular with particular groups. These efforts at pro-Union retribution were generally far less murderous than the acts of Confederate sympathizers, but they contributed to the disorder and fear that characterized post–Civil War society. The Loyal League, formed among Union advocates in Choctaw County, Mississippi, harassed Confederate supporters—including forced incarcerations and public beatings. Similar leagues formed in other counties across the South. The collapse of traditional authority meant the rise of vigilante justice, in the service of multiple political aims.[12]

The war came home with a vengeance in the months after April 1865. This was a period of state collapse when local strongmen filled power vacuums across the landscape. An atmosphere of terror touched citizens throughout the South. The months and years after the surrender at Appomattox witnessed a continual, and escalating, contestation of power in local communities as starving groups, frightened families, and overstretched Union soldiers struggled to assert control of their surroundings. Outside of the very limited areas of Union

Army concentration, power devolved to "paramilitary politics." As in other cases of state collapse, terror became the language of daily life.[13]

Complex Transformations

The chaos and violence of the postwar South set back hopes for a quick and deep transformation of the region. Despite Lincoln's call for a national effort to "mould" a new South and Douglass's demand for opening the "light of law and liberty," many scholars have pointed to the shortcomings of government policies. According to this general argument, Southern Reconstruction was a very limited, and perhaps disingenuous, form of nation-building. As early as 1909, W. E. B. Du Bois criticized Southern white leaders for their efforts to keep African Americans in a social position barely better than slavery. During the height of the civil rights movement, six decades later, historian Kenneth Stampp extended Du Bois's powerful argument: "In place of slavery a caste system reduced Negroes to an inferior type of citizenship; social segregation gave them inferior educational and recreational facilities; and a pattern of so-called 'race etiquette' forced them to pay deference to all white men. Negroes, in short, were only half emancipated." More recently, Eric Foner has agreed: "whether measured by the dreams inspired by emancipation or the more limited goals of securing blacks' rights as citizens and free laborers . . . Reconstruction can only be judged a failure."[14]

These are powerful reminders about the "unfinished" nature of nation-building, even within the United States. Integrating diverse citizens into a single people, with representation and security in a unified territory—that Madisonian goal remains part of an evolving political process more than a century after Lincoln and Douglass articulated their post–Civil War vision. Even the most "successful" nation-states fall short of their promises for popular representation, sovereignty, and prosperity. Even the most "successful" nation-states operate on the edge of failure. Building a common government for a united people is, in fact, a very precarious endeavor.[15]

Like other nineteenth-century nation-building enterprises, Reconstruction in the South was not the end of a process. Too often we treat these moments in this way. Instead, Reconstruction was "the beginning of the war"—an uncertain opening into a more extensive world of nation-states, and a closure for other hybrid and partial forms of governance from the past. For all its limits, Reconstruction set the American South, the United States, and many other parts of the globe on a new trajectory. It ended any serious effort at defining a "sectional" political system that challenged the unity of a single people, an integrated economy, and a common public culture that spanned such a large and diverse territory. Reconstruction affirmed that there would be only one American nation in rhetoric and in daily practice.[16]

The destruction of the Confederacy extinguished the claims that a large portion of the population could live a distinctive social and economic life—slavery amidst free market industrial capitalism, plantation aristocracy amidst individualism and corporate power. Diversity and exception within the larger body politic were no longer tolerated on this scale. Reconstruction created a more homogenous definition of the "people" and the "government" that could speak for them. It forced a universal model of the nation-state on the diverse communities of the United States. A more centralized federal government, with powers far exceeding those that Madison or Hamilton could conceptualize two generations earlier, now managed life across this vast nation.

This was the modern nation-state in action. National bureaucracy, a professionalized military, and a tradition of intervention replaced localism, antimilitarism, and isolation. Standardization and unity trumped diversity and independence. Reconstruction solidified order, stability, and growth among a single people tied to a single territory. The post–Civil War government would embody this people and territory, and the people and territory would constitute this government.

The newly constructed American nation-state became a global power, a global model, and ultimately a global promoter of its way of life.

The appropriate applications and adjustments for the newly centralized American nation-state would take generations—and many courageous acts—to negotiate. The same could be said for Argentina, Germany, Italy, Japan, and many of the other unified nation-states created around the same time. They were all deeply influenced by events in post–Civil War America. Reconstruction was a global moment in the alternatives that it foreclosed, the political directions that it pushed, and the difficult questions that it raised. It marked a new debate as much as a new set of institutions and practices.

After 1865 nearly every major society experienced its own Reconstruction moment. The competition to form integrated economies, mobilized publics, and large professionalized armies encouraged forced nation-building in recalcitrant ("backward") regions, on the model of the American South. The echoes of Lincoln and Douglass reverberated from the uprooting of the landed elites in Germany and Japan to the emancipation of wageless labor in Russia, Brazil, and other countries. To build what they perceived as modern societies, nation-builders from Bismarck to Sun Yat-sen followed the same patterns as their American predecessors. They fought internal opponents. They imposed a new political order from the center of the state. They narrowed the space for diversity and they increased the pressures for conformity. Most of all, they defined a new identity for their society—unified "Germans" and "Chinese," like post–Civil War "Americans." These nationalized identities, tied to clearly defined territorial boundaries, legitimized a more empowered and representative centralized government. In Lincoln's famous phrase, nineteenth-century nation-builders formed assertive governments that would be "of the people, by the people, and for the people." They presumed one territory, one people, and one government as few local predecessors had before.

If the American founding moment in the late eighteenth century created a new nation-building creed, the era of Reconstruction in the United States made that creed an almost irresistible model for ambitious leaders around the world. Madison and Hamilton found many followers within the most learned sections of foreign societies. Lincoln and Douglass exerted their greatest international influence among the men and women who built the modern states that still dominate the globe.

Leo Tolstoy, the monumental figure in nineteenth-century literature, provides the best evidence for this phenomenon. Traveling on the edges of the Russian state in the Caucasus Mountains, Tolstoy encountered startling testaments to the influence of Lincoln and the image of American nation-building far from North America. Tolstoy recounted how the Muslims he met treated Lincoln as the "the greatest general and greatest ruler of the world." Tolstoy remembered one determined group in the Caucasus saying: "We want to know something about him. He was a hero. He spoke with a voice of thunder; he laughed like the sunrise and his deeds were strong as the rock and as sweet as the fragrance of roses. . . . He was so great that he even forgave the crimes of his greatest enemies and shook brotherly hands with those who had plotted against his life. His name was Lincoln and the country in which he lived is called America, which is so far away that if a youth should journey to reach it he would be an old man when he arrived. Tell us of that man."

For Tolstoy and the people he met in the Caucasus, Lincoln's greatness came from his devotion to a cause that was much larger than himself. Lincoln's heroism was the defense and construction of a new nation-state. Even for Muslims on the edges of the czarist empire, this image had a certain potency. Despite all the violence of the Civil War, Lincoln's vision of a strong, inclusive, and prosperous nation-state was impressively humane—especially when compared to the available alternatives. Tolstoy put it very well: "His example is universal and will last thousands of years. Washington was a typical American, Napoleon was a typical Frenchman, but Lincoln was a humanitarian as broad as the world. He was bigger than his country—bigger than all the Presidents together. Why? Because he loved his enemies as himself and because he was a universal individualist who wanted to see himself in the world—not the world in himself. He was great through his simplicity and was noble through his charity." Lincoln's allure was the allure of the American nation-state, strengthened and extended by the complex transformations of Civil War Reconstruction.[17]

Making Freedmen

Lincoln's legacy drew on the inherited American nation-building creed, but it also began a process without clear guidelines or precedents. The abolition of slavery in 1865 meant the rapid creation of four million new American citizens. In other post-emancipation societies—Haiti, Jamaica, Russia, Cuba, Brazil, and others—the end of forced labor elicited a wide variation of halfway houses to full political rights. Slave abolition in these countries also initiated violent conflicts over the reallocation of land and wealth. Many post-emancipation societies suffered from persistent instability, lasting in some cases to the present, because of unresolved struggles over the rights and resources of citizenship.[18]

This is partially true for the United States after the Civil War. Conflicts, sometimes violent, over rights and wealth characterized much of the nation's history well into the twentieth century, and beyond. Unlike most other societies, however, the federal government invested heavily in creating new foundations for free, prosperous, and peaceful participation among former slaves. The government also invested in securing these possibilities for Southern whites who had lost much of their wealth in the war. Although American society accepted gross inequalities of rights and wealth, it embraced a common foundation for individual freedom in the ability of all male citizens to control their own labor and property. This was the "free labor" ideology that replaced slavery.[19]

Government efforts to develop former slaves and former slave-owners into productive parts of a post-emancipation society set the United States apart from other countries that did not do the same. These American efforts were always too limited in retrospect, but they were also more extensive than many could have imagined before. They were explicit, experimental, and frequently heavy-handed attempts at nation-building. Making freedmen into citizens who contributed to American unity and security—that became the model for transforming fragmented populations in other societies into contributors to more unified and purposeful nation-states. Reconstruction, citizenship, and government-sponsored social development went hand in hand. These became the common building blocks for nation-building at home and abroad long after the Civil War.

The U.S. federal government enforced the single largest nineteenth-century redistribution of wealth when it required slave-owners to free the human beings whom they exploited. The federal government then required the former slave-owners and their freed slaves to enter into new social relations that were designed to promote mutual benefits, regional stability, and even some interpersonal cooperation. These policies presumed freedom, but not equality. They presumed peaceful interactions, but not integrated lifestyles. Above all, the post–Civil War policies affirmed a commitment to making groups live together as a single American people in a unified nation. In ways more intrusive than ever before, the government would make this interracial union possible, and the existence of this interracial union would constitute the postwar government. Madison's vision of a sovereign American voice in the eighteenth century, embodied in the original Constitution, now expanded to include a broader American identity, with new institutions and a revised Constitution.

Like all American nation-building, Reconstruction efforts in the South centered on constitution-writing. The Thirteenth Amendment, ratified at the end of 1865, made slavery illegal. The Fourteenth Amendment, ratified in July 1868, replaced slavery with universal citizenship: "All persons born or naturalized in the United States and subject to the jurisdication thereof, are citizens of the United States and of the State wherein they reside." The Fourteenth Amendment broadly guaranteed "due process of law" and "equal protection of the laws" to all citizens in all states. The Fifteenth and final amendment in the aftermath of the Civil War, ratified in February 1870, guaranteed all male citizens the right to vote.

These amendments were paper guarantees. Their most expansive promises of due process, equal protection, and individual suffrage confronted immediate violations throughout the South, as well as parts of the North. Despite local resistance, the amendments articulated a vision of a single American nation that replaced the racial and class divisions of the Confederacy with a universal people. The amendments redefined the United States as a sovereign body composed of a single multiracial citizenry. As in the late eighteenth century, the American nation made a united people, and a united people made the American nation. The post–Civil War amendments extended Madison's creative fiction into areas that had formerly made exceptions of themselves.

Constitution-writing did not change immediate behavior, but it transformed expectations, national identity, and ultimately the reach and role of the federal government. Most of all, constitution-writing eliminated alternative visions of legitimate politics and authority. Many local actors and institutions could act contrary to the paper guarantees of the Constitution, but they could no longer claim national legitimacy, nor could they call upon protection from Washington, D.C. The acceptable and even valorized behavior of the Confederacy immediately became illegal, illegitimate, and treasonous against the United States. This political inversion—turning "normal" behavior into unconstitutional practice—created one single standard for national patriotism, just as it allowed hidden and criminal violations to fester in the local shadows. Constitution-writing remade the image of the nation-state; it stigmatized contrary behavior.

When acted upon by local and national agents over the next century, the post–Civil War amendments allowed government investment, regulation, and manipulation—often through quasi-military institutions—in the daily politics of diverse communities. The somewhat distant and elite nation-building of Madison and Hamilton became a deeply entrenched process of federal government negotiation with local groups and authorities. Leadership by inspiration and imagining became direct force, investment, and control. Nation-building in the South was about using the power of the national government to remake citizens, who in turn remade national government. It was Reconstruction from without and within. Every American nation-building endeavor after the Civil War followed similar lines.

A New Nation-Building Agency

The Freedmen's Bureau served as one of the first and most important tools in this process of government-sponsored social transformation. It began with the inherited American nation-building creed, and a recognition of the monumental barriers to its implementation within the destroyed Southern states. On 16 March 1863, less than three months after Lincoln issued the Emancipation Proclamation, Secretary of War Edwin Stanton charged a special Freedmen's Inquiry Commission of three distinguished Northern reformers—Robert Dale Owen, James McKaye, and Samuel Gridley Howe—to survey the Confederate territories under Union control, assessing the possible methods for freed slave inclusion in postwar society. Stanton understood that slave emancipation created profound sources of disorder in the South. He believed that the only solution was to make the freed slaves integrated parts of the newly governed states and the nation as a whole.[20]

Samuel Gridley Howe used his position on the Freedmen's Inquiry Commission to expand on Stanton's vision in ways that were motivated by practical concerns for postwar society and what his biographer calls a "radical" inclination to transform behavior in the South. Howe advocated government-supported public education for blacks and whites, broad land ownership, "wages for work," and equal protection under the law. "I want," Howe wrote, "to sink the differences of race and treat the blacks exactly as I would whites in their condition. I do not believe in black colonies, or black regiments. It is only in this way that we can leave free and unobstructed course to that natural law by which the weaker and poorer race is to be absorbed by the stronger and better one to the improvement of humanity and the glory of God." Howe was indeed radical for his time, but his ideas grew from the commitment to nation-building reforms that motivated Lincoln, Stanton, and the Freedmen's Inquiry Commission in the second half of the Civil War.[21]

Samuel Gridley Howe was part of the Freedmen's Inquiry Commission that surveyed Confederate territories under Union control during the Civil War. He helped to promote a vision of freed slaves as contributors to nation-building in the American South.
Samuel Gridley Howe, 1859, Boyd B. Stutler Collection, West Virginia State Archives

Howe was one of many figures committed to building a society unified around a single people, in a single territory, with a government that credibly represented all citizens. His vision did not affirm full equality between the races, but it assumed a united sovereign community after one of the bloodiest wars between peoples and states. Stanton and his commissioners recognized that the Union Army was directly responsible for occupying the Southern states. They realized that the army had to begin the process of transforming the former territories with slaves into units of the United States government with free citizens. Destroying the Confederacy would start the difficult process of building a new nation. The American military would eventually play this role across the globe, but it began in the American South.[22]

Owen, McKaye, and Howe traveled to the occupied Confederate territories during 1863 and 1864, interviewing Union commanders, emancipated slaves, and local residents. They also surveyed the scholarly literature on slavery, emancipation, labor, and education. Howe traveled to Canada to examine how that part of the British Empire adjusted to the emancipation of its slaves thirty years earlier. The Freedmen's Inquiry Commission explored numerous possibilities—contemporary, historical, and imagined—for restructuring relations among postwar Southern citizens.[23]

These Northern reformers fully imbibed the basics of the American nation-building creed. They viewed the Confederacy—including its white and black residents—as a backward society that required tutelage, development, and even some external discipline. To the astonishment of many observers, they contended that the former slave population would be a positive contributor to the Reconstruction process. The freedmen and -women were the formerly oppressed segment of the population that would embrace new forms of reform and representation. They were people who would build new bonds across geographic, ethnic, and religious lines. Most of all, the freed slaves were the men and women in the South who most strongly pursued the promise of a single American identity. Southern blacks, who had been denied political personhood for so long, now offered a powerful source of leverage for building a more inclusive, representative, and productive nation. In this context, Owen, McKaye, and Howe referred repeatedly to the key contributions of freed slaves to America's growth as a modern nation.[24]

The preliminary report of the Freedmen's Inquiry Commission argued that the former slave "is found quite ready to copy whatever he believes are the rights and obligations of what he looks up to as the superior race, even if these prove a restraint upon the habits of license belonging to his former condition." Owen, McKaye, and Howe wrote optimistically about the possibility of "civilizing" the former slaves, and the entire South, through targeted Northern aid and regulation:

> the African race, as found among us, lacks no essential aptitude for civilization. In a general way, the negro yields willingly to its restraints, and enters upon its duties not with alacrity only, but with evident pride and increase of self-respect. His personal rights as a freedman once recognized in law and assured in practice, there is little reason to doubt that he will become a useful member of the great industrial family of nations.[25]

Creating peace and prosperity in the postwar South would, according to the Freedmen's Inquiry Commission, require much more than the defeat of the Confederate armies. With freed slaves liberated from their plantations, the old economy destroyed, and traditional social relations severed, the federal government would have to take a direct and intentional role in creating new institutions across the region. That was the challenge, but that was also the opportunity. Nurturing the potential of the freed slave population to become full national citizens, the commission argued, the federal government could make rapid progress in the Reconstruction of the South in the North's image. The new black citizens would transmit the values for

American nationhood to a white population that had followed a degenerate political culture since the foundation of the first plantations. The freed slaves would cooperate with Northern reformers to build the newly united American nation.

The final report of the Freedmen's Inquiry Commission, submitted to Congress on 22 June 1864, contributed to a rancorous political debate. Massachusetts senator Charles Sumner and other Northern Republicans advocated the explicit "intervention of the National Government" in a "transition period" that would bring the South into conformity with the Union. Sumner made a direct analogy to the role of the government in building the infrastructure, laws, and habits of nationhood in other parts of the country. The same kind of government-directed nation-building was necessary in the South, he argued: "The national Government must interfere in the case precisely as in building the Pacific railroad. Private charity in our country is active and generous, but it is powerless to cope with the evils arising from a wicked institution; nor can it provide a remedy where society itself has been overthrown."[26]

Opposition to Sumner and the Freedmen's Inquiry Commission report came from Democrats and more moderate Republicans who distrusted a more intrusive federal government in postwar society. Northern Democrats, including Samuel Cox of New York and George Pendleton of Ohio, wanted to return to a small executive branch after the battlefields silenced. They feared that an active Freedmen's Bureau would allow for the erosion of local autonomy and the permanent establishment of broad federal controls. William Henry Wadsworth, a congressman from Kentucky, stated these concerns clearly: "I see no possible resurrection for the agricultural States in the South and West if the control of four million ignorant people be removed from those States to this Hall." Wadsworth accused Sumner and the Freedmen's Inquiry Commission of placing power over the former Confederacy "in the hands of the commercial and manufacturing parts of the country."[27]

Wadsworth was correct. An expanded federal presence in the South and the West would diminish local autonomy. A government agency working to reform and protect the freed slaves would encourage Northern-style industrial work, public education, and political inclusion. Wadsworth, Cox, Pendleton, and others supported the Union armies and they accepted the emancipation of the slaves, but they wanted to stop there. They opposed permanent new regulations. They wanted to demobilize federal authority, not create new ambitious plans. These early critics of the Freedmen's Inquiry Commission articulated the traditional and enduring opposition to nation-building, in the name of limited government.[28]

The congressional debate over the role of the government in postwar society produced a compromise that authorized new federal powers, but included strong constraints on resources and capabilities. On 3 March 1865, President Lincoln signed an act of Congress creating the new Bureau of Refugees, Freedmen, and Abandoned Lands. The legislation authorized only one year of work, and it placed the bureau under the authority of the secretary of war. The mandate for the bureau was broad, as Sumner and the Freedmen's Inquiry Commission suggested: "the supervision and management of all abandoned lands, and the control of all subjects relating to refugees and freedmen from rebel states, or from any district of country within the territory embraced on the operations of the army."[29]

The details of the legislation, however, made it virtually impossible for the bureau to address all of the stated issues. Congress authorized a commissioner with a skeletal staff, and assistant commissioners in each of the Confederate states. The bureau could allocate abandoned land (in forty-acre parcels or less) to freed slaves, but that was about all. It had no mechanism for administration over the large and diverse territory of the South. It had no means for enforcing its orders. Most startling, it had no budget. Under the congressional act, the Freedmen's Bureau would pursue an ambitious Northern Republican vision with woefully insufficient resources and a short calendar. Within a year, the bureau would be out of time.[30]

Renewed in 1866 by congressional Republicans despite a presidential veto, the government's most important nation-building institution in the South would last only until 1872. That was six years longer than the skeptics of Southern social and political transformation expected. It was, however, many years short of Howe, Stanton, and Sumner's vision for making full citizens of former slaves. The Freedmen's Bureau affirmed the lofty aims of the constitutional amendments passed after the Civil War, but it left them only partially enforced in the daily conflicts that followed emancipation. As in all nation-building endeavors, capabilities rarely match ambitions; deadlines rarely coordinate with local needs.

The Work of the Freedmen's Bureau

Secretary of War Edwin Stanton chose General Oliver Otis Howard to serve as the first and only commissioner of the Freedmen's Bureau. Howard was a graduate of West Point who had fought as the commander of the Union Army of Tennessee, directly supporting General William Sherman's infamous march through Georgia and the Carolinas at the end of the Civil War. Less than thirty-five years of age, Howard had also distinguished himself for his religious piety and his professional integrity. He was the "Christian General," who seemed an ideal candidate to bring the organizational skills of the army together with the beneficent aims of relief and reconstruction. Advocating for Howard's appointment, one of the most prominent Northern ministers and abolitionists, Henry Ward Beecher, proclaimed that the general "is, of all men, the one who would command the entire confidence of [the] Christian public."[31]

General Oliver Otis Howard
served as the first and
only commissioner of the
Freedmen's Bureau.
Gen. O. O. Howard, 1908,
Library of Congress

Howard would marry Christian mission to federal power in the postwar South on a scale without precedent in American history. He would also struggle with the difficulty of maintaining that marriage amidst competing claims, active resistance, and insufficient resources. As in the legislation creating the Freedmen's Bureau, Howard's ambitions were grand but his capabilities were constrained. General Sherman aptly described the impossible "Hercules' task" confronting his former comrade in arms: "it is not in your power to fulfill one tenth part of the expectation of those who formed the Bureau."[32]

Like other later cases of ambitious nation-building, things did not begin well for Howard and the Freedmen's Bureau. In his memoirs, Howard describes how, on his first day, the secretary of war handed him a "large, oblong, bushel basket heaped with letters and documents." "Here general," Stanton said to Howard, "here's your Bureau!" The new commissioner of the Freedmen's Bureau had access to offices and some assistants from the army, as well as a Washington, D.C., house confiscated from a former Confederate senator. That was all. Howard had to figure out what to do next.[33]

He began by building an organization. This included the appointment of representatives in various parts of the defeated Confederacy. Howard divided the South into nine sections, each with an assistant commissioner in charge of Freedmen's Bureau activities in the area. The assistant commissioners were all military officers who could bring army resources to the job. Howard did not have a budget of his own, so he had to rely on military requisitions, local confiscations, and charity. The Freedmen's Bureau scrambled to fill what was a broad and unfunded Reconstruction mandate.

Schooled in years of grinding warfare against the Confederacy, the assistant commissioners combined knowledge of the Southern terrain with organizational experience. They immediately began relief efforts, organizing the distribution of government and donated rations. Following Howard's orders, bureau agents attempted to assess the most dire health and nutritional needs, and they worked to move supplies accordingly. Basic relief and order were the immediate priorities. Howard articulated very simple guidelines and his assistant commissioners had wide latitude for local action. In the aftermath of the destruction wrought across the Southern landscape by the very "hard hand of war," Howard's agents faced pressing crises that differed from one county to another. The assistant commissioners drew on the military resources at hand, they made quick adjustments, and they communicated with Washington after the fact. Nation-building in this context was driven by the new bureau's men in the field.[34]

Thousands of blacks and whites throughout the South received basic sustenance through what became a new federally managed, but locally controlled, distribution mechanism. Although the process involved waste and corruption, it mobilized extensive supplies for serious needs in a way that would not have been conceivable without a central institution, connected to the necessary military resources. One historian explains: "The relief work of the Freedmen's Bureau was one of its foremost and most praiseworthy endeavors. In an era when the constitutional right of the federal government to engage in large-scale relief was questioned, the Bureau set a precedent for later periods of economic difficulty."[35]

Freedmen's Bureau agents also used the military resources at their disposal to encourage whites and blacks to return to productive labor, with some assurance of security and market compensation for their work. Howard recounted: "I stated that the demands for labor were sufficient to afford employment to most able-bodied refugees and freedmen . . . assistant commissioners were to introduce a practical system of compensated labor." The Freedmen's Bureau did not have independent capital to finance work on farms and in factories. Instead, Howard's order meant that the bureau commissioners would act as arbitrators in labor disputes, requiring employers to pay wages, but also encouraging workers to return to their jobs. Idleness was the enemy of freedom, according to Howard.[36]

The specific labor policies of the Freedmen's Bureau varied from state to state, and Howard never articulated a common position beyond the virtues of free wage labor. From the spring of 1865, however, this basic assumption led bureau agents to restrict the movement of former slaves from plantations where their labor remained vital. The bureau encouraged the negotiation and enforcement of labor contracts that guaranteed pay to workers, but often under conditions that belied the promises of a free life—with free movement—after slavery. Efforts to enforce wage employment in the South contributed to order and productivity in the months after the Civil War, but they also restricted the possibilities for economic transformation and a redistribution of wealth. The Freedmen's Bureau emphasized wage work that kept existing agriculture and industry intact.

Howard's free market vision made the Freedmen's Bureau a limit on the changes in economy that one might have expected. Market incentives and pressures kept thousands of people in place despite the end of slavery and the passage of the constitutional amendments. This continuity was a source of stability in the postwar South. Free wage labor, however, favored those with inherited access to wealth and influence, and it prevented radical unionization or collective bargaining among workers. The Freedmen's Bureau proclaimed political equality but it tolerated, and even encouraged, deep economic inequality.

A new form of postwar repression emerged, especially for former slaves, many of whom remained attached to their prior plantation homes as poorly compensated sharecroppers. The free men of the new nation were no longer tied to their masters; they were now tied to wages in a market economy dominated by white male property-holders. The Freedmen's Bureau was organized to facilitate, but not challenge, this part of the capitalist system imported from the North to the former slave South. Although the Freedmen's Bureau promised mobility, it did not provide an economic mechanism for those without property to escape the dominance of property-holders, most of whom were former slave masters. Many freed slaves managed to create economic opportunities for themselves through migration, self-help, and community-organizing. The vast majority, however, found that the end of slavery had still not made them free.[37]

Educating Citizens for the Nation

Public education was the one powerful lever the Freedmen's Bureau promoted to nurture new life choices among former slaves. In September 1865, General Howard appointed John Alvord as inspector, and later general superintendent, for public schools in the occupied South. Alvord was a Congregational minister who had served, along with Howard, in Sherman's army as it moved through the Confederate states at the end of the war. Alvord had witnessed the poverty and despair of Southern society. He recognized that stability, prosperity, and true Union in these conditions required investment in social transformation. He also recognized that much of the capital and assistance for social transformation would have to come from outside the war-devastated South.

Alvord spent the last months of 1865 traveling through the former Confederacy. He examined the possibilities for mass education in a region that was, before the Civil War, hostile to the schooling of poor whites, and especially black slaves. Alvord, Howard, and their supporters recognized that nation-building in the South had to begin with reeducating citizens to behave civilly, work cooperatively, and live side by side despite differences. A united people in a shared Union required a common foundation in language, literacy, and basic social norms. A united people also required common skills for productivity and sustenance.

These assumptions had underpinned the growth of public schooling in the Northern states during the mid-nineteenth century. After the Civil War, the federal government extended this process to the South. Government-sponsored institutions for public education—especially the "common school"—trained a broad citizenry across the expanding American nation from Massachusetts to Wisconsin. Public schools would begin to do the same from Richmond to Atlanta after 1865. That process continues a century and a half later. Public education is a vital part of nation-building.[38]

Combining his missionary sensibility with the agenda articulated by the Freedmen's Bureau, Alvord sought a mechanism for providing poor Southern citizens—including the newly emancipated slaves—with instruction in citizenship. The free labor logic that allowed for the continued inequality of the market also demanded the basic preparation of young men and women for productive participation in society. Capitalist competition presumed an ability to compete. It required productivity across a diverse workforce. Despite Southern traditions to the contrary, the Freedmen's Bureau proclaimed the immediate need to educate whites and blacks so that they could read, write, add, and work in a newly united nation. Focusing on schools for as many citizens as possible, the bureau explained that only "when Liberty is made complete, we shall have ground for faith in a perpetual Union."[39]

Alvord initially shared the common missionary belief, embedded in Freedmen's Bureau rhetoric, that Northern benevolence would guide the former Confederacy from ignorance and degeneracy to enlightenment and democracy. The American Missionary Association and other religious groups reinforced this assumption, espousing a paternalistic claim that they had the capability and the obligation to improve the dark children of the South. This was a natural corollary to the religious duty of abolishing slavery, asserted by abolitionists before the Civil War. Alvord was one of many pious abolitionists-turned-educators, attempting to bring God and "civilization" to a heathen, "backward" Southern society. Freed slaves appeared as passive receivers of imported wisdom and training, according to this long-gestating vision of reform. They were the population whom the missionaries would target for uplift and conversion.[40]

Alvord's travels in the South reinforced the need for Northern aid, but they also opened his eyes to a very different social dynamic. Freed slaves throughout Georgia, Louisiana, South Carolina, Alabama, and other states recognized the vital importance of education to their future standing in America. They demanded access to knowledge and training as full citizens. They desired full participation in the nation through educational attainment. Organized groups of former slaves called for assistance with their own educational efforts as early as 1864, and they continued to voice their commitment to schooling in later years. Alvord observed: "the surprising efforts of our colored population to obtain . . . education are not spasmodic." "They are growing to a habit."[41]

The emerging education "habit" of freed slaves, and their energetic efforts at self-organization, contributed to a network of diverse "negro schools" across the former Confederacy. Most of these schools had opened at the end of the Civil War through the labors of ex-slave communities, with some limited assistance from Union Army soldiers and Northern missionary societies. The schools were largely run by African Americans, for African Americans, by African Americans. Where resources allowed, they tended to emphasize a combination of vocational training and what one scholar calls a "classical liberal curriculum"—reading, spelling, writing, grammar, diction, history, geography, arithmetic, and music. Freed slaves had very few resources of their own, and their intellectual training was severely limited. Yet they pooled what they had to improve themselves. When the Union Army and then the Freedmen's Bureau arrived in many parts of the South, black communities were already hard at work educating themselves for full participation in the new nation. The freed slaves seized their own future through local schooling.[42]

Alvord and others were in awe. The post-emancipation "habits" of the former slaves were "crystallizing into a system, and each succeeding school-term shows their organization more and more complete and permanent." Black education in the South had many "self-sustaining" elements that belied the missionary assumption of Southern dependence on Northern beneficence. The assistant commissioner for the Freedmen's Bureau in Alabama captured the courage and dynamism of black citizens: "Too much cannot be said of the desire to learn among this people. Everywhere, to open a school has been to have it filled. Everywhere, a reciprocity of interest dictates facilities for education, and private and plantation schools are supplementing, and perhaps exceed, the more conspicuous efforts."[43]

The addition of the word "reciprocity" in the rhetoric of the Freedmen's Bureau is most revealing. It was absent from the language of missionaries and other Northern reformers who, before 1866, emphasized the importing of Enlightenment ideas into the former Confederacy, and their passive reception among suffering Southerners. Working on the ground to build schools, hire teachers, and enroll students, Alvord and others realized that they had to build on what the former slaves were already doing. The "Negro schools" were desperately short of resources, but they were functioning institutions, reaching a large number of former slaves. They trained blacks in basic skills and good citizenship. Most of all, they encouraged orderly behavior, self-improvement, and loyalty to the newly united American state. The black institutions were grassroots schools for the nation. The Freedmen's Bureau redefined its mission in 1866 to build on this foundation.

African American schools opened throughout the South following the Civil War. The Freedmen's Bureau helped to build many of these schools. *Hill School, Christianburg Institute, (CI003), Digital Library and Archives, University Libraries, Virginia Polytechnic Institute and State University*

Alvord and his assistants abandoned consistent school reform for a series of pragmatic case-by-case efforts. Effective nation-building always proceeds in this way, from simplistic doctrine to creative adaptation. Throughout the South, the Freedmen's Bureau invested in buildings, in teachers, and in mechanisms for getting more boys and girls into schools. The bureau emphasized access, inclusiveness, and local control. It drew on local organizers, many of whom were former slaves. It mobilized teachers from both local communities and the Northern aid societies. Most of all, the bureau left the details about hours of operation, teaching methodology, and curriculum to the community. Howard and Alvord did not create national or regional standards, and their regulations were minimal in content. In its best moments, the Freedmen's Bureau simply supported local education for all citizens, financed by a varying combination of community groups, states, and the federal government.[44]

This approach created a diverse mosaic of educational institutions. The schools did not make citizens for a new nation through common lessons. They taught many different things. Some institutions, like Booker T. Washington's famous Tuskegee Institute, provided vocational training for skilled work, practical science, and self-help. Other learning establishments, including the black colleges built throughout the South, offered a classical education that included European-influenced study in philosophy, history, and letters. Tuskegee empowered an African American working class; black colleges nurtured a new intellectual class, what W. E. B. Du Bois would later call the "talented tenth."[45]

Most schools did something in between. They trained students with widely varying (and unequal) life expectations, but they were all now American citizens. Freed slaves, poor whites, recent immigrants, and others had claims for belonging, participation, and respect that carried unprecedented political weight, despite continuing efforts to deny their realization. As one sympathetic observer noted, "the crying evil" was no longer the existence of separate laws, but instead the "non-execution" of national law created through constitutional amendments, congressional legislation, the Freedmen's Bureau, and courageous local acts after 1865. The problem centered on making the improved laws a source of better lives. That was difficult enough, but it was better than beginning from bad laws, as was the case before the Civil War.[46]

The schools opened by former slaves and supported by the Freedmen's Bureau constructed a new nation through mass education—an unthinkable proposition in the South less than a decade earlier. Former slaves articulated a public claim on education that the bureau affirmed as a necessary component of citizenship. An individual could be free and remain poor and property-less—as was true for many blacks and whites across the country—but one could no longer be free without access to some education, even at the public expense. Although many poor blacks and whites, a majority in some regions, remained uneducated for at least another half century, the Freedmen's Bureau promoted a nationwide presumption that all citizens should be trained for literacy, labor, and loyalty to the larger nation. Schools made a sovereign people of fragmented slaves, peasants, and immigrants. A sovereign people affirmed their unity in the schools.

Multiracial Americans

Madison and Hamilton's Constitution had created a single American people by designing the fiction of a United States that did not yet exist. Building on this experience in nation-building, the Freedmen's Bureau created a single multiracial American people by designing the fiction of a common education for citizenship that was not possible at the time. This dynamic for both periods of nation-building also worked in reverse. The existence of an eighteenth-century American people—affirmed in the Constitution and national elections—provided a legitimate wellspring for a United States government. Similarly, the existence of a post–Civil War American people—affirmed in mass education—provided a legitimate wellspring for a new national government with powers far greater than any of its predecessors.

Southern Reconstruction After the Civil War, 1870

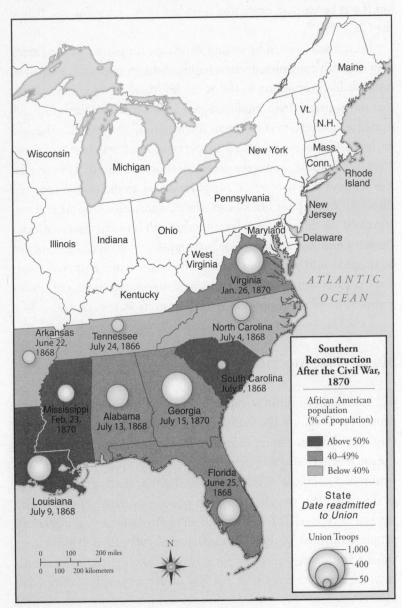

The federal government after the Civil War would not always deploy its expanded power. It frequently failed to enforce its own laws. That said, the federal government would never turn away from the claims of united representation and nationwide influence affirmed in the years after the first shots on Fort Sumter. By educating freedmen, the United States asserted a muscular sovereignty that made Lincoln's Union much more than the sum of its parts.

After the dissolution of the Freedmen's Bureau in 1872, racist Southern leaders began to reverse many of the African American gains of the postwar years. Public education in the former Confederacy, however, never returned to its antebellum emptiness. Freed slaves and poor whites had more access to education, mobility, and citizenship after the Civil War than before. That was an inadequate but still real accomplishment for the Freedmen's Bureau and American nation-building. That was also a source of hope for citizens looking to extend Lincoln's and Douglass's vision of "law and liberty" across the continent and beyond in the later decades of the nineteenth century. The Freedmen's Bureau set a precedent for similar efforts as far away as the Philippines.

Chapter 3

Reconstruction After Empire

Take up the White Man's burden—
Ye dare not stoop to less—
Nor call too loud on Freedom
To cloke your weariness;
By all ye cry or whisper,
By all ye leave or do,
The silent, sullen peoples
Shall weigh your gods and you.

Rudyard Kipling, February 1899[1]

The great agency to bring industrial activity and awakened enterprise
and prosperity and contentment to the country of the Philippines must
be, not a military government, but the same kind of individual enter-
prise which has built up our own country. With increased activity of in-
dividual enterprise and business will come the greater revenues necessary
for the performance of the proper duties of civil government, for harbor
improvements and paved and sewered streets and passable highways and
adequate schools and effective police.

Elihu Root, 24 January 1901[2]

In the last year of the nineteenth century the United States quickly became a major nation-builder in Asia. No one, not even the most aggressive promoters of expansion, had planned for this. No one, not even the most prescient policy-planners, was prepared for the new challenges.

Wrested from Spanish control by American military forces and local revolutionaries, the Philippines included more than seven thousand islands inhabited by more than seven million people, eight thousand miles from Washington, D.C. The United States had no experience exercising political authority in such a setting. Since its founding, and especially through the Civil War, the United States had built an effective continental state with powerful, but still limited, extensions of influence into other parts of the Western Hemisphere. Nineteenth-century American nation-building was continental and hemispheric, not global.

Many Americans wanted things to stay that way. Prominent figures—including congressmen, religious leaders, intellectuals, and businesspeople—opposed what they viewed as a misguided urge for American "imperialism." Asia offered economic promise, but it was unrealized. Asia was alluring in its exoticism, but it was also impenetrable in its cultural and racial complexity. Most of all, Asia was very far away. How could Americans imagine that their ideas about sovereignty, territory, and government would transfer across the vast Pacific Ocean? Even if some of these ideas did travel, how could Americans ever hope to manage their application by sail and steamship, eight thousand miles from home?

During the four decades of American occupation in the Philippines, the United States remained uncertain, unprepared, and deeply divided about its policies. There never was an American consensus on the Philippines. Instead, there was broad agreement about what the United States would *not* do.

Americans would not build a large standing military force to flex their muscles in Asia. The United States Army and Navy remained very small in comparison to their peers and their potential capabilities. Military doctrine continued to emphasize continental defense and harbor fortifications, not preparation for battle far from home. Grading the quality of the troops, the procurement of equipment, and the planning for conflict, American forces in the early twentieth century were "less prepared for war" than in decades past. The poor state of the U.S. military on the eve of the First World War made this evident to everyone, particularly those who remembered the much larger, better-organized, and battle-hardened Union Army of a generation earlier.[3]

Americans would not build a permanent colonial service or any other government institutions designed to rule a foreign people. Washington expanded the nation's diplomatic corps after the Civil War, but in 1900 the United States still lacked a modern bureaucracy for recruiting, training, and supporting effective representatives abroad. With few exceptions, American diplomatic efforts in the early twentieth century were small, shallow, and inward-looking. One scholar has shown that the spoils system of appointing representatives based on political loyalty, not qualification, continued to dominate American diplomacy. The nation's foreign actions were driven more by urban machine politics and rural crowd-pleasing than any serious calibration of strategy.[4]

Most of all, Americans would not replicate the European empires in Asia and other regions. A rising European state like Bismarck's Germany could extol its right to join the club of empires and find its place in the sun, but the United States never made the same claim. Americans of all political stripes instinctively reacted against such a notion and the accompanying image of foreign repression and exploitation. Americans wanted to see themselves as spreading freedom, prosperity, and modern nationhood, not empire.[5]

The most cosmopolitan figures in the United States thought in global terms, and they often called for more activism overseas. Their internationalism, however, was built around the experience and advocacy of cross-border cooperation, culture, and civilization— all concepts they defined against empire. From Jane Addams and W. E. B. Du Bois to John Dewey and Walter Lippmann, the keenest early-twentieth-century American interpreters of the world were self-consciously anti-imperialist. They wanted to serve American interests by changing the world and destroying the traditional forms of European rule. The American progressives commanded a broad and enduring following because so many of their fellow citizens agreed.[6]

There were, of course, contrary impulses among some advocates of American growth. Figures like Alfred Thayer Mahan, Henry Cabot Lodge, and especially Theodore Roosevelt frequently beat their chests about the manly virtues of American expansion in heathen corners of the globe. Businesspeople eager to sell their wares in China and other foreign markets sought points of entry into distant societies. "Scientific" promoters of social Darwinism and eugenics proclaimed that "backward" peoples needed new forms of external rule. Late-nineteenth-century American society surely had its share of militarism, greed, and racism. Thirty years after the Civil War, amidst a disorienting boom-and-bust economic cycle that accompanied the dominance of Lincoln's free labor capitalism across the continent, tensions over the uses of state power and the definitions of political purpose rumbled throughout the country. The dawning skies of the twentieth century looked ominous to many contemporary observers.[7]

Violent impulses existed in American society, but they frightened as many people as they inspired. Although popular figures like Theodore Roosevelt could advocate for a stronger, wealthier, "purer" America, these belligerent ideas would never win broad acclaim for empire. That was a step too far. Empire ran against the nation's self-image as a society that had broken free from dictatorship and aristocracy. Advocates of empire contradicted the faith citizens held that the American vision of nation and state was a viable, even godly, alternative to the repressive European politics of the past.

That was how Americans understood their own history. Facing a world of war, oppression, and poverty beyond their borders, the dominant American instinct was not to play the game of realpolitik like everyone else. Writers and policymakers offered the model of the United States as a way out—a proven system at home that could work abroad. The American nation-building creed hardened as citizens confronted impulses that both challenged its faith and increased its necessity.[8]

The American Nation-Building Burden

Rudyard Kipling's infamous poem about the "White Man's Burden" was never popular in its own time. Published in *McClure's Magazine* in February 1899, the poet's words were immediately controversial. They were also difficult to comprehend. Despite the apparent bravado in the title, Kipling's message was ironic, perhaps even tragic. The Indian-born British writer spoke contemptuously of the "sullen peoples"—"Half-devil and half child"—living in Asia and Africa. He immediately turned to the folly of European efforts to master distant lands:

> *The savage wars of peace—*
> *Fill full the mouth of Famine*
> *And bid the sickness cease;*
> *And when your goal is nearest*
> *The end for others sought,*
> *Watch sloth and heathen Folly*
> *Bring all your hopes to nought.*

Those who fought for "rule of kings" were quickly lost, Kipling exclaimed, near "The ports ye shall not enter" and "The roads ye shall not tread." For all the efforts at exporting "Freedom," the poet warned, "the silent, sullen peoples" would determine the proud Europeans' fate. "Go mark them with your living," Kipling warned, "And mark them with your dead."[9]

When read in the United States, these words were hardly a welcome introduction to empire. Quite the contrary, Kipling captured the hesitance, the anxiety, and the rueful discontent that accompanied debates about expansion at the end of the nineteenth century. Like the British poet, Americans were not deluded about the difficulties of applying their ideals in distant lands. If anything, Kipling reminded them of the costs, the sacrifices, and the probable failure. Although he glorified the urge to uplift "dark" societies, Kipling did not extol empire. As his biographers agree, Kipling's firsthand experience in India, and his ambivalent views of late Victorian England, informed his belief that foreign occupations were a terrible burden for the white man—probably not worth the death and destruction. Kipling's later writings, particularly his masterpiece novel, *Kim*, reinforced this sense of tragedy and loss—as well as personal uncertainty—in the exciting adventure of empire.[10]

By 1899 Americans came to believe they had no other choice. Expansion was an unavoidable ordeal in the face of worse alternatives. It was a burden and a challenge, not an easy opportunity. That was Kipling's real message to his readers, and it matched with recent experiences in the decades after the Civil War. The global reach of the United States had grown, but so had the accompanying difficulties and frustrations.

Limited American efforts at penetrating Japan, Korea, and China had elicited stiff foreign resistance, debilitating disorganization, and widespread disillusion. None of these adventures produced great profits or lasting glory for Americans. In 1853 and 1854 Commodore Matthew Perry's squadron of "black ships" forced the isolated Japanese islands to negotiate a treaty of "friendship and commerce" with the United States, but trade between the two countries remained negligible and the Japanese underwent a rapid internal modernization—the Meiji Restoration—that soon undermined American ambitions in the region. In Korea, Americans were even less successful. During 1866 and 1871 the subjects of the "Hermit Kingdom" rebuffed U.S. warships attempting to penetrate the peninsula. American diplomats did not suffer the same violent exclusion from Chinese society, but their influence remained constrained due to the competition of more established foreign powers, the resistance of imperial Chinese officials, and the general chaos of the vast, declining Middle Kingdom. The American record in Asia confirmed the pessimism of Kipling's purple prose.[11]

Under these circumstances, why didn't the United States abandon adventures in the Pacific? Why not use opposition to empire as a firm indictment of intervention in the region? Why not simply stick to the Western Hemisphere and limited trade relations with countries farther afield?[12]

These propositions made sense in light of America's hemispheric history, but they did not match the very real challenges of the late nineteenth century. For a large industrializing American economy that needed resources and markets, trade with Asia was vital. It did not amount to much at the time, but it was the future. Asia, especially China, had the potential consumers of American products— millions of them. In an age of steamships, Asia was not very far from the Pacific coast of the United States. Access to the region promised economic gain, and it also offered a measure of security against what military planners recognized as the growing vulnerability of the Western Hemisphere to foreign incursions. The rapidly expanding navies of Germany and Great Britain had already begun to increase their presence in Mexico, the Caribbean, and parts of South America. They did the same, with even more show of force, around the Philippines.[13]

During the last decade of the nineteenth century, American leaders had forestalled action, repeatedly rejecting foreign and domestic pleas for more muscular policies around Cuba, China, and other areas. President Grover Cleveland, in particular, turned down numerous proposals to send U.S. forces into troubled places beyond American borders. He and other American policymakers relied on the declining Spanish Empire to act as a buffer between the ambitions of the European and Japanese expansionists, and the more uncertain American reactions. The United States could wait to act because Madrid held off the other empires. For at least a few years, Spain contained nationalist revolutionaries in Cuba, the Philippines, and other territories.

Where Spain could not play this buffering role, the United States tried to stitch together international coalitions that would protect order and access, without creating new imperial possessions and conflicts. This was the genesis of Secretary of State John Hay's famous—and often misunderstood—"Open Door Notes" on China. Abraham Lincoln's former personal secretary had learned the virtues of strategic creativity from his old boss, a master of political maneuver. Under Hay's guidance, the United States endeavored to create an alternative to war, intervention, and empire in China that would still protect trade and investment. The Open Door emphasized territorial integrity and foreign access, just as it forbade the division of land, people, and resources among aggressive imperialists in Tokyo, Berlin, London, and Paris. The Open Door was a temporary buffer against the dominant trends of subjugation and warfare. It was a substitute on the Chinese mainland for surrogate Spanish authority in Cuba and the Philippines.[14]

By 1898 Spain no longer had the resources, legitimacy, or will to play its buffering role. Emboldened revolutionaries in Cuba, the Philippines, and other parts of the decaying empire openly revolted. Madrid's efforts to crack down were ineffective and they contributed to growing violence and disruption—all of which threatened American economic interests and encouraged foreign intervention from Germany, Japan, and Great Britain. By the end of the nineteenth century the Caribbean and Southeast Asia had become geopolitical cockpits of great power conflict.

Following a long and tortuous debate, on 25 April 1898 the United States declared war against Spain. Rather than an enthusiastic endorsement of militarism, the declaration was an act of frustration, fear, and frantic thinking. President William McKinley and his closest advisors had watched Spain's slow spiral for many years.

They recognized that the empire had entered a period of irreparable crisis that would only get worse with time. It was no longer an effective buffer against less attractive alternatives. American policymakers understood that the likely chaos of crumbling Spanish authority would inspire increased regional violence, reduced American access, and redoubled aggression from other powers. The geopolitical consequences of Spanish decline motivated American action.[15]

McKinley acted without a detailed plan. He sought to seize the initiative and forestall a likely escalation of violence that could trigger broader regional wars. The president wanted to redesign the strategic configuration of Asia and the Caribbean, to reverse existing trends. Like his predecessors at the founding and Reconstruction, he relied instinctively on an inherited set of American assumptions encapsulated by the belief that the United States could replace Spain's hemorrhaging authority with a new order of nation-states. What had worked on the North American continent after the removal of British and Confederate power would now apply in Cuba, Puerto Rico, Hawaii, and, most of all, the Philippines. American nation-building would bring peace, prosperity, and independence where Spanish rule and alternative empires promised more war, starvation, and repression. McKinley's inclination was to do abroad what Americans had done at home: create sovereign peoples, defined within specific territories, and governed by representative institutions favorably inclined to cooperate with the United States.[16]

This was the vision that McKinley shared with John Hay, Theodore Roosevelt, and many others. It was a powerful faith, reluctantly extended to foreign sites of crisis, rather than a careful architecture for rule and reform. It was an image for a new kind of foreign authority, navigating as Americans always do between opposition to empire and fear of chaos. In between these two extremes, Americans would build nation-states. The difficulty came in making these instincts a reality in 1899, after the United States gained possession of the Philippines, as well as Cuba and Puerto Rico.

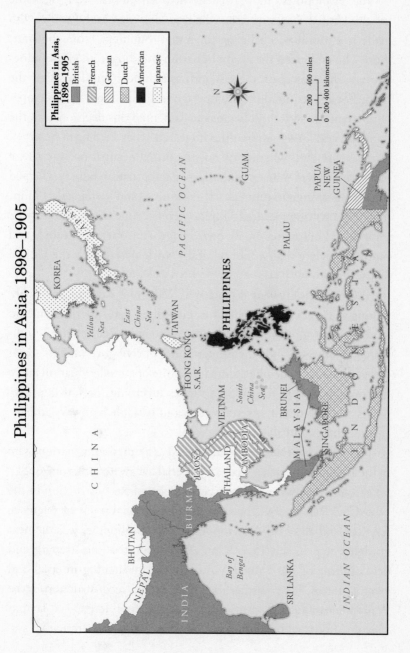

Philippines in Asia, 1898–1905

The Philippines, in particular, held enormous strategic value for the United States in Asia. The size, diversity, and distance also made it a profound challenge for nation-building. From the start, those who embraced the vision of nation-building in the Philippines also saw the project on these islands as a difficult burden. After the United States acquired the archipelago from Spain on 10 December 1898, many American policymakers lamented this decision, and the domestic and foreign difficulties it created. They held firm, however, to the belief that, whether or not the initial occupation was a wise move, the United States could improve the situation only if it helped to create a sovereign, unified, self-governing, and sustainable Philippine state, serving a united Filipino people. America would nurture a modern Philippines in its own image—an open, educated, and capitalist society that would naturally work closely with the United States.

This is precisely what Secretary of War Elihu Root meant when, writing to President McKinley, he emphasized that American aid and guidance must prepare the Philippines for "industrial activity," "individual enterprise," and "the proper duties of civil government." Root was very specific when he painted a picture of a modern nation and a functioning state in the Filipino future, including "harbor improvements and paved and sewered streets and passable highways and adequate schools and effective police."[17]

Building what Root vividly described as a functioning nation-state in the Philippines, rather than an imperial backwater or a zone of disunity and chaos, was a self-conscious repeat of Reconstruction in the post–Civil War South. That was the generational point of reference for Root and all of his contemporaries. The Philippines was the next grudging step in this Lincolnian effort to protect the strength and development of the United States against threatening internal and external forces. Like Southern Reconstruction, reconstruction in the Philippines was about ensuring mutual peaceful interests—at least as Lincoln, Root, and others perceived them—against alternative systems of repression, conflict, and degradation. This was the unavoidable "White Man's Burden" that Kipling described to Americans in 1899. It included all the tragedy, loss, and personal uncertainty that the poet expressed.

Americans were swimming against violent currents. Searching for an alternative to the dangerous shores of empire and chaos, they wished to return to their initial harbor, but they had gone so far to sea that they could no longer turn back. They had to swim with diligence and determination, searching for a new route to a viable nation-state amidst the dispersed Philippine lands.

From Circuit Judge to Civil Governor

William Howard Taft, the president of William McKinley's Philippine Commission and then the first civilian governor of the islands, captured the American sense of unwanted obligation in January 1900. President McKinley asked a very reluctant Taft to lead American efforts in the Philippines, as Oliver Otis Howard had led Union efforts in the post–Civil War South. Like Howard, Taft reflected simultaneously on the terrible burden and the political necessity for American leadership:

> I told him [President McKinley] I was very much opposed to taking them [the Philippines], that I did not favor expansion but that now that we were there we were under the most sacred duty to give them a good form of government . . . that I deprecated our taking the Philippines because of the assumption of a burden by us contrary to our traditions and at a time when we had quite enough to do at home; but being there, we must exert ourselves to construct a government which should be adapted to the needs of the people so that they might be developed into a self-governing people.[18]

Taft was not an expert on Asia, economics, or foreign policy. He showed very little interest in these subjects before 1900. Taft was a prominent legal mind, widely respected for his knowledge of the law and his astute judgment of its application to various local and national issues. Trained at Yale and the University of Cincinnati, a former United States solicitor general, and a federal circuit court judge in Ohio, Taft dreamed of serving on the Supreme Court, not in the faraway islands of a former Spanish colony. Taft's reluctance to take on the latter task was sincere; he was no swashbuckling imperialist of the late-nineteenth-century British or German variety. Just one look at his wizened professorial face and his enormous rotund body made the point!

President McKinley dispatched Taft to the Philippines with his unorthodox attributes in mind. The president could have sent a variety of full-throated, muscular advocates of American force, but he chose a sedentary expert on national law instead. Following two years of intensive military activities in the Philippines, and the rise of two prominent American military figures in the islands—Generals Elwell Otis and Arthur MacArthur—McKinley wanted to convert warfare to nation-building. He wanted not only to manage the continuing conflict with local insurgents; the president wished to begin the process of what he sincerely, and condescendingly, called "benevolent assimilation": "substituting the mild sway of justice and right for arbitrary rule." He called for "temperate administration of affairs for the greatest good of the governed" and "the strong arm of authority"—initially military, but soon civilian—"to repress disturbance and to overcome all obstacles to the bestowal of the blessings of good and stable government upon the people of the Philippine Islands under the free flag of the United States."[19]

Since McKinley first wrote these words on 21 December 1898, observers have criticized him for his offensive assumption that the "little brown" boys and girls of the Philippines should shed their "backward" ways and become more like the strong and intelligent citizens of the United States. The president and many other Americans did indeed subscribe to some of the common assumptions about racial inferiority among foreign peoples at the time. What made the phrase "benevolent assimilation" particularly noteworthy was the additional meaning that McKinley attached—the belief that public education, improved health, and good governance could make the Filipinos into a modern people with their own modern state. That was the purpose of American "benevolence" in the islands, as it had been in the post–Civil War South.[20]

After destroying the old and degenerate sources of political misrule, in McKinley's view, the United States would help build effective governing structures to serve the interests of all. Washington's representatives endeavored to "assimilate" different cultures and traditions into a common society of states. The government of the Philippines would look more like that of the United States, and the residents of the islands would continue to work with Americans, but they would not remain subordinated or repressed by a foreign ruler. The former Spanish colony would become a sovereign, self-governing society—a nation-state allied with the United States. This was an aspiration for racial uplift, on the model of the Freedman's Bureau. It was also a project for law and governance, precisely what Taft brought to the region.

The circuit court judge arrived in Manila on 3 June 1900 to direct the most detailed civilian review of social circumstances and the political future in the Philippines. Working with other members of McKinley's appointed Philippine Commission—Luke Wright and Henry Ide (both lawyers), Dean Worcester and Bernard Moses (both scholars)—Taft set out to devise a replacement for American military rule on the islands. He wrote to Secretary of War Elihu Root that the "cruel methods" of the U.S. Army helped the insurgents gain recruits. American civilian leaders in the Philippines had to make a concerted effort, in Taft's words, "to cultivate the good will of the people and to convince them of the purposes of the United States to give them a good government."[21]

The capital city of Manila was the focus of American
nation-building efforts in the Philippines.
*1905 Photograph by Harry Fowler Woods, Copyright 2006
by H. F. Woods Camp Trustees, Reproduced by Permission*

General Arthur MacArthur, the U.S. military governor in the
Philippines, led counterinsurgency efforts against nationalist groups
and ruled the country as a virtual dictator. He immediately recognized the Philippine Commission and Taft as challenges to his authority. The rapid rise of civilian control, despite continuing warfare,
was a testament to American efforts at progressive political and social
reform, rather than MacArthur's divide-and-conquer policies. Filipino rebels continued to challenge American authority in the islands,
and the U.S. Army increased its use of force—including instances of
torture—against the insurgents. Taft's arrival, however, built on the
general stability that military operations had created by the middle
of 1901, and the emerging belief that peace would endure only in
a context of consensual civilian authority. Practitioners of judicious

political bargaining, especially Taft, supplanted the more aggressive behavior of the military. To reinforce this transition, on 4 July 1901 Secretary of War Root relieved General MacArthur of his duties.[22]

The Philippine Commission assumed legislative authority in the islands. This meant control over the writing of laws, the design of new institutions, and, most important, the collection and disbursement of money. Appointed by President McKinley as the first American civilian governor of the Philippines, Taft became the supreme political figure in the former Spanish colony, designated to represent American interests, nurture Philippine nationhood, and construct a workable government. Taft was to be more than an ambassador or a viceroy; he was to be a pillar of civil society for a people and a territory emerging as a modern nation-state.

Taft worked to bridge historical precedent with contemporary circumstance. Like any skilled judge, now operating on a broader canvas, he applied and adjusted accumulated wisdom in government to new challenges. Although Taft's deployment to the Philippines represented a major career shift, his core competencies remained crucial to his activities. Civilian nation-building was strikingly similar to judicial adjudication. In many cases, they were one and the same.

Integrative Knowledge

Taft immediately brought a change of tone to the Philippines. Instead of isolating the population and intimidating potential enemies, the former judge reached out to Filipino civilians. He continued to view the natives as "ignorant, superstitious people" in general, but he also recognized: "One of the things we have to do here is to extend hospitality to Filipino families of wealth and position." Taft criticized "army circles" that "definitely and distinctly decline to have anything to do with them." McKinley's civilian representative called for a "different course" whose "political effect will be very considerable."[23]

Taft was optimistic about the prospects for his civilian administration of the Philippines. He reported: "The situation politically and from a military stand point is distinctly better than I had been led to suppose. The insurgent army is entirely dispersed and now there are nothing but small bands." Taft aimed to keep the pressure on the remaining insurgents, while winning over the plurality of the population. He pledged to "pass laws with a view to an improvement in the civil conditions here. Much has been left undone in this matter which the military governors have not been willing to undertake."[24]

The American civilian leader began his work by engaging numerous Filipinos in official dinners and meetings at his residence. This was a marked contrast from General MacArthur's tendency to isolate himself, and his commanders, from the population. Taft also participated in a series of what politicians would later call "listening sessions," where he heard appeals and grievances from diverse figures, including local religious leaders, businesspeople, and even opponents of American-sponsored governance. Most impressive, Taft traveled widely around the islands and to the interior of Luzon. He attended different ethnic ceremonies, participated in various religious rituals, met with regional chiefs, and paid his respects to various communities. His biographer recounts that he attended "elaborate banquets" throughout the islands, displaying his eating prowess, and he also danced in local festivals, as best as his bulking physique allowed.[25]

One of the leading Filipino historians of the period agrees that Taft gained local popularity from his "ability to listen to and deal with the Filipinos on equal footing. He seldom imposed his will on them and [he] made himself available to those who wanted to talk to him." "From the time he arrived in June 1900," Rene Escalante explains, "he continuously held public consultations every time he was confronted with a delicate issue. . . . During the hearings, he was tolerant, democratic, and gracious and his guests appreciated this." The former judge was a very effective public diplomat. That was crucial to what Escalante identifies as his "success."[26]

As the first American civilian governor of the Philippines,
William Howard Taft traveled widely and worked to build
productive relationships with local elites.
*1905 Photograph by Harry Fowler Woods, Copyright 2006 by
H. F. Woods Camp Trustees, Reproduced by Permission*

One should not exaggerate Taft's ability to bond with Filipinos.
For all his efforts to interact with the population, he remained a distant figure with very limited knowledge of the islands and their peoples. Taft did not speak Spanish, although he did try to learn, and he could not converse in Tagalog or other regional tongues. He traveled wide and far in difficult terrain, but he only scratched the surface of the vast archipelago. Most of all, Taft did not have the background, experience, or instincts to understand the complex and distant society he now governed. He had a deep familiarity with American law, but his judgments in the Philippines had to rest on a hurried understanding of his subject matter.[27]

Despite these serious limitations, Taft had one advantage over both his military counterparts and the local figures who frequently underestimated him. His years as a judge had taught him to assess personal character, weigh contradictory arguments, and build authority through processes that encourage consensus, even as their results do not please everyone. Taft had made his career through persuasion and compromise with antagonistic groups, not force or moral self-righteousness. Like all good practitioners of law, he understood that justice is imperfect and ever-evolving, not static or formulaic. Taft worked to elicit consent from influential figures in the Philippines, rather than craft perfect policies. The process of forming civilian consensus was the stuff of nation-building for the judge, near his bench in Cincinnati and far from his home in a strange land.

Taft's local knowledge was deficient, but his basic political skills were sharp. Scholars and area experts have a natural bias to value regional immersion in language, culture, and history above all else. To understand a time and a place, we are told, one must learn to speak and think like the natives, or one must come as close as possible. Although empathy and identification are certainly important, they can also debilitate judgment. How does one weigh different claims when one is invested in a particular perspective? How does one build compromises between local and nonlocal interests when one is clearly attached to the former above all? Most important, how does one maintain a critical distance when one's sympathies, identification, and even advocacy for the local become so strong?

Nation-building is a constant and tortured struggle to arbitrate between the local and the global, to balance competing claims, interests, and cultures. It requires integration more than immersion, accommodation more than advocacy. Despite the urge to fragment identity and knowledge into the infinite particularities of the human experience, nation-building requires a skill to construct unities and common attachments. Constitutions, laws, and procedures for civil government are sources of unity and attachment. These pillars of order are made from human habits, traditions, and relationships nurtured over time. Nation-building, in this sense, is about constructing civil society.[28]

Civil society, of course, is what courts are all about. That is precisely how Taft saw his task in bringing law, good government, and nationhood to the Philippines. This was a messy process of evolving justice, not rule by imperial imposition. The islands would have their own laws built *between* Filipino and American sensibilities. Taft's power came from his ability to operate at the intersection between multiple worlds. Connections among peoples were more important than immersion in any single group. As in the United States, nation-building in the Philippines was about integrative knowledge more than local expertise.

New political and social orders are not made by experts, technocrats, or advocates. These figures are crucial sources of inspiration, pressure, and even some guidance for change. The real work of building sustainable lifestyles is dependent on the creative synthesis, public persuasion, and courageous adjustment that experts, technocrats, and advocates generally disdain. Adjustment, in particular, often appears to advocates as "selling out." Taft was not a sellout, nor was he an expert. He was that rare but necessary political animal who could bring divergent ideas and peoples together in a new institutional framework.

This integrative process sacrificed perfection for pragmatism. It served many but pleased very few. Most of all, it created a workable but imperfect system of governance for the Philippines after 1900. If Jacob Burckhardt famously identified the state as a "work of art," Taft's Philippine state was much more of a multicolored collage than a focused portrait. Its strength and its dynamism came from the uncertain integration of various elements.[29]

Taft put it very well in his 4 July 1901 inaugural address as civilian governor: "Government is a practical, not a theoretical, problem and the successful application of a new system to a people like this must be brought about by observing closely the operation of simple laws and making changes or additions as experience shows their necessity." Integrative knowledge provided a basis for implementing political reforms, assessing effects on both local and foreign interests, and then adjusting policies. This was an unending process of change, learning, and adaptation for Americans and Filipinos working together.[30]

Hearts and Minds

Taft worked to integrate people, interests, and institutions across the Philippines. He understood that the capital city of Manila—also the sight of vicious fighting between American and Filipino forces—was the crucial place to start. In this dense and troubled urban context, Taft applied the lessons of urban boss politics from his native Cincinnati and other early-twentieth-century cities in the United States. Power came from deals negotiated with influential ethnic, religious, labor, and business interests. To rule, in this sense, meant to build relationships that would nurture mutual dependence, common benefits, and, most of all, support for a central political authority. Ideology meant far less than the effective distribution of goods and respect to local power centers. Lofty goals had less value than a process that made everyone believe they were better off. Urban politics was judicious bargaining. It was what Taft had learned as a judge and what he practiced as the highest-ranking American civilian in the Philippines. He quickly made himself the Boss Tweed of Manila.[31]

That was Taft's strategy for winning "hearts and minds" in the islands. He would cultivate, and if necessary buy off, various elite figures. He would choose the individuals, and invest in the institutions, that could then sell cooperation with the United States to larger groups of Filipino citizens. He would mix lucrative incentives with threats of damaging reprisals. He would build a new state around the personal Filipino networks that he constructed. These networks centered on extended families, rooted in regions and professions around the archipelago.[32]

A common identity for the Philippines would also emerge from the experience of negotiation, cooperation, and collaboration. The American civilian government, like the government of many big U.S. cities at the time, would forge a Filipino nationality through the web of relationships that it stitched together. The new nation-state for the Philippines would not emerge immediately, but it would grow—like the

United States itself—from the seeds planted and cultivated by energetic and strategic leaders. Nation-building, in this context, was a process of intensive education, as it had been in the post–Civil War South.

Taft reported to Washington that Filipinos were not, in his judgment, ready to manage a central government in 1900. They had to become stakeholders in one sponsored by the United States. This meant broader and more purposeful participation by Filipinos in new political institutions. Taft's report for the Philippine Commission began with this point. He lamented the favoritism, corruption, and incompetence that characterized municipal government under the Spanish. He also noted the temptations to corruption among Americans who had recently arrived on the islands. "To avoid the dangers presented by these conditions," Taft argued, "it is necessary, first, to banish all favoritism and political considerations from the selection of civil servants and rigidly to enforce the requirements of a competitive examination and a satisfactory showing by the applicant of his good moral character." Taft also argued for "adequate salaries," "liberal leaves of absence," and, perhaps most important, efforts "to awaken an enthusiasm in the service by offering as a reward for faithful and highly efficient work a reasonable prospect of promotion to the highest positions in the Government." Civil service was to become merit-based public work, promising social utility and personal mobility.[33]

The new civil service would constitute a new government, built around nonmilitary cooperation between diverse Filipinos and Americans. The Civil Service Act of the Philippine Commission, signed by Taft on 19 September 1900, gave preference to the hiring of qualified Filipinos over foreigners, and it established a board of overseers that would include Filipinos. The board, in particular, would ensure the effectiveness of the new governing body, and it would help to recruit and train citizens for cooperative work throughout the islands. The civil service would be the backbone of a Filipino state, and it would be the school of the nation, nurturing common bonds across society.

Under American direction, the civil service would do for the Philippines what the Freedmen's Bureau did for the American South, turning informal political institutions and social groups into a single state and nation.[34]

Two Filipino figures, brought on to the Philippine Commission by Taft in September 1901—Trinidad H. Pardo de Tavera and Benito Legarda—helped to further the effectiveness of the new civilian government in the islands. Both were elites ("ilustrado") who were wealthy, well educated, and well connected to Filipino, Spanish, and now American society. Both also had strong domestic credentials from their participation in the nationalist government of Emilio Aguinaldo before American occupation. Pardo de Tavera and Legarda were collaborators who benefited enormously from their flexible proximity to power. They also served as crucial glues for nation-state formation in the Philippines through partnership with the United States. They legitimized the civilian government formed by Taft, they brought it to the Filipino people, and, most important, they served as a key transmission belt for dialogue and mutual adaptation between Filipinos and Americans. This was not a democratic process—the average Filipino peasant did not have a powerful political voice—but it was a mechanism for the exchange of practical advice on policy, the sharing of knowledge for partnership, and the organization of groups around common aims. The elite-driven civilian government contributed to the formation of a functioning state with a unified population.[35]

As in other nation-states, political order required the formation of a popular party with a broad institutional base to coordinate local actors. The Federal (or *Federalista*) Party of the Philippines, formed in December 1900, played this role under the new civilian government. Pardo de Tavera was particularly influential in the creation of this party, and the publication of a newspaper, *La Democracia,* that supported many of its aims. The newspaper and the party advocated unity, modernization, and eventual sovereignty for the Philippines, with the help of the United States. Pardo de Tavera encouraged the formation of various Filipino political organizations with local competence and legitimacy, connected to a larger Federal Party umbrella.[36]

By May 1901, only five months after its founding, the Federal Party had 296 branches throughout the archipelago, including more than 200,000 members. This was still a far cry from a majority of the population, and the party remained dominated by elites. It was, however, more representative of Filipino opinion and more integrated in local politics than any other institution in the islands at the time. Although later reviled, the Federal Party provided an effective framework for American and Filipino collaboration.[37]

Taft leveraged this collaboration for broader policy purposes, defining the postwar Philippine nation and state. The Federal Party also shaped Taft, the Philippine Commission, and American policy as a whole. This was a process of mutual, although certainly unequal, influence. The Federal Party was representative of local needs and it was attentive to American interests. It was not democratic. The model was much more akin to an urban "machine" that attracted various neighborhood ethnic elites, rather than relying on the mass participation and the institutional checks and balances observers had come to expect from democratic politics.

At its core, the machine system behind the Philippine Commission and the Federal Party worked because it encouraged cooperation among empowered figures, it rewarded competence, and, most of all, it recognized the need for compromise among divergent interests. The machine system was a version of Madisonian pluralism in action—the balancing of diverse factions across a broad landscape, integrated within a federalist framework of overlapping authorities. The Philippine Commission played the role of the early U.S. national government—arbitrating between group differences, rewarding contributions to unity, suppressing threats, and negotiating with local power centers where the capabilities of central authorities were most constrained. This was a process for winning hearts and minds by balancing diverse local needs.

Emerging pluralistic governance was remarkably effective in the Philippines, especially considering the difficulties of the circumstances. Corruption was an obvious problem, and the local elites who informed Taft often served themselves more than their constituents. These flaws fueled a continuing small, but stubborn, insurgency, even after the American capture of the rebel leader, Emilio Aguinaldo, on 23 March 1901. In light of how recently the United States had arrived, how limited American resources were in country, and how strong the opposition to prior Spanish rule had been, the new system functioned with relative efficiency and even some elements of good government.[38]

The chain of political influence within the islands ran from Taft and the Philippine Commission, through the Federal Party, to the various local organizations. This system circulated ideas, capital, and personnel from the center to the periphery and back. Despite the obvious hierarchy, influence flowed in both directions. The different levels worked closely together forming a rich information network—the most sophisticated in its era, according to one scholar. The flow of resources constituted governments, managed economies, supervised development projects, built schools, and, perhaps most important, policed territories. The organized integration of information and resources, not public consensus, was the connective tissue for nation and state. American influence was preeminent, but unlike traditional empires, it was decentralized, distant from Washington's control, and highly dependent on Filipinos. Taft and other U.S. officials were deeply embedded in a Philippine-centered system of power, with very few global or regional manifestations at the time.[39]

Policing on the islands, for example, reflected the dynamics of pluralistic political power, designed to win hearts and minds, and destroy challengers. As always in nation-building, persuasion and force went hand in hand. The United States exerted frequent repressive influence against perceived enemies, but it did not impose a central model of authority. Policing, like politics in the archipelago and in the United States, involved overlapping offices, jurisdictions, and points of negotiation.[40]

The three tiers of Philippine policing matched the interwoven levels of government. The Philippine constabulary, composed of Filipino and American soldiers, patrolled the islands, under the direction of Taft and the Philippine Commission. The Manila Police, designed to secure the capital, also included a hybrid force with oversight from U.S. military authorities, but growing influence from the Filipino elites who came to run the politics and economy of the city. The ubiquitous lightly armed Filipino municipal forces, charged to patrol other cities and the countryside, were far less centrally governed. They answered to local officials, usually the figures who directed regional offices of the Federal Party. Authority in the archipelago was organized around diffuse, overlapping institutions that elicited local participation in broader national aims. Law enforcement was really about negotiating the rule of law for the diversity of Filipino experiences.[41]

The police forces were part of an elaborate nation-building apparatus that merged Filipino and American elites, secured local cooperation, and repressed challenges to a unified Philippines. Like the Federal Party, the police appealed to hearts and minds by a combination of ubiquity, flexibility, and coercion. They were everywhere, but in many different forms and combinations. They stitched the basic tissue of the state by encompassing all citizens in an organized set of authority structures. The police also contributed to a common national identity by making all citizens conscious of a shared set of laws. The police and the Federal Party were powerful schools for defining Filipino sovereignty during the American occupation.[42]

Educating Citizens for State and Nation

Nation-building needs police power, but it succeeds only when it concentrates on classrooms. As the nation-builders patrol the streets, they must also build more schools espousing progressive political change. This is exactly what the United States did in the Philippines. Education was the most enduring element of American influence. As in the post–Civil War South, the United States changed local attitudes by appealing directly to those young citizens with the most hunger for improvement in their lives.[43]

The U.S. Army began educating Filipino citizens in 1900, as it sought to manage a large population with very few public institutions for maintaining social order. On 30 March 1900, General Elwell Otis created the Department of Public Instruction to open new schools, recruit teachers, and acquire necessary books, supplies, and other items. Within a tightly constrained military budget, the general allocated almost $100,000—a very large sum at the time—for the purchase of classroom materials. Despite continued fighting against a Filipino insurgency, Otis gave high priority to education in the Philippines.[44]

The army schools relied on common educational practices from the United States. American soldiers re-created their own classroom experiences. The schools opened their doors to all young citizens, without tuition. Local communities, working with the Federal Party and the Philippine Commission, raised necessary funds from trade tariffs. Army schoolteachers gave their lessons in English, they emphasized basic literacy and numeracy, and they avoided explicit religious instruction. American-led education in the Philippines followed the general model of early-twentieth-century urban communities in the United States.[45]

By instinct, Americans brought public and secular education to a society that had little of either before. From the start, Americans assumed Filipino nationhood required that most members of society learn to read, write, add, think, and work like modern citizens. The United States would rely on elite local figures to manage the new institutions of the state, and it would mobilize young men and women across the islands to participate actively—and cooperatively—in a new economy and society. The Spanish and other imperial powers had never devoted so much effort and idealism to uplifting their occupied peoples.[46]

In May 1900 civilian authorities took control of public education in the Philippines from the U.S. military. Taft appointed Fred Atkinson, the principal of a high school in Springfield, Massachusetts, as the first general superintendent of public instruction. This was the third official act of the Philippine Commission, following appropriations for transportation infrastructure in the islands. Atkinson reported directly to the commission, and he sought to build upon army educational efforts, creating a Philippine-wide system of schooling. He emphasized primary education, aiming to establish universal access and "obligatory" attendance "for all children between ages of 6 to 12 years." Atkinson's goals matched those of urban reformers throughout the United States confronted with widespread juvenile truancy and pressures to train a skilled workforce for industrial jobs.[47]

On 21 January 1901 the Philippine Commission passed Act 74, written largely by Atkinson. It made civilian-organized education a cornerstone of governance in the islands. The legislation followed a series of commission decisions the prior year that appropriated funds for educational administration and increased teacher salaries. Act 74 created a centralized system of public primary schools for the entire archipelago, and it authorized Atkinson to hire new Filipino teachers as well as one thousand American classroom instructors. Using customs duties and other revenue sources, the Philippine Commission agreed to pay for American teacher salaries, textbooks, and other school supplies. Local municipalities would cover the costs of school buildings, as well as Filipino teacher pay. Atkinson, Taft, and the Philippine Commission made a very strong statement about the importance of public education, and their commitment to funding it generously. Few other parts of the civilian government in the Philippines received as much support. Educational institutions in the United States usually received less.[48]

Act 74 prohibited religious instruction during regular school hours (it could occur only as an "after school" activity). Public education would be secular, it would be practical, and it would prepare young Filipinos for the modern world. The act stipulated: "The English language shall, as soon as practicable, be made the basis of all public school instruction." Imperial powers in other parts of Asia restricted European language instruction to a narrow elite, for the purpose of controlling access to knowledge. The Chinese and Japanese governments traditionally followed similar policies, training only a small literate cadre of loyalists and scholars. The American model for the Philippines was radically different. It was open in its aspiration for universal participation, it was nonsectarian in its rejection of religious dogma, and it was, most important, keyed to citizen mobility through new knowledge acquisition in the language of political power. Americans pursued mass education in the Philippines for an emerging nation-state.[49]

One observer put it well when he explained: "Spaniards wished to involve a minimum of Filipinos in the political process." Through schools and other institutions "Americans aspired to involve as many as possible." English literacy and basic numeracy provided a foundation for a public voice among formerly voiceless peasants. These skills encouraged a widened sphere for political discussion. Most of all, they inspired a sense of belonging among educated Filipinos that allowed for the articulation of a national identity. English became, in this sense, a language of patriotism for modernizing Filipino men and women, seeking to improve their lives and build a prosperous society that would ultimately operate independently of the United States.[50]

Joseph Ralston Hayden, a former vice governor and respected scholar of the Philippines, quotes one Filipino who explained that American instructors "couldn't help teaching us patriotism and love of our own country. They did it with every lesson in American history. When, as a little, barefoot boy, I stood up before the class and recited, 'Give me liberty or give me death,' I wasn't thinking of Virginia and King George. I was thinking of the Philippines and the United States."[51]

The American model of mass education and political participation, when inculcated through public schools, was contagious. It did not alleviate deep problems of poverty, inequality, and injustice. It did, however, encourage efforts to unify people and organize institutions that would serve the population and territory of the Philippines. The same process was evident in other parts of Asia where American teachers traveled at the time. Educating young citizens for political participation served the American vision of nation-building, but it ran against imperial assumptions of controlling and limiting populations. Joseph Ralston Hayden put it very well: "Those who dream of empire regard this course as having been one of the capital errors of American colonial policy. American statesmanship, however, decreed that the Philippine public schools should be dedicated to the building of a Filipino nation."[52]

This radical model was an obvious one for figures, like Atkinson and Taft, who believed in an educated citizenry. They had watched John Alvord and others transform the Confederacy through the educational efforts of the Freedmen's Bureau. The Philippine Commission rejected imperial models of stratified school instruction for a free labor ideology that sought to create independent, active, and knowledgeable citizens of the new nation. In place of the ignorance that encouraged slavery and imperial savagery, according to Atkinson and Taft, universal primary education would nurture hard work and social integrity. Literacy would breed political organization, and numeracy would encourage economic activity. In this context, Booker T. Washington's Tuskegee Institute, and the model of African American "industrial education" that he espoused, inspired the nation-builders in the Philippines. The small Southern schoolhouse, with an eager and recently trained teacher standing before a diverse mix of poor but eager students—that was the aspiring vision for education in Philippine nationhood.[53]

American efforts departed from traditional imperial practice, but they continued to assume superiority for Western institutions, ideas, and habits. Although the United States encouraged active and universal Filipino educational participation, it also assumed that learning would occur largely on American terms. These characteristics of nation-building in the Philippines were evident to observers, and many criticized them at the time. Despite this shortcoming, American-led education in the Philippines created unprecedented opportunities for citizens to learn, to improve their circumstances, and even to seize the future of their society. The promise of mobility through mass education was real, and it was radical for many Filipinos.

Trinidad Pardo de Tavera captured this promise and its attraction for many Filipinos at the time. He spoke of a "redemption" for his countrymen and -women that would be "complete and radical." He advocated English-language instruction as an opportunity to bring the "American spirit" to the islands, allowing its citizens to make a brighter future for themselves. American-sponsored education might have departed from true equality in its prejudices, but it opened substantive opportunities nonetheless. American-sponsored schools offered a ladder to Filipino nationhood.[54]

Teachers as Nation-Builders

The builders of a new educational system were not the politicians. As in the United States, new schools in the Philippines depended on the courageous, tireless, and poorly paid work of young men and women recruited for their idealism more than their professional ambition. Filipino and American teachers who sought to open schoolhouses and enroll local citizens in full-time instruction faced many obstacles. They were short of funds, as always. They were outsiders—even the Filipino teachers—who generally did not understand the local communities where they worked. Most of all, they had very little institutional support. Atkinson, Taft, and the civilian government lacked a large skilled staff, and they were distant from the sites of most new schools, especially those outside Manila.

The young men and women who built the new education system in the Philippines followed the general guidelines derived from their experiences in the United States, but they had to adjust largely on their own. "[C]ommunication and transportation," Atkinson recounted, "were so poor that close connection between the central authorities and those in the field was practically impossible; on account of the lack of good roads the supervising officers were often unable to reach all their schools within the time prescribed; and for a long period the sending of supplies, particularly after the military officials were compelled to withdraw the aid that had become almost indispensable, was a matter attended with most serious delays and losses." "Epidemics, particularly of cholera, and also of other tropical diseases," Atkinson continued, "played havoc with the system; various pests threatening the crops from time to time kept the children away from school." Teaching, in this context, was a hardship, to say the least.[55]

Education reform in the Philippines required patience and perseverance. It was about flexibility and adaptation—making basic principles about citizenship, governance, and social order apply to difficult and diverse circumstances. Opening schools required as much political negotiation as classroom instruction. Teachers arriving in a community had to nurture interpersonal relationships for their work, and their survival too. They had to establish trust and authority on local terms. They also had to devise mechanisms for motivating student attendance. Teachers were foreign political actors working to build new local constituencies, despite vast social and cultural differences. Few were prepared for this arduous task.[56]

Most difficult of all, teachers had to recognize and respect the boundaries of acceptable and unacceptable opinion in their communities. American-style schooling was a radical project in a society that was neither secular nor universalistic in its approach to knowledge. In contrast to imperial educators who largely affirmed and manipulated local authority structures, teachers in the Philippines after 1900 worked to define a more united, standardized, and sovereign system—a system for a nation-state. This was profoundly threatening for traditional elites. The teachers sent by Atkinson and Taft to the islands had to strike a very precarious balance between challenging local authorities and attracting their support for the promise of a better life. Again, the teachers did not possess the military or economic muscle to coerce. They had to persuade key figures and cooperate creatively with skeptical citizens. Education, in this sense, was a microcosm of American efforts in the Philippines as a whole—mutual dependence and constant adjustment for mutual benefit.

Hundreds of young American teachers traveled to the Philippines after 1899. They helped build schools and create the first system of mass education in the islands.
Photograph of several "Thomasites" with (Maj. Gen.) Leonard Wood, Governor General William Taft, and young students from the Cordillera, Philippines, American Historical Collection Foundation, American Association of the Philippines, Inc., Manila

Arthur Griffiths was an example of the more than one thousand American teachers who traveled to the Philippine islands in the cause of nation-building education. He later remembered: "September 1901 unexpectedly found me a Superintendent of Schools with headquarters at Bucay, Province of Abra, North Luzon. I had been sent there directly by the United States Philippine Commission fresh from my graduation from Yale College. William H. Taft, then President of the Commission, was also a Yale man. That is the reason that I, and two others [from Yale], were called to the Philippines. They [Herbert Lucker and Walter Gilliam] died in service."[57]

Like his counterparts from Yale and other American universities, Griffiths was self-conscious about the poor legacy of empires in Asia. He traveled to the Philippines with a deep belief that the United States had to be different. He contrasted what he viewed as the "Spanish purpose to keep the Filipinos in ignorance" with the American aim to share "the uplift and education that has been given me." "For only upon knowledge," Griffiths explained, "is any progress made. The strength of democracy is knowledge and the power of serfdom is ignorance."[58]

Griffiths was attentive to the growth of American economic and strategic interests across the Pacific, but he saw his work as part of a broader progressive mission to serve his own country and others. He pursued a common global "uplift" of peoples to prosperity, nationhood, and good governance—built around friendship and cooperation, not permanent foreign rule. Griffiths left New Haven in 1901 for the Philippines on a most American quest to use his knowledge, energy, and goodwill to create an alternative to empire and chaos. This was not a religious mission or an imperial adventure. It was, for Griffiths and so many other young teachers, a noble experiment inspired by America's own noble experiment. There were few detailed plans or assurances of success, but many inspiring visions of a new society of states, built around a modern Philippines.

Griffiths spent two years in the poor and mountainous interior of

North Luzon—the large northern island of the Philippines. He also traveled extensively in other areas, including the Sulu archipelago. He worked with little military protection, and he relied upon hospitality from local elites. What Griffiths offered in return, he recounted, was a promise of local improvement on terms that matched both American and Filipino interests. He opened small schools that taught English and basic math. He gave lessons in the experience of government within the United States, especially as modeled by "great American men," from Washington to Lincoln. Griffiths condemned slavery and other forms of human bondage, espousing the virtues of a market society with wage labor, industrial production, and large-scale agriculture. This was the Union free labor vision from the Civil War transported to the Philippines.

Griffiths found a receptive audience, with little resistance. As he admits in his memoir, his successes in building schools and attracting students were not because of his special skills as a teacher. In fact, he was pretty mediocre in the classroom from his own description. Griffiths's successes came from his ability to contrast his work with that of previous foreigners, including some of the Filipino insurgents who were equally foreign to the areas where Griffiths worked. In all of his statements and activities, the American teacher emphasized that he sought to help the Filipinos prepare to rule themselves rather than remain under another's dominion. "To my mind," he announced on his arrival in the town of Bucay, "the chief besetting sin of man has been the totally selfish desire to rule others." Griffiths pledged—"as a representative of the principles of our Constitution, of our Washington and of our Lincoln"—to make education a source of local empowerment, not continued repression at the hands of Manila and foreign capitals.[59]

His first school in Bucay followed this model. Griffiths opened it in a small building, formerly used by local teachers. He attracted students from families that wanted their children to learn useful knowledge for social and economic advancement. Griffiths's simple lessons emphasized just that: communication in English, basic arithmetic, and appreciation for good government as representative of the people. The local teachers whom Griffiths hired in Bucay and other towns added specific trades to their curriculum. They worked to connect lessons about great American leaders, like George Washington, with figures students could claim as part of their own past, including the charismatic Filipino poet and novelist José Rizal. The idea was simple: build a version of the New England "little red schoolhouse" for young people in the Philippines. Griffiths believed this was the way to "emancipate" the Far East.[60]

The schools in Bucay and other towns did indeed play an emancipatory role in local society. Unlike the religious and private institutions that dominated education in the past, the public schools admitted everyone, regardless of faith or financial capabilities. They did not seek to convert the heathen or prepare future chosen elites. To the contrary, they gave all children a chance to improve their economic prospects. The public schools also made education more accessible, situating it in local neighborhoods. Griffiths recounts how he and his counterparts re-created the "common schools" of their own childhood, bringing classrooms close to family settings so that students of the most modest means could still attend. After opening two schools in town, Griffiths established "schools in the barrios or small settlements dependent upon and contiguous to Bucay." These areas were "little, jungle-surrounded hamlets that knew nothing of the outside world, and no one of which had ever seen a white man before. I was the object of an immense amount of gentle and not unpleasing curiosity on the part of the jungle folks."[61]

Despite the obvious cultural distance between Griffiths and local residents, he found citizens of interior communities "eager to learn" and "avid" to acquire useful knowledge from his schools. Of course, there were still many moments of suspicion, awkwardness, and misunderstanding. In his memoir, Griffiths warns later observers not to exaggerate social barriers. He comments, perhaps

Early American Occupation of the Philippines

Early American Occupation of the Philippines

Number of United States troops per 1,000 people

12.5   9   3   2

PHILIPPINES

1900 First legislative action by the US commission in the Philippines
Port of Manila, road and bridge construction

Province of Abra

Cagayan

L u z o n

1905 Road building projects
Albay and Laguna, beginning of bridge construction between islands

1898 First public school opened by American authorities
Island of Corregidor

• Manila

1901 Arthur Griffiths,
an American teacher, traveled to Bucay Island.

Mindoro

VISAYAN

Bucay Island

ISLANDS

Panay

Negros

Sulu Sea

N

Mindanao

MALYASIA

Sulu Archipelago

0   50   100 miles

0   50   100 kilometers

to his own astonishment: "How widely and how broadly good will spread."[62]

The local demand for education grew so great that adults in numerous communities requested their own access to the classroom. Despite Atkinson's and Taft's emphasis on primary education, Griffiths opened a series of "night schools," catering to Filipino men and women who wished to learn English, math, and various skills. They often met late in the evening, long after dark. Their studies brought together families that would not normally socialize together. Most of all, the night schools replaced some local forms of nighttime entertainment with more focused self-improvement and productive cooperation. Local neighborhoods became more orderly and forward-looking, and perhaps a little less traditional.[63]

Griffiths believed that he and his fellow teachers were building a modern Filipino nation-state. They brought citizens from various religions, ethnicities, and classes together for learning as a single people. In their classrooms they established a model of secular governance. Most of all, they equipped large numbers of young men and women with some of the skills necessary for mobility in the twentieth century: literacy, numeracy, and basic modes of civic cooperation. The American-sponsored schools in the Philippines created a framework for dialogue across the wide terrain that separated citizens on the islands from one another, and across the even greater social divide that separated Americans from Filipinos. The schools did not supplant tradition or local particularism. They nurtured a broader institutional setting for cooperation.

That was the experience of Arthur Griffiths and many others. The American teachers entered a foreign land with little training and local knowledge. They emerged from their endeavors as skilled relationship-builders. The teachers did not change the Philippines, but they built enduring connections between the residents of the islands and citizens of the United States. These connections catalyzed new forms of unity in the archipelago, new kinds of cooperation with Americans, and new expressions of political identity. Twentieth-century Filipino nationalism emerged in the context of American-sponsored nation-building, just as twentieth-century American internationalism gestated in the context of building schools for the Philippines.

Power, purpose, and people were redefined for both societies. Arthur Griffiths and most of his counterparts returned to the United States with a clearer vision of their country as an international nation-builder, and a deeper appreciation for the difficulties this entailed. Griffiths's students remained in the Philippines, conscious of the value that their modern education offered, but also aware of the need to push this education forward for attaining fuller independence from their American overseers. Schools became a primary site for political contestation in later years.[64]

Relationships between Filipinos and Americans included a mix of alliance and resistance. The creation of the Philippine Assembly in 1907, modeled on the U.S. House of Representatives, provided a forum where both of these perspectives were aired for the next three decades. Within the United States, the American role in the Philippines also drew serious debate, especially among critics of the nation's alleged foreign adventurism during periods of growing domestic needs. Filipino-American relations deepened during the early twentieth century, and they drew ever-greater attention from observers on both sides of the Pacific Ocean.[65]

As elsewhere, nation-building in the Philippines remained controversial. Its benefits were not evenly distributed. Its promises of reform were only partially realized. Most of all, the Filipino demand for national independence—largely encouraged by the United States—met repeated delays as Americans, despite their commitment to this goal, continued to deem the islands and their people unprepared for the burdens of governance. A proliferation of regional threats after the First World War encouraged this American judgment. From 1898 to 1941 the Philippines were, from Washington's vantage point, too valuable to leave to other powers, but too important to keep in a position of subordination. Like Taft, every American policymaker struggled to find the correct balance between security and independence through nation-building.[66]

This difficult balancing act produced the most significant shortcoming of American nation-building in the Philippines: it was a process with a clear aim, but not an agreed measure for when it had been achieved. From William Howard Taft and Arthur Griffiths in 1901, to Franklin Roosevelt and Douglas MacArthur in 1941, Americans felt they were making progress. It was, however, never enough for them to leave, and it was never enough to meet the rising expectations of Filipino citizens.

Legacies

Nation-building in the Philippines was frustratingly incomplete. To call it a success would exaggerate the influence of American actors and the endurance of their innovations. To call it a failure would neglect the powerful relationships, institutions, and forms of common identity implanted with American support. After the early years of the twentieth century the former Spanish colony began to resemble a modern nation-state, on the model of the United States.

The Philippines developed a centralized civilian government, representative institutions, reliable law enforcement bodies, and most of all, a universal public education system. The archipelago had none of these things before. In the context of the American occupation, one could begin to speak sensibly of a shared Filipino nation and a functioning Philippine state. Working from their own precedent at home, American leaders helped to define a recognized Philippine territory, constituted by a united Filipino people, and represented through a legitimate government. The new Philippines constructed in the shadow of Taft and his successors was neither imperial nor chaotic. It was unprecedented and in between.

Americans, including President McKinley, had never intended to become nation-builders in Asia. They were wary of any "White Man's Burden." Quite the contrary, they sought to limit American military commitments and the costs of occupation. They hoped to invest in civilian projects and partnerships that would produce a self-contained, self-governing archipelago—free from the control of other powers, and open to trade and cooperation with the United States. Americans wanted to replace war and empire in Southeast Asia with their vision, drawn from their own history, of a peaceful and prosperous society of states.

The Philippines became the bridge from continental to global nation-building for the United States. In their efforts to spread influence without empire and protect order against chaos, Americans replayed their experiences with Revolution and Reconstruction. This time the process of nation and state formation occurred in a distant terrain, separated by thousands of miles of water, climate, and cultural difference. That distance raised many new challenges for inherited American political assumptions, but it also reinforced their perceived necessity for navigating the unknown.

For all its frustrations, nation-building in the Philippines reaffirmed American beliefs about the deep connection between a people and their territory, and the indispensable role of good, representative government. In their achievements and their shortcomings, men like Taft and Griffiths learned that the United States could contribute to unity, security, and political order in a society they only superficially understood. They could not rule, but they could lead and educate, at least temporarily.

Americans recognized that, even at their best, their impact on the Philippines was limited and controversial. There was little triumphalism after 1902. In a conflict-prone world, observers from William Howard Taft and Theodore Roosevelt to Herbert Hoover and Franklin Roosevelt anticipated that the United States would have to pursue similar nation-building activities again, somewhere else. If the Philippines were a bridge from the post–Civil War decades to the early twentieth century, the islands also opened a route to more intensive reconstruction a generation later in Germany and Japan.

Arthur MacArthur's military career began in the Civil War, and it peaked in the Philippines. Dwight Eisenhower served as a young officer in the Philippines, and he finished the Second World War as a decorated hero of the Allied liberation of Europe, especially Germany. In the twentieth century, Americans found themselves fighting to destroy ever-more-threatening enemies. Their victories meant ever-greater nation-building duties.

Chapter 4

Reconstruction After Fascism

That the present quadripartite administration of Germany has been a failure from the U.S. standpoint is almost universally acknowledged. The machinery has been called upon to perform labors inconsistent with its original purposes. It was always intended, at least by the U.S. and British, that the Allies should direct and control Germany. It was never envisaged that they should govern, and the present system has proved unequal to this unforeseen task.

Robert Murphy, U.S. Political Advisor for Germany, January 1947[1]

Our policy toward Germany has been based on the total illusion that the way to keep Germany from being a threat to the peace is to eliminate its industrial war potential. . . . The major problem is to develop German export industries so that Germany will be able to pay for its food imports and relieve the American and British taxpayers of the burden.

Former President Herbert Hoover, April 1947[2]

In 1947, two years after the great Allied victory against fascism in Europe, it appeared that the United States would, once again, lose the peace. The *New York Times* reported that the average daily food ration in Germany was 1,200 calories—less than half the daily consumption in neighboring Scandinavia, perhaps a third of the daily consumption in the United States. Even the Poles were eating more than the Germans! One traveler observed that the "average German adult has lost from two to ten pounds in the last three months; he now is thirty pounds underweight, and his wife is almost twenty-five pounds below normal weight for her age. Children have not lost weight in recent months because of a school feeding program, but they are nine per cent below the pre-war normal weight scale."[3]

Food shortages were undermining political order in the American and British occupied zones of Germany. They were the "basis of nearly every problem before United States Military Government," according to one observer. General Lucius Clay, the commander of American forces in Germany, agreed. Hunger motivated labor unrest, public disillusion, and communist agitation. Clay referred to Germany as a "bankrupt" society, desperately in need of new direction from without as well as within. Work stoppages and demonstrations in the coal-rich Ruhr Valley only reinforced this anxiety about Germany's political future. Asked by an American journalist about labor resistance, one coal miner explained: "we don't really care. Right now we get more to eat if we mine more, but the coal itself doesn't do us any good. Part of it is exported to Lord knows where, and what should go to our industry doesn't—we're not allowed to produce all the things we need. Where is the stuff to rebuild our homes? Where are the clothes I need for myself and my wife and children?"[4]

Meeting with local German trade union and political figures in the burnt-out cities of Frankfurt, Stuttgart, and Munich, the American political advisor for Germany, Robert Murphy, observed: "Except for the immediate post-combat period in 1945 when Germans were stunned by events, I have not found German morale any lower than it is today." Murphy warned that after the winter of 1946–1947, "the German people physically and psychologically will be unable to stand another winter of hunger and cold under miserable housing conditions in destroyed cities and in economic and political hopelessness." Murphy closed his analysis with an ominous prediction: "It is apparent that German sentiment is increasingly troubled. The shock of the combat period has subsided. Under pressure of economic misery German determination to survive will undoubtedly be manifest in future political action."[5]

The destruction of the Second World War left much of Germany in
ruins. This photo shows some of the damage in Bamberg, Germany.
Tubby Abrahams © Hulton-Deutsch Collection/CORBIS

The phrase "future political action" referred to growing Communist
Party influence, manipulated by the Soviet Union, within trade unions
and other social groupings throughout the American, British, and French
occupied zones of Germany. While the Allies appeared stymied and ineffective, the communists offered a dynamic program. They promised to
redistribute wealth to ordinary citizens. They pledged to remove dangerous militarists and greedy capitalists from German society. Most of all,
the communists created hope for citizens who endured an "inadequate
diet, acute commodity scarcity, crowded housing conditions, and uncertainty" under American occupation. Moscow's allies gained political
momentum from postwar German suffering and disorganization.[6]

Murphy and his colleagues spent much of the spring of 1947 re-
porting to Washington on the growing numbers of Germans who be-

came disillusioned with Allied policies and started to believe, or at least contemplate, communist promises. Feeling that they had lost control of their lives, many citizens who had rejected communism in the past looked anew to its claim that greater worker dominance of the occupied German state would bring economic recovery. Despite Soviet plans to remove resources from Germany, rather than invest in internal development, the failings of American-led relief and reconstruction efforts made Moscow's alternative to market capitalism increasingly attractive. After all, the communists reminded desperate German citizens, it had been the capitalists who supported the fascists in the 1930s, and allegedly brought on the horrors of the Second World War.[7]

Widespread hunger motivated labor unrest, public disillusion, and communist agitation in postwar Germany. This photo shows a German mother cooking for her family at the side of a road in Berlin.

© Hulton-Deutsch Collection/CORBIS

127

George Kennan, then chargé for the American embassy in Moscow, had warned of this very combination of postwar suffering and propaganda enabling communist subversion. Kennan contended that "What the Russians want in Germany is the dominant power over the life of the country." "Moscow can hope to achieve this power only if the German Communists succeed in penetrating, paralyzing and bending to their will the German Social Democrats and bringing about the suppression of the bourgeois parties." "If we continue," Kennan explained, to "remain relatively passive and neutral toward German internal politics, [the] Russians will see clear sailing for [the] German Communist Party."[8]

Kennan was one of many American officials in 1947 to call for containing Soviet aggression through a combination of force, propaganda, and direct investment in Western Europe. American policymakers had to devise an unprecedented set of policy instruments that simultaneously excluded foreign communist influences, empowered a devastated and fractured population, and ensured limits on the activities of that population. The United States contended with this ambitious agenda at a time when it faced nearly unlimited global and domestic demands on its resources, and it sought to avoid a return to military conflict in Europe and Asia. American policymakers were pulled in many directions, with few historical or institutional foundations for coherent strategy.[9]

Containing Soviet aggression was, in fact, only one element of a broad strategic matrix adopted hastily in Washington after months of uncertainty, disorganization, and worsening conditions. American policymakers mounted a somewhat desperate response to a palpable sense of crisis—a widespread perception of postwar policy "failure." Vulnerabilities in Central Europe—starvation, political unrest, and a directionless Anglo-American occupation—motivated an unplanned and radical decision: a long-term commitment by the United States to fund, through grants *not* loans, the rebuilding of the European economies by the Europeans, under the ownership of the Europeans.

Washington would pay to reconstruct the nations—allies and adversaries—destroyed in war. Washington would help prepare them for international stability and competition. This was the strategic purpose of the European Recovery Program (the Marshall Plan), formulated in the spring of 1947 by a small group of American figures, and announced in very general terms in June 1947.[10]

As we have seen, self-conscious "nation-building" by American leaders had strong historical precedents in the founding of the United States, the Reconstruction of the post–Civil War South, and various twentieth-century interventions, especially in the Philippines. Americans are—above all else—a "nation-building people." Navigating for two centuries between the opposite shores of disengagement and empire, Americans have invested in creating self-governing states that they expect to trade harmoniously with their neighbors out of enlightened self-interest. Americans have consistently expanded their foreign activities, but they have just as consistently substituted investment and local institution-building for the kinds of external control emphasized by traditional empires. This was precisely the early American vision for a "society of states" supported by wealth and ingenuity, not force of arms.

Early American hopes sustained policymakers confronting a complex and violent world in 1947. What made the decisions about postwar Germany so significant was their strategic importance for the future of Europe, as well as the risk and expenditure they entailed for Americans after decades of economic depression and war. Despite contrary domestic and international pressures, Americans made a radical policy choice about postwar Germany, in line with a long tradition of radical nation-building.

Nation-building in postwar Germany is not a model for other American activities. Chronological, geopolitical, and cultural context matter enormously. That said, the process of adjusting and adapting policy, as exhibited in postwar Germany, is instructive for other cases. The policies that contributed to the transformation of Western

Europe—particularly the Marshall Plan—were not planned or even fully thought out. They emerged from constant political give-and-take, negotiation and compromise, adjustment to circumstances, experimentation, and strategic risk-taking. Nation-building in postwar Germany was political horse-trading, often of a dirty and unsavory variety. The will and ability of Americans to undertake politics in this form, with consistency, are a necessary part of nation-building. Policymakers and citizens must embrace complex relationships, whether the focus of American activities is the former slaveholding South, the Philippines, postwar Germany, Vietnam, Iraq, or Afghanistan.[11]

Germany and America's Long History of Nation-Building

Scholars have analyzed the Marshall Plan in great depth, debating its purposes, effects, and legacies. Some writers have pointed to the Marshall Plan as a model for occupation and reconstruction elsewhere. Others have argued that the Marshall Plan was limited in its impact, and inapplicable to different cultures and societies. There is no reason to rehearse these debates, except to note that they turn on assumptions about how unique (or not unique) German conditions were after the Second World War. Was German society particularly well suited—by culture, war experience, and economic circumstances—for democratic reconstruction? Was German society particularly well served by an enlightened, or at least effective, set of American occupation authorities?[12]

In addressing these debates, scholars have neglected a number of other issues related to the adjustment (and readjustment) of American policies, especially after initial postwar failures. Most accounts of reconstruction in Germany and other societies are static and ahistorical, even if written by historians. They assume inevitable disappointment ("doomed to failure") or exceptional local conditions (the "luck of circumstance"). Neither is an accurate point of departure in thinking about postwar reconstructions. War-ravaged societies are not blank slates for imposed transformations. They generally are not settings of irreversible sectarianism either. If nothing else, war creates uncertain and contingent circumstances. Inherited authorities are defeated and discredited; new authorities are made and remade, often quite rapidly. Reconstructions are short-lived moments of great sensitivity to external influence. The question is not *whether* foreign actors can make a difference, but *how* they can intelligently react to circumstances and nudge a destroyed society in a new direction. Those were the key questions in the former Confederacy after 1865 and the Philippines after 1898. The same questions reemerged in postwar Germany.

In place of the paternalistic language about "reeducation," one should think about these diverse reconstructions in market terms. Powerful and rich external actors have the ability, if they act wisely, to change incentive calculations at a moment of market failure. The United States, in particular, also benefits from the ability to deploy significant human and capital resources into multiple projects simultaneously because of its vast domestic reservoirs of talent and material. Contrary to conventional wisdom, from the constitutional founding and the Civil War through the occupations of the Philippines, Germany, and contemporary Afghanistan, the historical record indicates that American society will sustain decades-long commitments of soldiers and treasure across diverse regions of perceived national interest. These state-building projects, at home and abroad, reinforce the sense of American nationhood; American nationhood drives citizens to pursue the creation and expansion of similar states.

The American experience in Germany is part of a long and mixed history of postwar nation-building that points, above all, to potentials for change—both good and bad—in occupied societies. The United States has a unique and consistent approach to nation-building that makes the transformation of the defeated Nazi regime after 1945 far less exceptional than it appears. As in other cases, postwar German reconstruction was a process of constant adjustment amidst contradictory possibilities. It involved frustrating half measures, repeated failures, and some startling successes.

Transitional Diplomacy

The political vacuums created by the destruction of war are openings for new actors. The breakdown in traditional governance empowers informal and semi-official figures with access to knowledge, networks, and resources that can replace destroyed institutions. With little planning or guidance, in postwar Germany a series of individuals took action into their own hands, shifting American policy in crucial ways. This was not grassroots social change, but it was not elite diplomacy either. It was creative adaptation by figures who found themselves positioned to exert political leverage. "Transitional diplomacy" filled the crucial space for reconstruction in Germany.

"Transitional diplomacy," as I use the term, involves a broad, ecumenical, but still focused mobilization of talent for addressing difficult international problems. In the case of America's policy toward Germany, this process did not coalesce until after the Second World War and the first months of chaos, uncertainty, and near starvation. The impetus to turn these terrible circumstances around did not come from the highest echelons of government, or from some nonexistent groundswell of grassroots opinion in Germany or the United States. Instead, a widespread disappointment with policy outcomes and a strong commitment to improvement among figures with diverse intellectual, political, and economic perspectives drove new initiatives. Groups assembled around the Council on Foreign Relations and other nongovernmental bodies (what observers would later call think tanks) reexamined pressing problems and proposed new solutions. More important, they defined themselves as part of the policy process, not outsider critics, following their suggestions with concrete, often informal, efforts at implementation.[13]

Transitional diplomacy was about knowledge (what some scholars call "epistemic communities"), interpersonal connections ("social capital"), common commitments, and creative (often unofficial) action. Successful nation-building requires a process that nurtures these attributes. Innovation, adaptation, and creative adjustment demand more intellectual synthesis than research genius, more clever collaboration than individual investigation.[14]

Middle-level diplomatic figures with some of these "transitional" attributes began to proliferate in late 1946 and early 1947. At the Council on Foreign Relations, for example, they formed "study groups" that included men with extensive foreign policy experience, deep intellectual knowledge, and influential political connections across party lines, such as: Allen Dulles (former OSS station chief in Switzerland, later director of central intelligence), John J. McCloy (former assistant secretary of war, contemporary president of the World Bank, and future U.S. high commissioner for Germany), economist John Kenneth Galbraith, historians William Langer and Carl Schorske, and theologian Reinhold Niebuhr, among others. These men were not the most powerful politicians or policymakers of the day, but they drew attention to American shortcomings in Germany, they experimented with new ideas, and they lobbied for policy change. They aided Herbert Hoover, Lucius Clay, Dean Acheson, George Kennan, and eventually George Marshall in devising the European Recovery Program and selling it to skeptical observers. They helped nation-building work in western Germany through trial and error, cooperation and cajolery, even wish and prayer.[15]

"Civilization"

The importance of transitional diplomacy raises questions about its purposes. What did these figures aim to accomplish? What consensus constituted them as a group? What role did transnational ideas about culture and "civilization" play in their activities? The latter term is ubiquitous in the records surrounding the reconstruction of western Germany. Speaking to the Council on Foreign Relations in April 1947, former president Hoover echoed a common postwar view when he explained: "If Germany falls, the western world falls. Germany is the frontier of western civilization." Hoover also referred to Japan as the only "ideological dam in Asia" against communism, atheism, and civilizational degeneracy.[16]

Nation-building is always about much more than strategy and economics. It turned in Germany, and elsewhere, on perceptions of commonality and difference. Despite the experience of war, successful occupation involved the building of trust between peoples. Trust required common ground—"civic space"—hinged upon some assertion of a shared mission. The existence of a Soviet enemy helped construct a common anticommunist position, but that was not enough. In the case of postwar Germany, reconstruction was about more than rebuilding a single society defeated in war. American policy aimed at constructing a wider social and cultural space that connected countries on both sides of the Atlantic Ocean. German "nation-building" became transatlantic "community-building."[17]

The transatlantic alliance forged by soldiers, politicians, and ordinary citizens in the years after 1945 was a community of diverse actors committed to common goals. Mutual security interests in denying communist expansion and mutual economic interests in building markets for prosperity initially brought former enemies on both sides of the ocean together. Beyond that, the horrors of the Second World War convinced many observers that the promises of modern progress—with new technology, new institutions, and new ideas—needed careful management to prevent a replay of recent events. Transatlantic community was a necessary alternative to transatlantic warfare.

Exploiting what a young Henry Kissinger called the "psychological weaknesses" of large ambitious societies anxious for rapid advancement, demagogues like Hitler and Mussolini had channeled modern power for policies that produced mass destruction. That was the conventional understanding of fascism in the postwar years. To avoid a replay of this disastrous movement, Kissinger was one of many to counsel for transatlantic partnerships around a firm commitment to "civilization." The inherited wisdom of the past, accompanied by the strong hand of enlightened leaders, provided political ballast against threatening extremisms.[18]

The postwar "West" needed a foundation of shared ideas that would encourage change while prohibiting excesses after two world wars. Common West European traditions rooted in civil society, secular justice, and representative authority could discipline a fast-moving and violent modern world. Ideas of freedom and responsibility could discourage dangerous utopias. Policymakers in Washington and various postwar European capitals encouraged unity on both sides of the Atlantic around a useful past that drew on the history of cooperative nation-states in the nineteenth century, rather than the fragmented and antagonistic mass movements of recent decades. The history of "Western civilization" helped to outline a preferred future.[19]

This was not an inevitable outcome. It ran against the emotion of recent experience. After a half century of political competition, economic dislocation, and warfare, neither Americans nor Europeans saw themselves as part of a common "West" or a single "civilization." President Franklin Roosevelt had pushed his listeners in the late 1930s to recognize what he called the "solidarity and interdependence about the modern world," and the need to cooperate with foreign allies to defend the imperiled "foundations of civilization." After 7 December 1941 Americans accepted this argument, but they never embraced commonality with the Europeans and Asians they joined on the battlefields. Americans certainly did not identify with their fascist enemies or even their temporary communist friends.[20]

Citizens of the United States self-consciously perceived their individualist democracy, free market capitalism, and anti-imperialism as an alternative to the hierarchical aristrocracies, communal economies, and far-flung empires of the Old World. Most Europeans, including Winston Churchill, found these American assumptions naive, self-serving, and a barrier to long-term cooperation. Americans remained upstart children in the eyes of their cousins across the Atlantic, incapable of mature partnership. Woodrow Wilson's failure to persuade American citizens to participate in his own international League of Nations had reinforced this point. In war and in peace, the Atlantic Ocean remained a divider of peoples and their ideas about society.[21]

If anything, feelings of difference and separation only grew with American participation in the war. The United States fought, in President Franklin Roosevelt's terms, as an "arsenal of democracy," freeing Europe of fascism and, later, communism. Roosevelt and his fellow New Dealers blamed traditional European politics for the rise of fascism, the spread of degenerate empires, and the extreme violence of the battlefields. As the president carefully nurtured a "Grand Alliance" with his British and Soviet counterparts, he also prepared to build a new international system of American-style law, economy, and nation-states at the end of the conflagration. From the Atlantic Charter of August 1941 to the United Nations Charter of June 1945, the U.S. government challenged traditional European politics, injecting American assumptions about representativeness, sovereignty, and a cooperative society of states into discussions about territorial adjustment and the balance of power.[22]

In contrast to these divergent war aims, leaders and citizens forged meaningful partnerships during the postwar German occupation. Common goals emerged through patterns of action *after the war*. They reflected responses to challenges and opportunities during the period of dislocation, confusion, and uncertainty that characterized the years between 1945 and 1947. Too often observers assume that strong transatlantic connections preexisted this period or that they were somehow produced primarily in the realm of culture and ideas. Quite the contrary, the enduring emphasis on "pastoralization" and "demilitarization" (rather than reconstruction) in American discussions of postwar Germany, and the continued assumption that U.S. forces would soon extricate themselves from Europe, show that cultural presumptions ran against deep transatlantic partnership. As late as 1947 many prominent Americans wanted to reestablish a "normal" prewar pattern of politics, which involved a return of U.S. soldiers and treasure to the western side of the Atlantic, and vigilant efforts to prevent the rebuilding of challengers to American interests in Europe—Russian, German, or British. By this logic, the postwar nation-states of Europe should have been small, self-absorbed, and separate from one another and the United States. This was not "isolationism," which never really existed in practice, but a traditional streak of American unilateralism.[23]

The transformation in assumptions and behavior on both sides of the Atlantic came from the *practice* of cooperation in efforts to address pressing postwar problems. A transatlantic "civilization" did not exist independent of action; it was the product of concrete and immediate actions. In similar ways a transpacific sense of common purpose emerged between American and Japanese partners, as it did in other postwar regions, when encouraged by daily behavior. Civilizational bonds are made and unmade by political practice, not the other way around.[24]

Civilizational bonds also do not follow rigid theoretical paradigms or canonical models of thought. War-ravaged people do not learn to trust their enemies because they share language, literature, or traditions any more than they go to war with each other for reasons of cultural difference. Civilization is as civilization does. Acts of partnership, commitment, and even beneficence build more of the same. Credible sacrifices for a larger common purpose encourage respect and reciprocation. The World War II generations in the United States and western Germany defined each other as civilizational enemies for half a decade, but then quickly built a new edifice of commonality through intensive daily interactions. The density of interpersonal contacts contributed to the resilience of postwar bonds.[25]

Reconstruction along the lines of a common civilization was not planned. It was hardly conceptualized in 1945. Common goals were not even articulated clearly and consistently. They lacked simple and catchy labels. Instead, a joint sense of German-American (even European-American) mission emerged from weeks and years of constant, intensive, and adaptive interactions. Germans and Americans learned from each other. Americans in different branches of the military, the diplomatic corps, business, and politics also learned from one another. Nation-building in war-destroyed Germany became an open-ended process of trial and error, with the daily pressures of starving civilians and threatening foreign adversaries. This was not war, but a scramble for survival.[26]

Ideas about Western civilization were crucial for American nation-building in Germany because they provided a new prism for viewing the former enemy. As U.S. Army soldiers shifted from shooting at Germans to helping them rebuild their cities and feed their families, a claim to a common civilization justified this behavior—especially when Americans had pressing needs elsewhere, including at home. As U.S. officials forged working relationships with former Nazis for the purpose of governing postwar Germany, rhetoric about the shared West legitimized this political turn. Most of all, as American and German citizens nurtured interpersonal relationships—professional and conjugal—the image of a common Western civilization helped erase the preexisting boundaries of separation, replacing them with a new acceptance of fraternization, familiarity, and friendship so soon after the world's bloodiest war.[27]

The practice of nation-building in western Germany required a new ideology of transatlantic cooperation. Leaders and citizens on both sides of the ocean worked to imagine this possibility. Western civilization, an amorphous and largely unpersuasive concept amidst depression and war, emerged as a hinge for unprecedented cooperation after 1945. It was a creative fiction—like James Madison's late-eighteenth-century "American people"—that helped to build unity among fragmented citizens and states. As a phrase, Western civilization moved traditional boundaries to reflect the postwar division of the world, and it reinforced the American commitment to reconstruction in former enemy territory. As a promise, it legitimized the continued investment, experiment, and sacrifice necessary to rebuild Germany. The postwar imaginings of Western civilization were a vital instrument in European-American nation-building.

Herbert Hoover

Our language about German reconstruction and nation-building is misleading. Despite the self-contained image of the "nation" and the engineered implications of the term, successful nation-building is never about closed borders or the technical management of people and institutions. Quite the contrary, it is the interconnections between societies and the experimentation with different forms of authority that make transitions from destruction to reconstruction so fruitful for creative change. The politics of nation-building might look predetermined in retrospect, especially in the case of postwar Germany, but the process functioned effectively only because it was contingent—even somewhat serendipitous—in practice.

This was certainly the case as the United States contended with what had become a failed reconstruction in Central Europe by early 1947. American and German opinion was nearly universal in this negative verdict. Widespread starvation, disorder, and confusion made it clear that assumptions about the need to break up economic power in postwar Germany and limit American financial commitments were wrongheaded. For good historical reasons many Americans (and even some Germans) remained committed to preventing the reconstruction of a strong industrial Germany.

Open debate about the limits of this approach produced a powerful push for policy change. Reform did not come from the most informed and dominant figures. It came from men who had sat on the sidelines for the initial planning, but now entered to reassess, redirect, and rethink reconstruction. This was the politics of nation-building—bridge figures operating across societies to create a new German-American partnership that was a hybrid of forms, rather than a blueprint of power and empire.[28]

A close reading of the historical record reveals the surprising role of Herbert Hoover. The former president was the hero of food relief in Belgium, Russia, and other parts of Europe at the end of the First World War. Within the United States he had been disgraced by the image of his feeble leadership during the early years of the Great Depression. Despite the political recriminations, however, he remained deeply connected to events in various societies. He was one of the most internationally minded figures in the United States, drawing on unmatched experience traveling the globe, negotiating business deals, and organizing distant movements of people, resources, and relief supplies. In an era of hyper-nationalized institutions for technology and economy, Hoover was a vestige of an earlier cosmopolitan internationalism—the turn-of-the-century world of traveling scientists, activists, and businessmen rather than the secret atomic projects, bloated militaries, and government-managed corporations that dominated mid-twentieth-century politics.[29]

In the wake of the destruction wrought by the nationalist violence of the Second World War, Hoover sought to open new avenues for international cosmopolitan reforms. He pushed an agenda that emphasized cooperation, volunteerism, and increased interpersonal contact between societies. As he had done after the First World War, Hoover focused on the creation of new transnational organizations and the distribution of famine relief. He pushed for more border crossings, more informal associations, and more nongovernmental innovations.

Hoover had not been a figure of major influence between the Pearl Harbor attack and the German and Japanese surrenders. His cosmopolitan principles made little sense when Americans were mobilizing resources behind an expanding federal government, fighting enemies on two fronts. Hoover reemerged, however, in 1946 as a recognized and respected expert on postwar societies. He began a new career, traveling to Europe and Japan to assess the possibilities for reconstruction after all the war damage.[30]

President Harry Truman relied on former president Herbert Hoover to help address scarcity and dislocation in postwar Europe. *1950, Corbis*

At the urging of his Republican supporters, including General Lucius Clay in Germany, Hoover embarked on another fact-finding tour of Central Europe in early 1947, authorized this time by a somewhat desperate President Harry Truman. The White House faced mounting criticisms for its combined failure to build a secure order in postwar Germany and extricate American soldiers from a costly occupation. Truman's anticommunist critics—including two newly elected figures: Senator Joseph McCarthy and Representative Richard Nixon—accused him of allowing the Soviets to exploit the chaos, suffering, and uncertainty of postwar Europe. Those more focused on the American domestic economy, including Senator Robert Taft, contended that the administration's ineffective policies in Germany were prolonging the flight of U.S. capital abroad, at precisely the time when investment was needed most at home. The president confronted demands for more results at reduced costs, more nation-building in Germany that simultaneously served American interests.[31]

Truman (a New Deal Democrat) and Hoover (a conservative Republican) were longtime political opponents, but they shared one common goal in the winter of 1947: to explore new policy options in Germany. They both imbibed the American nation-building creed. Germany, or at least the Allied-occupied western half of Germany, had to become a self-sustaining, sovereign nation-state with representative institutions, a market economy, and a united people. It had to govern and feed itself, working cooperatively as part of an American-led society of states. That was the image of a postwar Western civilization that both Truman and Hoover wanted to build, rather than a prewar system of rival societies or a British-style empire. Truman believed that Hoover's extensive international experience, particularly at the end of the First World War, could help with this difficult but necessary endeavor. He also recognized that if Hoover failed, then the Democrats could pass at least some of the blame to the Republican Party. A bipartisan nation-building effort in Germany made good political sense.[32]

Hoover was happy to undertake this difficult mission because he longed to redeem his reputation. He also had supreme confidence in his ability to solve complex global problems with an intelligent combination of government, business, and citizen-based solutions. Nation-building for Hoover was about creating new associations of capable people, committed to common material ends, working through representative institutions. As he had done throughout his long career, Hoover would try to show Germans and Americans the possibilities for reconstruction and growth in these terms, countering contrary claims about the need for more authoritarian, socialist, and communist alternatives. The former president was seventy-two years old in early 1947, but he remained an energetic zealot for American-style nation-building.[33]

Germany After the Second World War

Germany After the
Second World War

Hoover's Travels

Boundary,
American Zone
of Occupation

Total Population by
Province:

Over 5,000,000

3,000,000–5,000,000

1,500,000–3,000,000

Less than 1,500,000

DENMARK

Baltic Sea

Schleswig-
Holstein

Mecklenburg-
Vorpommern

Hamburg

NETHERLANDS

Bremen

Lower Saxony

Brandenburg

POLAND

Berlin

North Rhine–
Westphalia

Saxony-Anhalt

Saxony

Hesse

Thuringia

Rhineland-
Palatinate

Frankfurt

CZECHOSLOVAKIA

LUX

US ZONE
(38,000 US Troops)

Saarland

Wurttemberg-
Baden

Bavaria

FRANCE

Stuttgart

Wurttemberg-
Hohenzollern

Baden

AUSTRIA

SWITZERLAND

Hoover arrived in Frankfurt, Germany, on 4 February. He toured Berlin, Hamburg, and Stuttgart, among other areas, before traveling to Rome, London, and then back to New York on 23 February. During these arduous travels, the former president met with American military and political administrators, their British counterparts, former German officials, and various local figures. He did not conduct a democratic assessment of German society, and his contacts with "ordinary" Germans were indeed limited. That said, Hoover completed one of the most thoughtful, self-critical, and informative surveys of social conditions in the destroyed nation at the time.

The former president's experience in international business equipped him very well to locate the individuals who commanded local authority and possessed the competence to address the most pressing problems. Hoover also had a good ear for those who could speak accurately about the daily challenges confronting citizens. Instead of espousing easy political slogans or economic formulas, the former president engaged in detailed and informed conversations with diverse German figures. He listened as much as he spoke. He asked for cooperation as much as he offered American aid. Most of all, he showed a sincere commitment to basic problem-solving, with respect for German opinions, traditions, and aspirations. Local newspaper coverage immediately noted this productive and promising attitude. In recognition of Hoover's public impact, a number of German cities—including Berlin and Stuttgart—renamed schools in his honor. President Truman and General Clay, despite their more powerful positions, did not receive the same honors.[34]

Hoover's visit to the bombed-out city of Stuttgart captured his approach to his mission, and nation-building in general. The former president arrived in Stuttgart on 12 February. He began the day meeting with a variety of officials from the U.S. military occupation. Hoover then talked with a small group of local German political figures who had served in the government of the former Nazi regime, but had also proven themselves willing to work with foreign forces after the war. These were men of status and capability, committed to improving the circumstances in Stuttgart and surrounding areas. According to a German newspaper account at the time, Hoover talked with the right people. He engaged in a "conversation with German experts" and he responded thoughtfully to their explanations. Hoover promised "new assistance" along the lines that the Germans requested.[35]

This was a give-and-take dialogue, which ranged from a detailed discussion of potato crops and milk production, to an analysis of Europe-wide economic trends, international finance, and industrial strategy. Hoover showed knowledge on a par with the German experts, he listened carefully to their statements, and he asked informed questions. Most of all, he did not offer easy answers or promote empty promises. Hoover did not make any threats either. He approached the Germans he met as a civilian and an entrepreneur, interested in negotiating mutually advantageous arrangements for citizens on both sides of the Atlantic.

In bold terms, Hoover warned that things would get worse before they got better. The food shortages were too great and American resources were too overstretched. What Hoover advocated to his small group of interlocutors in Stuttgart, and the thousands who read about his visit, was the beginning of a long-term partnership. Working together, they could address common problems, mobilize available capabilities, and craft practical solutions that were *both* German and American in formulation. The relationship between the two societies would not be equal—the Americans were the occupiers, after all—but soldiers, diplomats, local experts, and various citizens would engage in a shared process. In the business terms that Hoover deployed, the different groups would act as stakeholders in a common enterprise. Hoover's experience, his rhetoric, and especially his demeanor in postwar Germany embodied this "associative," rather than imposed, attitude toward nation-building. In this way, Hoover echoed William Howard Taft's earlier activities in the Philippines.[36]

Hoover's Vision

Hoover's vision for Germany was not new. It drew on the history of American efforts in other places, especially since the Civil War. The United States would not dictate strategy and tactics in occupied western Germany. Neither would Washington offer to "save" a suffering people. Like the Freedmen's Bureau in the American South, Hoover worked to avoid excessive expectations and the creation of long-term dependencies. He counseled for targeting American investments in food, education, and industry. That was what he promised his German counterparts he would advocate with President Truman. That was also what the Northern Republicans had done, two generations earlier, in the former Confederacy. This was a tried-and-true American strategy for nation-building that promised to build a new kind of German sovereignty. The "new" Germany would have the basic characteristics Americans associated with nation-building: the unity of a single "West German" people; the attachment to a fixed "West German" territory, managed by a representative state; the development of a capitalist free wage economy; and the nurturing of a strong national bond to the American-led society of "civilized" states.

Hoover's visit to Stuttgart and other parts of Germany in February 1947 connected postwar reconstruction efforts to the American nation-building creed. Hoover followed a distinguished line of transitional figures who sought to build influence abroad without empire. These figures tried to empower local self-governance while preserving a broader political order. The former president extended a tradition of American action pioneered by James Madison, Oliver Otis Howard, William Howard Taft, and others.

Hoover's German hosts in Stuttgart and other cities were not mere collaborators with his nation-building vision. They were nationalists, many with dark fascist pasts, and they had reasons to resent American power. They also had a legitimate claim to represent the basic interests of many German citizens, suffering after the war from deprivation and indignity. In their conversations with Hoover, the experts in Stuttgart were respectful, but not deferential or obsequious. They pointed to the severe deprivations of their city and they made a strong case that the United States needed to work with them in improving basic conditions. They spoke, with real foundation, as the "German people."[37]

Hoover understood this dynamic better than almost any other American of his generation. Nation-building in postwar Germany would rise and fall on those who could speak, with some authority, for the larger body of citizens. Reconstruction would succeed or fail based on the ability of local figures to mobilize and allocate resources, partially provided by the United States, for productive purposes. Hoover and other Americans had to invest in flawed but competent German nationalists, rather than vague ideas of democratization or imported authorities who lacked internal legitimacy. Hoover and other Americans would have to build influence through long-term relationships that were dominated by compromise and adaptation, not exclusion or imposition.

The United States faced multiplying demands after the Second World War, and it had very limited direct experience with reconstruction in Europe. Then as later, Americans felt an understandable urge to limit their foreign commitments and focus on their immediate security and economic needs. Hoover sympathized with these sentiments. He also recognized that the United States possessed the resources to invest in long-term relationships with a region that was crucial for stability and prosperity across the globe. In addition, Hoover shared an inherited belief that Americans could improve the world by helping to build representative nations and effective states—in place of empires, dictatorships, and other militaristic alternatives. Like African Americans in the South after the Civil War, German citizens after the Second World War would prove the continued resonance of the American nation-building creed.

The Hoover Report

Hoover's trip to Germany pointed to new nation-building possibilities. The former president now had to persuade Americans who might share his principles to institute policies, and take new risks, in this same direction. Hoover made a strong public case as soon as he returned to the United States. Working tirelessly, he published three separate documents—collectively known as the "Hoover Report"—on social conditions in Germany and Europe.[38]

The *New York Times* called the report a promising combination of "practical humanitarianism and humanitarian practicality." British officials, who joined French diplomats in their anxiety about American efforts to rebuild a strong German nation-state, acknowledged that Hoover "showed a remarkable grasp of the situation" on the ground. The British and French feared that the former president was too heavily invested in the German people he visited, and too detached from the needs of America's other European allies. Politicians in London and Paris focused extensive attention on the Hoover Report, and they immediately sought to revise it for their own economic and security purposes.[39]

Hoover focused on his American audience—the domestic citizens and politicians who would have to invest in his plan. He began his public efforts with clear language about the challenges confronting Germany and the United States. For Americans, this was not what they expected after defeating their enemies in a long and hard war: "It may come as a great shock to American taxpayers that, having won the war over Germany, we are now faced for some years with large expenditures for relief for these people. Indeed it is something new in human history for the conqueror to undertake."

Hoover called for an end to all major de-Nazification efforts. Instead, he advocated immediate and extensive American loans, assistance opening German factories, and large shipments of foodstuffs from the United States. The stakes were high, according to Hoover, in ensuring that a stable, productive, and sustainable German nation succeeded the chaos of the postwar years:

> Our determination is to establish such a regime in Germany as will prevent forever again the rise of militarism and aggression within these people. But those who believe in vengeance and the punishment of a great mass of Germans not concerned in the Nazi conspiracy can now have no misgivings, for all of them—in food, warmth and shelter—have been sunk to the lowest level known in a hundred years of Western history. If Western Civilization is to survive in Europe, it must also survive in Germany. And it must be built into a cooperative member of that civilization. That indeed is the hope of any lasting peace.[40]

Hoover's recommendations rejected both American handouts and American impositions. His report outlined the severity of German needs and the importance of successful German reconstruction for American interests. Hoover offered no step-by-step plan for accomplishing this end. Instead, he called for more extensive U.S. resource commitments, deeper German manpower efforts, and stronger partnership between the two societies. With resources and manpower, Germans and Americans would learn together to build a peaceful and prosperous nation in Central Europe.

Hoover's vision for Germany was industrial, capitalist, and pro-American, but it remained open beyond that. He emphasized participation, adaptation, and mutual interest. He assumed a united, sovereign people in the western half of Germany, represented by a single competent government. Hoover also focused, as he had in Stuttgart, on German leadership at the local level. This was to be a German recovery as much as an American one. It had to include true partnership—with serious German stakeholding—in order to keep American costs down and nurture a sustainable economy. "German industry must be operated by Germans," Hoover explained.[41]

In contrast to continued assumptions about divergent American and German interests, Hoover's report went furthest in making a case for long-term interdependence, and the possibilities for German nation-building in an American image. Despite the recent history of militarism and fascism, Hoover described the former home of Nazism as a major part of a remade Western civilization. "We can keep Germany in these economic chains," Hoover explained, "but it will also keep Europe in rags." Out of self-interest, Hoover contended, the United States had to act as a long-term economic, political, and cultural ally in Central Europe. Working together, Americans and Germans would build the instruments, institutions, and habits necessary for prosperity. They would resurrect civilization from the ashes of destruction. "I assume," Hoover wrote, "in our own interest and that of Europe, that we wish to restore the productivity of the continent, that we wish to revive personal freedom, honest elections, and generally to reconstruct the German people into a peace-loving nation cooperating in the recovery of Western Civilization."[42]

Hoover pressed Secretary of State George Marshall, in particular, to recognize that Germany was one of "the major fronts of Western Civilization." This meant for Hoover that despite the tortured history of German militarism and authoritarianism, the nation was a core element of future American activities. Germany was geographically, economically, and culturally fundamental to peace and prosperity. "We need," Hoover wrote, "a larger vision of the primary basis of world peace, which is productivity. Otherwise, there will be a disintegration of Western Civilization everywhere." This language was strident, but it resonated with many listeners.[43]

Hoover promoted his vision of a shared German-American nation-building mission throughout the United States. His report was only the beginning of a massive public relations campaign. Hoover testified before Congress. He briefed high-ranking government officials—including Undersecretary of State Dean Acheson, Secretary of State George Marshall, and President Harry Truman. Hoover also spoke extensively to the press, educating the public about the challenges in Europe and the importance of renewed American commitments, despite the calls for retrenchment at home. Acheson reported to Marshall that Hoover's ideas, although strongly stated, were no longer unfamiliar to listeners. In March 1947 Hoover's words received prominent newspaper attention, generally accompanied by praise from experts and editors.[44]

As a very nontraditional influence on a Democratic administration struggling with postwar policy, Hoover's advocacy helped move a fiscally conservative President Truman to embrace massive aid and economic reconstruction in Europe. Hoover's arguments—reiterated soon by Acheson, Marshall, and Truman—persuaded a reluctant American public to rebuild across the Atlantic, rather than turn away. Most significant, Hoover's tour of Germany and his communications with local American and German officials created a model for deeper and more extensive transnational partnerships. Hoover was seen as a credible figure in both Europe and the United States because of his experience with war relief, his acute recognition of the immediate problems in Germany, and his calls for enduring collaboration, despite his own misgivings about America's expansion abroad. Hoover pushed policy in a direction it otherwise might not have taken.[45]

The former president did not offer easy solutions. He did not promise quick results. His contribution came from his efforts to mobilize the resources and relationships for creative problem-solving. Hoover also drew on long-standing American assumptions about nation-building, showing how the United States could apply them in a new context.

The Marshall Plan

In the four months after Hoover published his report the United States and Germany turned an important corner. Secretary of State

George Marshall made his own trip to Europe, and he accepted the key elements of Hoover's analysis—especially the sense of urgency. Marshall retraced Hoover's steps and he reaffirmed the need for a shift in U.S. policy toward deeper commitment. As a response, Marshall formed the State Department Policy Planning Staff, under the able leadership of George Kennan.[46]

Kennan focused immediately on the problems of German reconstruction. Dean Acheson also turned his attention to these matters, arguing in a major public speech on 8 May 1947 that communist containment was not enough. Echoing Hoover, Acheson explained: "we must take whatever action is possible immediately, even without full Four Power agreement, to effect a larger measure of European, including German, recovery. European recovery cannot be complete until the various parts of Europe's economy are working together in a harmonious whole. And the achievement of a coordinated European economy remains a fundamental objective of our foreign policy."[47]

On 5 June 1947 Secretary of State Marshall gave this policy official standing. Speaking to an audience of graduates and alumni at Harvard University, Marshall announced that the United States would redouble its reconstruction activities in Europe, "not against any country or doctrine but against hunger, poverty, despotism, and chaos." He advocated a "revival of a working economy in the world so as to permit the emergence of political and social conditions in which free institutions can exist." In what listeners remember as a quiet, confident voice, Marshall promised that this commitment would include strong U.S. efforts, and it would be open to all countries of Europe (including the Soviet-dominated communist states), but it also "must come from Europe." "The role of this country," Marshall explained, "should consist of friendly aid in the drafting of a European program and of later support of such a program as far as it may be practical for us to do so. The program should be a joint one, agreed to by a number of, if not all, European nations."[48]

After two years of acute economic difficulty in postwar Europe, Secretary of State George Marshall sought to invest in the continent's recovery. He announced the European Recovery Program when he delivered the commencement address at Harvard University in June 1947. The Marshall Plan drew on many suggestions from Herbert Hoover.
Marshall Enters Harvard, Ref: 47-4/67-10-40 © OECD

The Marshall Plan eventually transferred more than $13 billion to Europe as grants, rather than the loans that Hoover had initially advocated. The Marshall Plan also increased the guiding role of the United States in creating new European currencies, industrial facilities, and consumer markets. It nurtured a liberal-capitalist order in Western Europe, closely tied to American economic interests. These are the topics that have received the most attention from scholars.[49]

Beyond these important observations, the Marshall Plan's greatest innovation was its emphasis on long-term partnership and its open-ended vision. As Marshall's biographer notes, no one—including Hoover, Kennan, Acheson, and Marshall—"had or proposed to have a specific plan for Europe to accept; that was to be worked out." William Clayton, the American undersecretary of state for economic affairs, informed his British counterparts that the Truman administration "had not considered in detail what such commitments should be, and *it was for Europe to make the plan.* Any plan, however, would clearly have to embody concrete proposals for European economic cooperation and European self-help," assisted by the United States.[50]

That was the genius of the effort. Europeans and Americans had to collaborate; they had to create new solutions to new problems; they had to adapt and reinvent. The United States would provide money and support. The Europeans would take the lead on local implementation.

The Marshall Plan was not a program for "Americanization." It created a new hybrid of German-American and West European–American cooperation. It nurtured a new West German nation-state that drew on American assumptions about sovereignty and representativeness, but also reflected local needs, desires, and traditions. The Marshall Plan was, as Hoover recommended, an investment in a self-sustaining Germany that would also serve wider European and American interests. In the process, it would help build a common "civilized" society of states in the West that promoted prosperity and undermined communist detractors. The Marshall Plan empowered American-style nation-building across the ocean. The Marshall Plan provided a political and economic foundation for an evolving European Union, composed of peaceful nation-states.

George Kennan echoes this perspective in his memoirs. He and his colleagues on the State Department Policy Planning Staff worked to help the Germans and their neighbors construct stable postwar societies. The United States offered assistance and support through a diverse range of local partnerships, financed and encouraged from Washington, but shaped on the ground. Kennan followed "the principle that the Europeans should themselves take the initiative in drawing up the program and should assume central responsibility for its terms." This was a regional effort at nation-building, connecting local and international figures on both sides of the Atlantic.[51]

What the Marshall Plan Did

Measuring the precise economic and social effects of the Marshall Plan is impossible. Many factors contributed to the improvement in West German and West European living conditions after the terrible winter of 1947. Many of the key sources of change were not connected directly to the Marshall Plan, including more temperate weather, better farm harvests, and local infrastructure repair. In addition, the focus on rebuilding national industrial capabilities that came with the Marshall Plan was almost unavoidable. The Soviet-dominated countries that refused U.S. aid also invested in big factories, heavy machinery, and mass production. The Marshall Plan was hardly revolutionary.[52]

Following the advice of Herbert Hoover and others, the United States structured its aid to western Germany in ways that incentivized positive developments already under way, discouraging negative alternatives. The local German leaders Hoover met in Stuttgart and other cities were already investing in feeding their citizens, rebuilding their communities, and planning for future export-oriented industrial production. Marshall Plan money, distributed to West European governments through an American-staffed Economic Cooperation Administration office in each country, encouraged a continuation of all these efforts. It seeded local initiative, self-help, and business. It discouraged handouts, restrictions on innovation, and the hoarding of resources. The Marshall Plan financed capitalist development and it undermined alternative modes of social organization.[53]

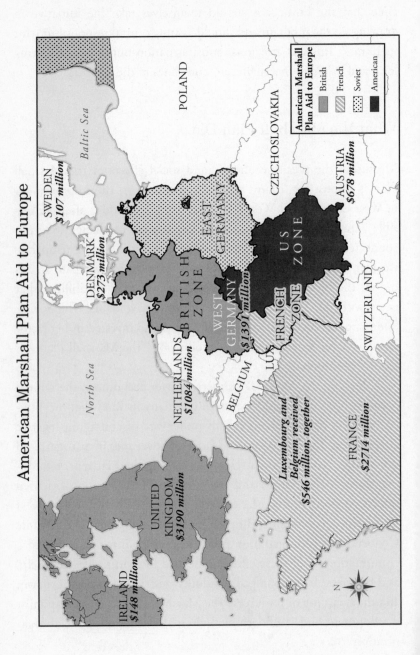

American Marshall Plan Aid to Europe

In addition to the disbursement of financial capital, the Marshall Plan created new markets for trade. Breaking down the old protectionist policies pursued by European nations before the Second World War, the United States pushed for an integrated European market, where countries could circulate industrial products and agricultural goods with minimal restrictions. Free trade, in these terms, would allow Germans to sell an industrial surplus to the French, for example, in return for imported food. Despite its own long history of protectionism, the United States opened its economy for German and other West European imports, providing the countries on the other side of the Atlantic with precious dollars that they could use for purchases and investments. Capitalist development and free trade, managed through the nation-states of Western Europe, empowered leaders to offer their citizens a common stake in a growing consumer economy. Everyone could benefit if they played by the same "civilized" rules.[54]

This was a system inspired by American capitalism and fears of communist collectivism, but it was also much more. Secretary of State Marshall and his supporters in the United States and Western Europe were investing to nurture what they envisioned as a continent-wide society of stable trading states. This meant an end to punitive postwar measures and a new emphasis on work and profit—what Americans had called free labor after the Civil War. The Marshall Plan helped to redirect political legitimacy in Western Europe from claims of postwar justice and retribution to promises of state-managed production and growth.[55]

In the case of European energy resources, particularly the iron and coal deposits in the Ruhr Valley, the United States encouraged their return to German nation-state control for extensive mining and factory use. These were the indispensable resources for fueling West European industrial economies, and they found their most efficient market distribution if regulated in a single state, Americans contended. The experiment with "international control" of the Ruhr Valley after the First World War had proven the impracticality of a nonnational overseer—one that had inspired both local resistance and national resentment against foreign occupiers. The United Nations, or some subset of this new organization, was not any better prepared for this regulatory task than the League of Nations and its affiliates had been twenty-five years earlier. American officials wanted to see the Ruhr Valley integrated firmly within a new German nation-state, bound to the postwar West European and transatlantic society of states.[56]

Although the British and the French continued to advocate international control of German resources, the United States used the Marshall Plan to favor nation-states over transnational or imperial institutions. In April 1949 the United States, Great Britain, France, Belgium, the Netherlands, and Luxembourg agreed on an interim international authority to supervise West German mining of the Ruhr Valley. By 1952 the new European Coal and Steel Community replaced this authority, built around agreement and trade among the postwar governments in the region. The United States helped finance the equipment and institutions necessary to share energy resources in Western Europe, but it encouraged this process to occur through negotiation between newly empowered nation-states, including the Federal Republic of Germany—the government, created in 1949, with the strongest postwar claim to the Ruhr Valley.[57]

Undersecretary of State William Clayton explained this vision to French economic planner Jean Monnet in terms that resonated with America's long tradition of nation-building: "I said that my view is that all Western Germany should be put under one administration with all [occupation] zonal boundaries completely eliminated." The iron and coal of the Ruhr Valley, Clayton continued, "should not be internationalized or detached from Germany." The undersecretary did acknowledge that an "international authority" should work to make sure that the resources are distributed widely and not hoarded. The resources should be used for business and civilian purposes, not remilitarization, Clayton argued. According to this American approach, the reorganization of the Ruhr would occur within a cooperative framework of integrated European economies, built around territorially sovereign nation-states, protected and supported by the United States.[58]

George Marshall articulated similar views, but with more pointed language about the productive use of the Ruhr Valley and the need for an integrated Europe of independent nation-states, not occupying powers. Clayton recounted: Marshall "asked me to make it quite clear to [British foreign secretary Ernest] Bevin that he regarded the British management of the Ruhr coal problem as pathetic; that the production of coal in the Ruhr is essential to European recovery as we all know, and that we cannot participate in any big new commitments to help Europe get back on its feet unless we know that the problem of producing coal in the Ruhr will be licked and quickly." To underscore his point, Marshall "added that we could not sit by while the British tried out any ideas which they had of experimenting with socialization of coal mines; time does not permit of experimentation."

The secretary of state wanted to use American aid to empower exactly the kinds of people Hoover had met—German, French, British, and other West European citizens who were willing to work hard as contributors to productive economies managed by well-governed, representative nation-states. Marshall believed the United States was investing in political order and economic prosperity, not postwar restitution or justice. Speaking of both Europe and Japan, he told Clayton, "we cannot longer stand for punitive interference by the British (or others) in our programs there."[59]

As Marshall's comments imply, the British, the French, and others had strong inclinations to oppose investment in European economic growth, centered on the creation of a prosperous West German nation-state. After all, German wealth had underwritten war and destruction for so many Europeans (and non-Europeans) over the last century. Representatives from Germany's western neighbors believed that their security and prosperity should be prioritized over a broader, and perhaps idealistic, vision of a society of "civilized" West European nation-states. American calls for German nation-building and West European integration sounded shallow, and even self-serving, when they came from across the Atlantic.

French foreign minister Georges Bidault made this point clear: "We have never wanted either to starve Germany or to let her resources lie dormant. But if on the morrow of the Paris Conference, at a time when we are still filled with uncertainty regarding ourselves, there is a certainty for Germany, the consequences of this priority cannot be escaped." Bidault warned on this occasion and many others: "I hope that our friends will attach at least equal importance to French psychology. I am compelled to say that to ignore that psychology when or because the French Government has committed itself will in all probability reopen the question of France's interior equilibrium and, through other men, the very choice she has made." Bidault was threatening French collapse or defection to the Soviet bloc in the face of rapid West German nation-building.[60]

The Marshall Plan did not persuade Bidault and others that their reservations about a revitalized Germany were misguided. Those reservations were based on sound historical memory. American aid after June 1947 did not deny that searing experience. Instead, the United States invested its resources in giving all the nation-states of Western Europe—Germany and her neighbors—the capital for building wealth and stability at home on terms that were compatible with a wider transatlantic trading system. Under this scheme, citizens would feel secure because they were part of cohesive nations, with representative governments and growing economies. They would expect peaceful relations with their West European neighbors because they were part of an emerging society of European and Atlantic states—independent and interdependent at the same time. Former belligerents were "civilized" by their incentives for trade and negotiation, not war or isolation. In the terms of James Madison and Alexander Hamilton, the Marshall Plan invested in an integration of local sovereignties—a federal system of sorts, perhaps a "United States of Europe."[61]

As in all cases of American nation-building at home and abroad, the Marshall Plan was not primarily about democracy or equality. It was a strategic investment in local organizations that would serve larger regional and American purposes. It prioritized political unity and economic production above other values. It also legitimized elite state institutions to act in the name of particular peoples, just as it defined particular peoples as sovereign groups with legitimate interests.

The Marshall Plan was not a design, a blueprint, or even a coherent project. It played an enormously influential role in postwar Germany, Western Europe, and the United States because it promoted a society of self-contained but interdependent nation-states on two sides of the Atlantic. This society of nation-states, like its eighteenth-century predecessor on the North American continent, was a fiction of sorts, but it was a fiction that made a new reality—especially for citizens in Stuttgart and other cities who longed for something other than depression and war.[62]

Lessons

The making of the Marshall Plan was a very messy process. The same can be said for the policies pursued by the United States in occupied Japan and South Korea in the same period, as well as the prior American experiences in the former Confederacy and the Philippines. Nation-building in all of these societies always operated on the edge of failure. Local populations were devastated by war, difficult to organize, and terribly deficient in basic resources—especially food. American officials were always ignorant of local cultures, unprepared for the gargantuan tasks of reconstruction, and distracted by other priorities. These are the "normal" conditions whenever the United States enters another society, in any form. The successes of the Marshall Plan, and U.S. policy as a whole in postwar Germany, grew from the relative adaptability and openness of the key actors both in Washington and in western Germany. Nation-building worked, in this case, because it constantly changed to match local needs and global interests.[63]

Nation-building involved much more than imposing or even suggesting institutions and ideas for a society emerging from destruction. External assistance was necessary for a scorched landscape, but foreign figures could not control activities inside distant countries. They knew that. From Hoover to Marshall, Americans worked from the ground up, closely partnering with local actors. This is how a sense of common civilization was constructed—in the daily interpersonal deals that got the water running, the roads repaired, the buildings rebuilt, and the economy functioning. This was also how authority was remade, in the practice of local politics, defined more as ad hoc compromise and dirty deal-making than the moral stridence of ideological proselytism or the chest-thumping of overwhelming military power. In postwar Germany and elsewhere, Americans entered towns less as all-knowing victors than as soldiers and entrepreneurs seeking partners among the people.

Partnership, in these terms, is not about transferring ideas and institutions from one country to another. Nation-building is never about replicating experiences and planting foreign models. Words like "Americanization," "Sovietization," and even "globalization" are misleading. If anything, the urge to make one society conform to another is the surest route to failure—witness the terrible record of "modernization" efforts in the middle decades of the Cold War. An external actor always lacks sufficient knowledge and power to make over an occupied society.[64]

Cultures and traditions define local meaning, they constrain change, and they influence expectations. They do not, however, determine outcomes any more than the weapons of a foreign occupier. Cultures and traditions constitute the paths through which foreign-influenced change can be brought to an occupied society. Rather than through imposition, reform emerges from locally informed negotiations on the application of new institutions and ideas to a still traditional society. This is a process of mixing, adaptation, and compromise. This is a process that is both foreign and local, traditional and modern. Nation-building, in its most common and often necessary form, involves just what the term implies: helping a society to emerge from a period of destruction with new institutions and practices that promise its people a better life. In the process, the new nation evolves as a hybrid, defined by unprecedented—and uncategorized—institutions, practices, and populations.

That was the genius of the postwar West German nation-state: the Federal Republic of Germany. It was German in its culture, its institutions, and its leaders. It was also influenced by the United States in its greater openness, representativeness, and integration with its neighbors. The West Germans continued to define themselves by blood, but they also embraced a vision of a single people formed within a constitutional state. The state, in turn, drew its legitimacy from representing a single people. This was the Madisonian image of the American nation-state, reformulated in Central Europe.

The nation-building creed proved so successful in its West German form that it made East German and other alternative communist visions untenable. In 1990 German nation-building reached fruition as the Soviet-dominated eastern half of the country enthusiastically embraced full participation in an expanded West German state. The West German nation became the all-German nation, with broad public consensus on both sides of the former divide. The economic and social costs of rapid unification were serious, they inspired many regrets, and they continue to manifest themselves in inequalities across German society during the early twenty-first century. Nation-building is always a contentious process, even in the best of circumstances.[65]

The stable continuity of the postwar German nation-state attests to the enduring relationships nurtured by Germans and Americans, started in the starving depths of a cold and desperate winter in 1947. For almost fifty years, German nation-building was difficult and dangerous. Germans played the crucial roles, and they made the most significant sacrifices on both sides of the Berlin Wall. The process was also part of a longer American nation-building tradition, transported in unexpected ways to an old Europe made anew. This nation-building tradition did not travel with the same results to Southeast Asia.[66]

Chapter 5

Reconstruction After Communist Revolution

Indo-China should not be given back to the French Empire after the war. The French had been there for nearly one hundred years and had done absolutely nothing with the place to improve the lot of the people.

Franklin Roosevelt, 1943[1]

Vietnam has the right to enjoy freedom and independence, and in fact has become a free and independent country. The entire Vietnamese people are determined to mobilize all their physical and mental strength, to sacrifice their lives and property, in order to safeguard their freedom and independence.

Ho Chi Minh, 1945[2]

Franklin Roosevelt was a war leader who valued flexibility and elusiveness, often to a fault. His closest advisors could rarely get him to take a firm position on divisive strategic issues, like the opening of the Second Front against Hitler, postwar control of Eastern Europe, and future cooperation with Stalinist Russia. Unlike many of his successors in the White House, Roosevelt avoided the temptation to articulate categorical positions on controversial issues with no easy point of resolution.[3]

On the future of Southeast Asia, however, the president departed from this pattern. Although he had little personal knowledge or interest in Indochina, Roosevelt committed the United States to the postwar removal of French colonialism from the region. He consistently pushed for "national independence" in what became Vietnam, despite strong British urgings to the contrary. Roosevelt warned Churchill that all inherited European empires in Asia were sources of instability and violence, as they had been in the Western Hemisphere a century earlier. They offended moral claims to freedom, retarded economic development, and, most dangerous of all, encouraged extremist politics—fascist and communist. These were the lessons Roosevelt had learned from his observations of the twentieth-century world. These were very American assumptions about the evils of empire. Roosevelt was firm and consistent in his anticolonialism.[4]

Before the Second World War, Americans were already accustomed to dismantling what they perceived as degenerate and inhumane empires. These included the British North American imperium of the late eighteenth century, the Southern slave aristocracy of the 1860s, and the Spanish Empire at the end of the nineteenth century. In each of these cases, Americans had acted to destroy established political power and replace it with a more open, representative, and "modern" alternative. The United States substituted American-style nation-building for inherited empire. Roosevelt perceived French Indochina in precisely these terms. Paris was the degenerate colonizer of Southeast Asia. The French Empire had contributed to violence, poverty, and chaos, according to the president. Americans would replace empire with nation-states for the sake of peace, stability, and development in the region.[5]

Roosevelt's hatred of French imperial rule influenced his war strategy. Until early 1945 he resisted British suggestions to work with French figures against Japanese forces in Southeast Asia. Instead, the president favored collaboration with Chiang Kai-shek's Nationalist (Guomindang) Chinese forces. Roosevelt perceived

Chiang as a more reliable and effective actor than his French counterparts. The president felt he could use Chiang for positive transformation, rather than a return to the prewar status quo. Most of all, Roosevelt assumed that he could control Chiang, and limit the Chinese Nationalist leader's abusive behavior, because of his near complete dependence on the United States. Despite French weaknesses, the president could not control the representatives of Paris's prior empire in the same way. French actors had too many sympathizers, including imperial officials in London, whom they could manipulate against Washington.[6]

American president Franklin Roosevelt worked closely with British prime minister Winston Churchill to defeat the Axis powers in the Second World War. Roosevelt pushed a reluctant Churchill to support plans for national independence in many former colonial territories, including the French colony of Indochina. This photo shows Roosevelt and Churchill in Casablanca, Morocco, January 1943.
Fox Photos, Hulton Collection, Getty Images

Roosevelt resisted joint military operations with British and Free French forces in Southeast Asia under British commander Admiral Lord Louis Mountbatten. U.S. Army and Air Forces around Indochina established direct relations, where they could, with Vietnamese fighters—including Ho Chi Minh's Vietminh nationalist organization (officially, the League for the Independence of Vietnam, founded in 1941). For most day-to-day military operations in the region, Roosevelt worked through the Chinese Nationalists and General Joseph Stilwell, the American commander of the China-Burma-India Theater. Roosevelt did not consult the European Allies, nor did he give them a veto over U.S. strategy in Indochina. As best he could, the president preserved independence for American anticolonialism, even as he fought alongside the colonial powers.[7]

In his meetings with Winston Churchill, Joseph Stalin, and other war leaders Roosevelt pushed for Vietnamese independence. At the Tehran Conference in late November 1943 the president assured Stalin that Allied sacrifices in war would not provide a source of sustenance for discredited French colonialism. Roosevelt observed that "after 100 years of French rule in Indochina, the inhabitants were worse off than they had been before." The president knew that the British prime minister (his closest ally) disagreed, but Roosevelt did not care. His personal commitment to anticolonialism in the region trumped his loyalty to Great Britain.[8]

On this contentious issue, Roosevelt had a broad group of supporters within American society. Opposition to empire, particularly the French Empire, was a default position among many citizens. Access for American businesses in Asia after the Second World War required the destruction of imperial trading regimes that excluded the United States. In place of empire, American entrepreneurs wanted to create open, independent national markets that allowed free trade. Prospects for peace and stability in the war-torn region called for a system of collective security. American observers looked to the model of the independent states in South America since the early nineteenth century, rather than the continuation of imperial conflicts in Southeast Asia begun during the same period.[9]

With proper guidance from the United States, an independent Vietnamese nation-state would, in American eyes, work much better than the inherited empires. One State Department official captured this perspective when he observed in June 1944 that the Vietnamese were more capable of political rule than the French. They are, he explained, "as able as the Thai, their independent neighbors to the west, and as the Filipinos." Like William Howard Taft in the Philippines, American officials who studied Vietnam expected a postwar period of transition—fifty years or less—to nurture a "self-governing nation." Policymakers in Washington hoped to bring Indochina into the American-led society of states on the ashes of Japanese (and French) defeat.[10]

Americans were well intentioned and often quite prescient about the end of empire. They recognized the importance of regional actors, and they understood that they could not build a postwar order on the strained and discredited shoulders of the old French imperium. Americans looked forward to a future of political independence and open markets in Southeast Asia. They had a vision, but they did not always know how to implement it in a very complicated, and overburdened, postwar world. American policy in Vietnam after 1945 reflected an unresolved struggle between clear anticolonial aims and a contradictory mix of actions that pushed for and against those goals, simultaneously. U.S. nation-building in Southeast Asia was often self-defeating.

Roosevelt and his successors tried to do too many things at once. As a consequence, Americans often undermined their deepest purposes. Less than two decades after the Japanese defeat, policymakers in Washington found themselves defending interventionist policies that prohibited the formation of the very nation-state in Vietnam they hoped to nurture. Americans were not destroying the village to save it, as one soldier notoriously claimed. Americans were trying to build too many different villages at once. They lost sight of their fundamental—and basic—nation-building goal in the region. More meant less, in terms of outcomes for American effort, especially when Washington confronted a skilled political adversary in the Vietnamese Communist Party.[11]

Trusteeship

The proposed American route to nation-building in Southeast Asia was what Roosevelt called "trusteeship." First proposed by the president in 1939 as a scheme to keep European possessions in the Western Hemisphere out of Nazi hands, trusteeship was a rejection of continued empire. It recognized the nationalist claims to independence voiced by former colonial subjects, and it created an obligation for a temporary occupying power—usually the United States—to help manage the transition to viable statehood. This meant cooperation with local citizens, not repression. It meant investment in security, economic development, and education, not exploitation. Most of all, trusteeship called for an end to foreign rule. Colonies would become sovereign states with representative governments, united peoples, and clear territorial boundaries. They would come to look like the United States.[12]

The Philippines was Roosevelt's model for Vietnam. He had followed the efforts of William Howard Taft and his successors in the archipelago. Although American nation-building had many limitations, and it encountered continued resistance, the president believed that the United States had helped the former Spanish colony to become a united, representative, and reasonably well-governed society. He was proud that his administration had, through the Tydings-McDuffie Act of 1934, pledged to recognize full Philippine independence by 1946. After the Japanese attacked the archipelago in December 1941, Roosevelt was also proud that the United States remained committed to expelling the attackers from the island and restoring security, good governance, and promised independence. Unlike Japan, Spain, France, or Great Britain, the United States converted its occupations into nation-states, not permanent colonies. From Roosevelt's perspective, the United States had acted as a trustee for Philippine nation-statehood during what was, after centuries of colonial rule, a reasonable transition to full membership in the society of states.

"Since this development worked in that case," Roosevelt argued, "there is no reason why it should not work in the case of Indo-China." The region needed a trustee to replace the institutions of French colonial repression with the good governance, public works, and education that had contributed to nation-state formation in the Philippines. Indochina needed external resources, assistance, and some guidance. It needed new partnerships and new incentives. It needed, above all, a coterie of cooperating elites—local and foreign—who would construct common public institutions for a united people. Washington would "hold Indo-China as trustee," Roosevelt explained. "This word cannot be translated into some languages. It means to hold for the benefit of the owner."[13]

According to Roosevelt's blueprint for trusteeship, Americans would nurture a transpacific elite, composed of Western-educated Vietnamese officials who could build a strong representative government in their homeland while maintaining good relations with the United States. As in all prior cases, nation-building would serve mutual interests. It would encourage transnational partnerships, productive economies, and popular stability. It would replace long-standing conflicts over colonies and other exploitative systems of rule with peaceful relations between diverse national peoples residing in similar sovereign states. The Kantian world of American-style governance promised progress from the Hobbesian system of empires.

It is hard to criticize Roosevelt's plans. Despite the pressures of more important theaters in the war, and the contrary preferences of his allies, the president took a stubborn stand for nation-building in a region far from the United States, where Washington had relatively minimal strategic and economic interests. Roosevelt recognized that a return to empire was counterproductive and immoral. He also understood that the obvious alternative—the immediate departure of all foreign powers and the affirmation of national independence, as Ho Chi Minh demanded—was also counterproductive and immoral. Local institutions were not yet constructed to hold the society together. Fragmentary impulses along religious and ethnic lines were powerful—more powerful than unifying political claims. Other regional actors—particularly the Chinese Nationalists, the Chinese communists, and the Soviets—were poised to exploit Indochinese fragmentation for their own benefit.

The United States needed a path to Vietnamese nationhood that navigated between the extremes of empire and anarchy. That was the point of trusteeship. That was also the point of the American nation-building creed, going back to the eighteenth century. Roosevelt's choices in 1945 renewed an inherited American position.[14]

Many observers have noted that trusteeship presumed hierarchy. The United States would act as a mature, "civilized" parent, holding the hands of ignorant "little yellow" Vietnamese children as they learned self-rule. They were not "ready" to govern themselves, Roosevelt and other Americans believed, because they were racially and culturally "backward." This racist attitude and the basic ideas for trusteeship were nourished by the experience of occupation in the Philippines. The American nation-building creed had its narrow-minded, condescending, and cruel qualities—especially after a half century of deadly wars.[15]

Roosevelt was a product of his times and the common racism of his contemporaries. He was also a realist in his recognition that societies were unequal, for whatever reason, in their preparation for governance. There were nonracist reasons to believe that after a hundred

n of War

he Second World War, Roosevelt's anticolonial de-
na did not disappear. They did, however, become
ever-greater demands on American resources. After
bbed direct possession of Indochina in March 1945,
ed for American military assistance to British and
fighting enemy forces. More than three years into
with casualties mounting and the Japanese military
to resist American attacks on Okinawa and other
es pushed to end the long conflict in Asia. Indochina
dor for the movement of Japanese soldiers and it thus
l site for defeating the last gasps of Tokyo's expansion-
g the isolation of the island empire, and forcing the
ntemplate surrender. British and French leaders called
tion to the opportunity that joint action in Indochina
ger war aims. Debates about colonialism now seemed
t.[17]

me minister Winston Churchill asserted an Allied obli-
the French. Following years of collaboration between the
regime and imperial Japan, patriotic French forces now
Tokyo's soldiers occupying Indochina. The Free French
ighting on behalf of the Allies, they sought American assis-
ey were overmatched against a stronger, battle-hardened
rchill made a moral and strategic plea to Washington, one
ficult to ignore: "The Prime Minister feels it would look
history if we were to let the French forces in Indo-China be
s by the Japanese through shortage of ammunition, if there
we can do to save them." The former colonial overseers of
ere now part of the team shedding blood on behalf of Great
l the United States to defeat Japan.[18]

eep misgivings, Roosevelt agreed to provide the British and
n with short-term American aid in Southeast Asia. We do

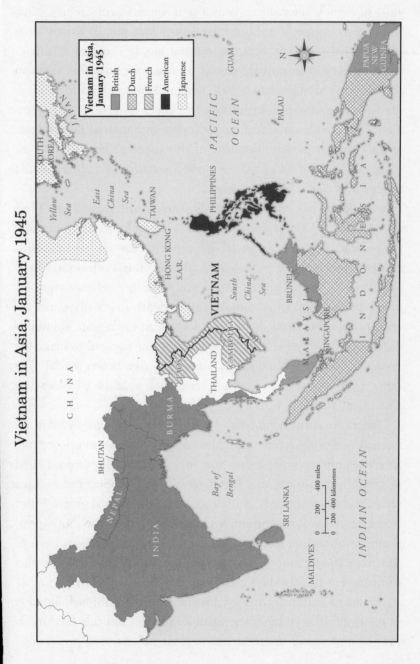

Vietnam in Asia, January 1945

years of French colonialism, centuries of imperial tribute to China, and an even longer history of fragmentary localism, "Vietnam" was an imagined political construct without strong roots to sprout in what was very rocky postwar terrain. To make the imagined Vietnam real, the United States had to help nurture a common national identity with representative institutions and effective agencies of government. The president rejected the racist presumption that the residents of Southeast Asia were incapable of this modernizing task, but he accepted the standard proposition that Vietnamese capability would emerge only under foreign tutelage.

More than sixty years later, we still struggle with these issues. How do we avoid the condescension of racial hierarchy without ignoring the presence of profound social inequalities? How do we aid political development while respecting racial and cultural autonomy? Roosevelt knew these dilemmas would not solve themselves, magically, if left alone—especially considering the deprivations of twentieth-century Indochina and the foreign designs on the region. Roosevelt also knew that if the United States did not take the lead to make the imagined Vietnam into a reality, another foreign power would. The other alternatives did not look any better than what the United States could hope to offer.

American aims during the 1940s and subsequent decades remained noble. Roosevelt and his successors did not seek to restore an old empire or build a new one in Indochina. They endeavored to create nation-states that better served their people, and in turn served the larger interests of the region and the United States. From Roosevelt to Lyndon Johnson, Vietnam always drew the most attention from American leaders who believed they had a vision, born of America's unique history, to transform the world. Vietnam became a recurring test case for the American nation-building creed.[16]

American endeavors in Vietnam often failed not for lack of effort or goodwill. If anything, these qualities made it difficult for Americans to understand the resistance to their policies. The problem in

not have the president on record at this time—just weeks before his death—but his chief of staff, Admiral William Leahy, conveyed the shift in U.S. military policy. During the second half of March 1945 American aircraft launched thirty-five bombing and supply missions over Indochina to support Allied ground capabilities. The U.S. military lifted its prohibition against direct collaboration with colonial forces, integrating French advisors, ships, and other personnel in their anti-Japanese maneuvers. For the first time after more than three years of war, American soldiers worked hand in hand with the European colonial officials in Southeast Asia. Washington distanced itself from the alternatives—the Chinese Nationalists and Ho Chi Minh's Vietminh.[19]

American leaders continued to emphasize the "obligations of a trustee" in the region, and Roosevelt demanded that returning French forces work toward Vietnamese statehood, not colonial control. In this way, the president and his closest advisors sought to solve their strategic dilemma by supporting old authorities for new purposes. In an echo of collaborations with former Southern confederates and German fascists, Americans hoped to transform the discredited conservatives into agents of change through engagement, support, and continued pressure. This was what one scholar calls a "reformist intervention" by an ambitious but overburdened U.S. government.[20]

As in other cases where Americans collaborated with the old oppressors to build new forms of political autonomy, the process often undermined its deepest purpose. Washington's direct aid to French colonial forces hindered reform. French officials, and their British supporters, were firmly committed to rebuilding empire. They saw a viable Vietnamese state as a direct threat to their postwar status, security, and prosperity in Paris and London. If anything, the burdens of war had convinced the West European powers that they needed to cling to their foreign possessions for any chance at restored national power. The countries of Europe had, quite literally, destroyed themselves; their colonies were their only remaining source of global leverage. The United States underwrote efforts at West European restoration for obvious military and strategic purposes, but Washington never figured out how to maintain momentum for the reforms in Southeast Asia that the West Europeans were dead set against.[21]

The French and the British were indeed allies *and* adversaries for American aims. The two qualities went together. How do you work with a discredited but indispensable ally, without becoming tainted by that ally? How do you strengthen a regime while also maintaining pressure for that regime to reform? These are, of course, recurring questions for American foreign policy—from Germany and Vietnam after the Second World War to Iraq and Afghanistan a half century later. There are no easy answers for a powerful American government, with global military and economic interests, as well as a sincere commitment to nation-building. The Roosevelt administration's decisions of March 1945 marked a significant turning point for the United States and Vietnam because they sharpened this dilemma between colonial allies and anticolonial aims. Americans never found a satisfying or workable solution. The Vietnamese communists, and Ho Chi Minh in particular, proved far more effective at matching power to principle.

Vietnamese Nation-Building

Japan's surrender on 15 August 1945 left a political vacuum throughout the territories that Emperor Hirohito's armies occupied at the end of the war—including parts of mainland China, Indonesia, the Korean Peninsula, and especially Vietnam. The former French colony became a cockpit for competing groups. Japanese military forces remained in place until the last months of 1945. They continued to provide basic order, and they maintained an important influence over daily life. French colonial officials, with very modest military capabilities, moved into the region with the clear ambition of reestablishing their control. Paris's representatives viewed the presence of defeated Japanese officials as an impediment to the reconstruction of the French Empire. Chinese forces under the authority of Chiang Kai-shek and other regional warlords also operated in the area, particularly near the northern boundary of Vietnam. Chiang hoped to expand his regional influence and use access to Indochina as a mechanism for strengthening his hand against communist challengers on the mainland.

These foreign actors—Japanese, French, and Chinese—had competing claims and interests. They each saw Vietnam as a target of opportunity, a point of leverage for larger geopolitical aims. Each foreign actor sought to expand its influence at the cost of the others. The recession of Japanese power meant that this competition would only increase.[22]

New internal power centers also emerged within the region. Through the Vietminh and other loosely affiliated Vietnamese groups, the Indochinese Communist Party pushed for independence from Japanese, French, and Chinese Nationalist interventions, arguing that the end of the war should also mark the end of colonialism. A classic political front organization designed to mobilize citizens, the Vietminh had strong foreign communist connections, particularly with the Soviet-dominated Comintern and the Chinese Communist Party. Its strong and consistent advocacy for Vietnamese independence, however, made the Vietminh a powerful magnet for support among diverse anticolonial actors—communist and noncommunist—in Southeast Asia. As one scholar observes, the Vietminh was probably the sole organization capable of building a "nationwide movement for national independence, one that could not only win the support of the mass of the Vietnamese population but even earn the sympathy of progressive peoples around the world." Although this "popular front" strategy of mobilizing a broad spectrum of anti-imperialists was more of an aspiration than a reality, it changed the political dynamics in and around Vietnam.[23]

Ho Chi Minh was the communist-trained figure who had done more than anyone else to bring international attention to Vietnamese nationalist aspirations. He had petitioned for Vietnamese independence from French rule as early as 1919, he had spent the subsequent decades in exile working toward "national liberation" with an international coterie of communist revolutionaries (including Mao Zedong and Zhou Enlai), and he had collaborated with those groups (including Americans) fighting against Japanese domination in Southeast Asia after 1942. Ho had earned his nationalist credentials, even as his communist connections deepened.

Ho Chi Minh created a communist government in Vietnam after the Second World War. He proved to be the most effective nation-builder in the region.
Picture dated March 1951, somewhere in Vietnam, Getty Images

Ho had unparalleled charisma and credibility among independence activists, but he did not control the Vietminh or any of the other postwar Vietnamese movements. His decades of exile had made that impossible. Instead, Ho used the Vietminh, with great skill, as a platform for asserting his claim to native rule. The threats of Japanese, French, or Chinese occupation in Vietnam lent domestic legitimacy to Ho's anticolonial claims. The work of domestic and foreign activists, especially those nurtured by the Soviet and Chinese communist parties, provided an organizational foundation for Ho to grasp power.[24]

Ho Chi Minh therefore emerged in the summer of 1945 as a figure uniquely situated to build on a vast network of local political organizations, broad international recognition, and almost unimpeachable credentials as a tireless advocate for his country. He was a communist ideologue, but also a sincere nationalist. He was a revolutionary, but also a pragmatic political operator. Most of all, he was a leader with a vision for a postcolonial Vietnam that would expel the imperialists, erect domestic authority around the Communist Party, and manage diplomatic relations with powerful noncommunist countries, especially the United States. Since at least 1944, Ho had shown a willingness to work constructively with Americans in what he hoped would become a joint effort to eradicate empire. He even convinced representatives from the U.S. State Department to plan a trip for him to the United States at the end of the war—a proposal ultimately rejected for fear of antagonizing America's French allies.[25]

Ho Chi Minh's combination of nationalism and communism did not necessarily undermine American nation-building aspirations. Despite their many differences, Franklin Roosevelt and Ho Chi Minh shared a hatred of empire, a commitment to national independence, and a vision of peaceful independent states in Southeast Asia. They both advocated territorial sovereignty, popular unity, and representative government in the region. When Ho Chi Minh famously quoted from the American Declaration of Independence on 2 September 1945, he did not embrace American individualism, democracy, or free enterprise. He did, however, pay homage to the American model of self-governing political institutions that united a people and a territory in peace and prosperity. Ho recognized that American nation-building had saved its people from the recurring colonial divisions, exploitations, and wars that had plagued Indochina. Ho wanted to build a powerful nation-state of his own—one with Vietnamese, communist, and even some American characteristics.[26]

If the large regional and colonial powers converged on Vietnam in 1945, a small but organized group of Vietnamese was poised, as never before, to make its voice heard. Ho Chi Minh, the Vietminh, and the Indochinese Communist Party worked to create a Vietnamese nation-state as a bulwark primarily against France, China, and Japan—the historic powers in the region. Although the new Vietnamese nation-state would draw on Communist Party institutions, ideas, and influences, it would also replicate some basic assumptions about government, representativeness, and sovereignty derived from the American nation-building creed. The American model influenced communists as well as capitalists after the Second World War.

American Retreat

The United States helped to shape events in Vietnam during the summer of 1945. The direct American role in the region was, however, quite constrained. Although Washington's representatives on the ground attempted to nurture close relations with a range of actors (including both Ho Chi Minh and his French adversaries), the United States did not play the role of king-maker.

After almost four years of exhaustive warfare on two fronts, American policymakers were overwhelmed by the seemingly endless pressures that came with the final surrender: the growing demand for American resources to fuel postwar reconstruction around the globe; the powerful calls for retrenchment within the United States among citizens who wanted to reap the rewards of war sacrifices; the stubborn Soviet claims for access to resources and territory in the name of postwar security; and, perhaps most jolting, the poorly prepared transition in American leadership after Franklin Roosevelt's death on

12 April 1945. The end of the war created a widespread feeling of relief, but it also renewed anxieties. What would come next?[27]

Roosevelt's anticolonial commitments, his self-confidence, and his foresight led him to devote extensive attention to Vietnam amidst all the challenges of a world war. During the second half of 1945, and subsequent years, President Harry Truman and his closest advisors would lack the same focus, confidence, and clarity of vision. They would remain committed to anticolonialism, but they would look far beyond Southeast Asia. Overburdened with commitments in Germany, Japan, and countless other countries—as well as growing evidence of Soviet opportunism and aggression—Truman allowed Vietnam to fall through the cracks. For good reason, the new president felt crushed by an "avalanche of things." After Roosevelt's death, the United States did not have a real postwar policy for Indochina.[28]

The Truman administration relied on a combination of sincere but superficial platitudes about support for national independence, and hesitant efforts to maintain order in the region through existing Japanese, French, and Chinese forces. The White House worked, above all, to minimize its direct postwar commitments in Southeast Asia. As a consequence, the political initiative devolved to actors on the ground—the very groups whose conflicting goals and limited capabilities produced a power vacuum in the first place. The United States inadvertently contributed to additional instability, uncertainty, and frustration: American rhetoric encouraged Ho Chi Minh and other nationalists; American diplomatic cooperation with Paris encouraged French imperialists; Amercan support for Chiang Kai-shek encouraged Chinese Nationalist aims in the region; and American efforts to collaborate with Japanese conservative leaders, especially the emperor, encouraged the defeated country's continued interests in Indochina. Washington's postwar efforts to reduce costs and play all sides in Vietnam raised expectations among regional actors and set the stage for near universal disappointment with the United States.

In neglecting the hard policy choices, the Truman administration allowed conflict in the region to expand. Determined to avoid disappointing anyone, Washington antagonized everyone.[29]

Too often scholars look for organized plans and clear intentions where they do not exist. Too often observers assume that government actions reflect careful forethought and serious calculation. Contrary to these assumptions, the most powerful policymakers frequently fall into decisions that they did not anticipate, advocate, or even recognize at the time. Burdened by heightened commitments and limited attention, even the strongest international actor often finds itself reacting to circumstances it does not control. In the case of Vietnam, Washington's distraction and disinterest meant that the geopolitcal vacuum created by Japan's defeat opened an opportunity for the weaker groups more committed to the region. American half measures enabled the small to punch above their weight.

Ho Chi Minh and the Vietminh recognized these circumstances better than anyone else. They also had the advantage of clear focus, despite their relative weakness. If the French had a domestic nation and a huge overseas empire to rebuild, the Vietminh had only one area for its operations. If the United States had a vast postwar world to police and reconstruct, Ho Chi Minh had only one country and one people who mattered for him. Ho Chi Minh and the Vietminh turned global complexity into a startling, and successful, revolutionary opportunity.

The Vietnamese Communist Revolution

Revolutions are inspired by ideas and planned by people, but they are made by the circumstances of a society undergoing profound transitions. This was true for Vietnam in the summer of 1945. Years of war and misgovernance had produced famine conditions, especially in the northern parts of the country. Floods around the time of the Japanese surrender made matters worse. Dikes on the Red River—flowing southeast from Yunnan province in China, past Hanoi, and emptying into the Gulf of Tonkin—broke in August 1945, destroying at least 300,000 hectares of rice fields. Adding to the previous strains on the insufficient Vietnamese food supply, the country now lost about one third of its seasonal rice harvest. As many as one million people had already died of starvation in 1945, and the floods promised that thousands more would perish. Vietnamese citizens throughout the countryside and cities began to take matters into their own hands, seizing food supplies and other resources, denouncing local authorities (Japanese and Vietnamese), and claiming power for themselves. Amidst famine, floods, and a full political collapse, the country entered a period of "social revolutionary behavior, the consequences of which no one could predict at the time."[30]

The Vietminh did not make these conditions. In fact, local citizens frequently blamed Communist Party officials for their problems. Ho Chi Minh, however, saw an opportunity in tragedy. This was the secret to his political success. His opportunism and tenacity set him apart from other actors at the time.

Under Ho's leadership the Vietminh moved decisively to provide relief, order, and hope to the citizenry. It launched an organized country-wide insurrection on 12 August to capitalize on disorder and discontent, and establish new institutions for authority. Most political groups—Japanese, French, Chinese, and Vietnamese—were hesitant to act so decisively. The circumstances were too dire, the future too uncertain. Pulling the trigger on revolution—even in the most propitious circumstances—is scary. There are few points of retreat once a group risks everything for power.[31]

Ho had spent three decades waiting for this moment, and he would not let it pass. In contrast to most of his fellow activists, he pushed for the Vietminh to take control of events "immediately." "The situation is about to change very rapidly," he told his Communist Party members. "We can't lose this opportunity." The Vietminh deployed this precise language in appealing to suffering citizens of various backgrounds: "The decisive hour in the destiny of our people has struck. Let us stand up with all our strength to liberate ourselves!"[32]

Liberation, in this context, meant freedom from foreign oppressors, unity in pursuing common Vietnamese interests, and, most of all, control of resources and power by self-selected representatives of the people. Ho Chi Minh and the other leaders of the Vietminh were Leninists who had studied the Bolshevik "liberation" of czarist Russia at the end of the First World War. Ho Chi Minh had lived in Russia—an "apprentice revolutionary," in the words of his biographer—while the communist regime consolidated power from 1923 to 1924. He would follow Lenin's model two decades later, exploiting war conditions, mobilizing popular aspirations, and building a new state to manage his society. As in the Soviet Union, the revolutionary Vietnamese state would assert firm control over territory. The Communist Party would embody the united will of the people. The new Vietnamese nation-state would be a Leninist party-state. It would promise food and land to all loyalists from a newly empowered governing center.[33]

This party-state building process began in August 1945 with the army, as it always does. Ho Chi Minh persuaded the Vietminh to increase the size of its very small Vietnamese Liberation Army (VLA). With only five thousand soldiers, this paramilitary force served as the initial shock troops for a wider insurrection. They attacked French and Japanese positions, they asserted control over selected local areas, and they requisitioned "volunteer" soliders and supplies throughout the country. The VLA became a symbol of Vietminh power and the possibilities for Vietnamese citizens to control their own destiny. As in other Leninist settings, the volunteerism of the troops became a conduit for asserting Communist Party control through various settings and institutions. Loyalty and patriotism were redefined as service in the Liberation Army. The growing reach of the VLA was the growing reach of the party-state.[34]

Factions in Vietnam, 1945

In September 1945 150,000 Chinese Nationalist soldiers (largely poor peasants) arrived in Hanoi. They looted the city and the villages they encountered during their movements.

In August 1945 the Vietnamese Liberation Army included only 5,000 soldiers. Ho Chi Minh relied on a much larger collection of revolutionary committees, self-defense forces, and guerrilla units. Ho and his supporters drew on a force of 200,000 armed citizens.

In July 1945 3,000 guerrilla soldiers supporting Ho Chi Minh operated in Tonkin.

In October 1945 French general Jacques-Philippe Leclerc arrived in South Vietnam with 35,000 soldiers. French forces expelled the Vietminh from Saigon.

Vietminh "revolutionary committees," composed of Communist Party officials and volunteers, quickly sprouted with centralized support throughout the country, particularly in the north. This network of small organizations addressed local problems, combated challengers to Vietminh authority, and, most important, built a new fabric of loyalty to the Communist Party throughout Vietnam. The revolutionary committees made ordinary citizens feel the state. They provided people with a sense that their voices mattered, that their problems would find redress. The revolutionary committees also intimidated and attacked those who offered alternatives. Postwar Vietnamese identity emerged from the mix of volunteerism, problem-solving, and coercion spun around the new institutional tentacles of the Communist Party web. Ho Chi Minh had learned to manage this process firsthand, during his years in both the Soviet Union and communist-held territory in China.[35]

Leninist party-state–building was not democratic, but it was effective. In response to the famine, floods, and postwar dislocations, the Vietminh offered the most direct relief to citizens. It began with a mix of symbolic and pragmatic measures. Ho Chi Minh announced that he would forgo food once every ten days, donating his unconsumed nourishment to poor citizens. He called for reductions in consumption across the population—rich and poor, urban and countryside. Contrary to communist dogma, the Vietminh also broke up communal lands, dividing arable territory into small parcels for family cultivation. The Vietminh opened vacant lands for agriculture, and it established a small credit bureau to provide local capital for farming. Ho Chi Minh claimed governing authority for these actions in the name of the people, but his ability to seize the initiative reflected the broad organization of the Vietminh, its decisiveness, and its reliance on a combination of volunteerism and coercion throughout the country. In addressing the needs of Vietnamese citizens, the Vietminh filled the postwar vacuum in domestic society.[36]

Ho Chi Minh's power did not come from a persuasive ideology

or a set of miracle solutions to difficult problems. Quite the contrary, most Vietnamese citizens were illiterate and few saw any immediate benefits from Vietminh policies. What made Ho Chi Minh and other communists effective at building mass support was their ability to give ordinary men and women a feeling that they had political voice. Vietnamese, not foreigners, were now implementing policies in response to the needs of Vietnamese. An organization now existed to serve the people, not vice versa. A leader now appeared who understood the people and had shown, during three decades of struggle, that he would stand up for the people. The Vietminh possessed popular credibility that no other organized group could match. It offered a persuasive revolutionary promise: political voice for the voiceless masses.

Japanese soldiers, still in Vietnam at the end of August 1945, recognized that they could no longer maintain order in these tumultuous circumstances. Witnessing the organization and effectiveness of the Vietminh, the Japanese turned over their positions to what became Ho Chi Minh's provisional government. Tokyo's commanders ceded police power, control of government buildings, and even protection of the French governor-general's palace to the Vietminh. Ho Chi Minh could now claim mass support, policy momentum, and possession of basic governing infrastructure. In a time of great uncertainty, these became anchors for state-building. The Vietminh assumed power in symbol and action, on the ashes of the old authorities destroyed by the war and the revolution. In this context, those who looked most ready to rule gained the initiative. "Ho and his colleagues," in the words of one historian, "presented the world with a fait accompli."[37]

For the next three decades, Ho Chi Minh and his fellow revolutionaries never lost their advantage acquired in the summer of 1945. Even an anticommunist critic of the Vietminh recognized: "The majority clearly welcomed Ho and his men—the mysterious and awesome figures emerging from prisons, jungles, mountains, and foreign countries." Ho Chi Minh worked to build a "united front" government—the Democratic Republic of Vietnam—that initially included various groups. He continued to reach out to the United States, and even the French on occasion. Ho understood that he had to translate his personal charisma into institutions of national governance.[38]

He spoke authoritatively for the Vietnamese people as a whole, most famously on National Independence Day, 2 September 1945: "Vietnam has the right to enjoy freedom and independence, and in fact has become a free and independent country. The entire Vietnamese people are determined to mobilize all their physical and mental strength, to sacrifice their lives and property, in order to safeguard their freedom and independence." These words were autobiographical and aspirational; they spoke to popular hopes and demands in a language most Vietnamese could easily understand. More than 400,000 citizens attended Ho Chi Minh's National Independence Day speech in Hanoi, and they closed the occasion by pledging a public oath to defend the new nation and implement the policies of the Vietminh. Personal sacrifices were valorized as signs of patriotism and enlightenment. Rhetoric, symbol, and volunteerism bound a new people to a fusion of nationalist-communist politics.[39]

Despite its international communist connections, the Vietminh became the most recognized and legitimate political party for Vietnamese national dreams. This was a difficult point for anticommunist French and American observers to appreciate. In his spare peasant attire, Ho Chi Minh was the almost unimpeachable symbol of a united Vietnamese people. One scholar explains that he fulfilled "the need of people for a just, invincible leader, projecting the collective dream, weaving the new myth." The Ho Chi Minh myth became the founding postwar Vietnamese national myth. All nation-states are built on myths and the institutions that they support. Vietnam was no exception.[40]

After 1945 Ho Chi Minh and the Vietminh made the most persuasive claim to embody the new nation. A Vietnamese sovereign people existed because of the partial unity provided by Ho and the

Vietminh. Ho and the Vietminh could exercise political power because they represented a united people in aspiration, if not always in practice. Postwar Vietnamese nation-state–building, in this sense, was a replay of James Madison's constitutional fiction 150 years earlier—the people made the government and the government made the people.[41]

Although many Vietnamese, particularly in the south, opposed his leadership, Ho rapidly built a powerful state infrastructure—dominated by the Vietminh—to support his personal popularity. He converted the Vietnamese Liberation Army into the National Defense Guard, with a Vietnamese Political-Military School. In true Leninist fashion, the new school combined military training with Communist Party indoctrination. The size of the National Defense Guard quickly grew to include eighty thousand soldiers under arms. Ho's government requisitioned gold from the citizenry in 1945 and 1946 to finance weapons and other supplies. In the coming years the size of the army, and the requisitions from the public, would grow considerably. A national Vietnamese army, under Vietminh control, would make the nation-state.[42]

Although the Democratic Republic of Vietnam was dominated by the Communist Party, it created a new National Assembly, first meeting in downtown Hanoi on 2 March 1946. To some extent, this was a charade—Ho Chi Minh and the Vietminh leadership made all the key decisions. The National Assembly remained important, however, as an enactment of united national self-determination. The representatives in the assembly were all Vietnamese. They were chosen by the citizens in nationwide elections that, for the first time in the country's history, gave all citizens above the age of eighteen the right to vote. The national act of voting for representatives, even if their power was seriously constrained, asserted the existence of a united people and the right to rule for a state composed of elected representatives. The National Assembly affirmed the nation in its composition and its daily performance.

The collection of Vietnamese voices in the National Assembly legitimized government decisions. They debated and voted, but they really did not legislate. On key questions of policy, Ho Chi Minh and other communist leaders provided them with decisions that had already been made to deal with foreign threats and domestic needs in a time of pressing emergency. Instead of changing policy, or proposing new actions, the assembly provided a mechanism for nationwide implementation. Elected representatives brought decisions from the center back to their home districts. They suggested points of effective compromise between national need and local opinion. Most significant, elected representatives made citizens feel included—that their interests were addressed—even if they did not like the government's substantive decisions. The National Assembly created a credible process of national participation that justified, and sometimes motivated, popular sacrifices for the emerging nation-state.

This process of inclusion had real tangible effects. The national government and the army became recognized parts of people's lives. National holidays, elections, tax collections, and other state rituals became ordering events in the daily routine of citizens. Ho Chi Minh's picture and other images of the Democratic Republic and the Vietminh became ubiquitous, even in the countryside. When leaders spoke of an independent Vietnamese nation, as they did all the time, most residents of that territory understood what they meant. The national defined the local.

As in other cases of nation-building, education was a particularly important site where families felt their new nation-state at work. Ninety percent of Vietnamese citizens were illiterate in early 1945. French colonialism, like Spanish colonialism in the Philippines, reinforced an inherited tradition of educating only the most elite, leaving the vast majority to toil with very limited intellectual horizons. Educational deprivation was a form of social control. The new Vietnamese nation-state abruptly changed educational expectations. As part of the government's efforts to create an active, mobilized, and productive citizenry, it invested its scarce resources in schools for all citizens—especially those in poor rural areas. Mass education was a communist priority in Vietnam.

The Communist Party sent young members to the countryside to live off the land, bond with the people, and teach them to become "modern." This meant basic literacy and numeracy, a self-awareness about the nation, and a familiarity with concepts of public health, political participation, and communist economy. Rural education often took place in local pagodas, hospitals, and marketplaces hastily converted to schools. Instructors often received little pay, but became important figures in local communities. Although education disrupted many indigenous hierarchies, it offered new forms of hope and belonging to suffering people. Unprecedented in Vietnamese history, mass education created the rudiments of a modern mass citizenry, tied to Ho Chi Minh's nation-state. By late 1946, more than two million Vietnamese had gained literacy they did not possess before. These newly empowered citizens were the popular foundation for sustaining the Vietnamese communist revolution and its successor, the Democratic Republic of Vietnam.[43]

The Vietnamese communist revolution did not succeed in many of its aims. It did not evict foreign powers quickly from Indochina. It did not build a communist state where the peasants and workers governed the society. Most significant, it did not bring freedom and prosperity to many citizens who continued to suffer repression and poverty. Ho Chi Minh's power came from the popular hopes he inspired—hopes that remained largely unfulfilled.

Despite these limitations, the great success of the communist revolution was the foundation it built for a united Vietnamese identity and effective institutions of Vietnamese governance. Neither had existed before. After 1945 they became the most significant features of the political landscape. They gave birth to the only real Vietnamese nation-state.

After the Revolution

French, Chinese, Soviet, and especially American policymakers confronted a Vietnamese nation-state that they could not wish out of existence. The new government had strong nationalist and communist credentials. Ho Chi Minh and the Vietminh were the earliest and most earnest nation-builders in Indochina; they benefited from a first-mover advantage. Unlike in the Philippines, American policymakers had to compete with an established and effective alternative. Unlike in the post–Civil War South or Germany after the Second World War, American representatives had to contend with more recognized and empowered sources of local legitimacy.

Although Vietnam was a political vacuum in 1945, it quickly became a space dominated by non-American nation-builders. In contrast to prior experiences, the United States was *not* the most committed modernizer in the region. The United States also was *not* the agenda-setter for national reforms. After Vietnam's communist revolution, American ideas about governance, representativeness, and citizenship were *not* revolutionary. Despite its enormous power, Washington had to adjust to a position of dependence, perhaps even subordination, to Ho Chi Minh's primacy on the ground.

This was an adjustment that Americans, accustomed to leadership as nation-builders, were never able to make. Policymakers in Washington read their own history of nation-building in other places wrong. They assumed that either through allies or alone they could overpower organized local actors with a compelling political vision. They assumed that they could contain and destroy communist alternatives to American-style nation-building. The defeat of fascism and the emerging conflict with the Soviet Union raised the stakes for policymakers seeking to assert preponderant American power across the globe. The complexities of political persuasion were often lost in the pressures of communist containment.[44]

The history of American nation-building since the eighteenth century should have warned against strategic simplicity and stubbornness. It should have warned against excessive ambition and political hubris. The United States operated most effectively when it isolated discredited actors, coopted empowered groups, and displayed its commitment to local self-improvement through direct, often nonmilitary, actions. From Southern Reconstruction through the transformation of postwar Germany, nation-building pivoted on the American capacity to adapt, to change course, and to remake its relations with allies and adversaries. Dogmatism and self-righteousness were never favorable attributes for U.S. policy.

Americans had to win the Vietnamese people over by building their own credibility as providers of mutual benefits. That is, of course, the essence of nation-building—all the major players must have a stake in the course of political change. After 1945 this could not happen without Ho Chi Minh and the Vietminh. If anything, repeated efforts to deny the reality of the Vietnamese communist revolution reinforced its domestic significance as a touchstone of independence. Americans were operating in a region *after revolution*—after the international Communist Party and its local affiliates had fused their ideas and organization with the most powerful forces for national self-determination. American anticommunism undermined the possibilities of American anticolonialism.[45]

Failed Counterrevolutions

President Truman and his successors in the White House believed that they were continuing Franklin Roosevelt's policies in Southeast Asia. They opposed permanent colonial empires in the region. They embraced nation-building, hoping to create stable, sovereign, and open states that would resist external domination from the Soviet Union, and soon Communist China as well. Most of all, they sought to make the United States a force for progressive, modern change in the region through various forms of military and nonmilitary assistance. From Harry Truman to Lyndon Johnson, policymakers followed the inherited American formula of serving themselves by acting in ways they sincerely believed would also serve citizens of new nation-states. As elsewhere, Washington consistently invested in supporting a society of states, rather than empires or anarchy in Southeast Asia.

This consistent nation-building effort ran aground because its progressive qualities in American eyes appeared counterrevolutionary to many Vietnamese viewers. For citizens who had experienced the deprivation, dislocation, and determined Vietminh leadership of 1945, the United States looked out of touch in its priorities, suspicious in its allies, and misguided in its actions. Washington's hesitance to embrace Ho Chi Minh, and its apparent comfort with French colonial officials, discredited promises of positive change. Distancing itself from the Vietnamese communist revolution, the United States took on a counterrevolutionary identity in Southeast Asia. America's progressive intentions did not matter. Standing against Ho Chi Minh and the Vietminh threatened the most promising path to nation-building in the eyes of many. As was the case after the Russian Revolution in 1917, the United States appeared to be on the wrong side of history. Citizens in Southeast Asia reacted accordingly.

American leaders recognized that their options in Vietnam were limited after 1945. During the first years following the Vietnamese communist revolution, Washington lent minimal support to French efforts at reestablishing political control in the region. Paris's representatives used American supplies left over after the Second World War, and they relied on the United States to give some public support for their continued presence in Vietnam. President Truman and his advisors encouraged the French to play a stabilizing role in the region, but they also consistently voiced their desire for compromise with the Vietminh. Dean Acheson, undersecretary of state in late 1945, put it well: "the willingness of the U.S. to see French control reestablished assumed that [the] French claim to have support of the population is borne out by future events." In practice, this meant that Washington would wait and see—offering little tangible support to the French and avoiding antagonistic moves toward the Vietminh.[46]

French leaders resented American anticolonial sentiments and pressures for reform. As Cold War tensions between Washington and Moscow deepened, Paris's representatives appealed to the Truman administration's anxieties about Soviet expansion. They warned that a rapid collapse of the empire in Southeast Asia would undermine strength and stability in Western Europe. How could a humiliated France stand up to Soviet aggression? How could an economically destitute France restrain internal communist agitators if it lost its external sources of wealth and status?

France's lobbying paid off when Americans came to fear imminent communist advances in Europe and Asia—an apparent extension of the "satellite" regimes Stalin had created in Eastern Europe and North Korea. During the years after 1945 American policymakers grudgingly accepted a partial restoration of French power in Vietnam as a temporary, but necessary, evil. "We are not interested," Secretary of State George Marshall explained, "in seeing colonial empire administrations supplanted by [the] philosophy and political organizations emanating from and controlled by [the] Kremlin." From his tireless wartime leadership and his extensive efforts to mediate between groups in China, Marshall understood the Vietminh's nationalist appeal in the region. Nonetheless, he valued a continued French presence because, he wrote, "Ho Chi Minh has direct Communist connections."[47]

Events in 1949 and 1950 made these communist connections increasingly threatening for American policymakers. The growth of Soviet power (especially the testing of Moscow's first atomic bomb in August 1949), the triumph of Mao Zedong's Chinese Communist

Party in China, and the North Korean invasion of South Korea—all within less than twelve months—convinced many Americans that they had to do more to hold the line against what appeared to be an aggressive communist "monolith." Global communism was now the empire that drew the most militant opposition in the United States. The vestiges of colonialism in Asia were an easy target for the advancing communist armies. American policymakers believed they had to invest more heavily in regional stability and security so that nation-building—rather than Soviet and Chinese expansion—could take its course. A perceived global threat, and the searing failures of appeasement in the face of a similar threat ten years earlier, convinced Washington to front-load nation-building with more direct force.[48]

Americans continued to stand by their nation-building creed, hoping to create a society of representative, independent, and open states in Southeast Asia. They continued to defend territorial sovereignty and its connection to united and distinct peoples. Combining anticolonialism with militant anticommunism, however, converted American nation-building into a much more counterrevolutionary force than it had ever been before. Instead of finding avenues for cooperation with *some* communists—as Americans had with *some* Confederates and *some* fascists in the past—Washington's representatives now made communist isolation a near universal requirement for all positive reconstruction. Anticommunist absolutism alienated Americans from the progressive and popular urges embedded in communist activism throughout the region.[49]

The United States never embraced a return of empire, but it now set itself as strongly against the most powerful forces for change as the colonialists of old. With the simultaneous growth of American power and vulnerability in the Cold War, nation-building efforts after 1950 became far too rigid, too self-centered, and too counterrevolutionary. Beset by a proliferation of crises abroad, and McCarthyite recriminations for perceived weakness at home, Americans once again misread their history. They valorized absolutism and rigidity, rather than the compromise and flexibility that had contributed to past achievements.[50]

Neglected Diplomacy

Criticizing communist containment policy at the start of the Cold War, Walter Lippmann foresaw this tragic consequence of misdirected American power. "The history of diplomacy," he wrote, "is the history of relations among rival powers, which did not enjoy political intimacy, and did not respond to appeals to common purposes." "For a diplomat to think," Lippmann warned, "that rival and unfriendly powers cannot be brought to a settlement is to forget what diplomacy is about." American nation-building had always involved realistic diplomacy—in North America and abroad. That was the legacy of Oliver Otis Howard, William Howard Taft, and Herbert Hoover. It was a legacy Americans painfully rejected in the Cold War, especially around Southeast Asia.[51]

Instead of reaching out to the only credible nationalists in Vietnam—the Vietminh—American leaders threw their support to anticommunist stalwarts with little connection to the population, and little skill at state-building. Beginning in 1949, the United States increased its economic and military support to French forces, and it gave diplomatic recognition to the French puppet emperor in Vietnam, Bao Dai. At the same time, Washington refused to open official relations with Ho Chi Minh and the Vietminh. The Korean War triggered a massive upsurge in American aid to France and Bao Dai, and a further reinforcement of efforts to alienate local communists. By the time of the Korean cease-fire at Panmunjom in July 1953, the United States bankrolled the activities of the colonialists and the royalists in Vietnam. Both of these groups inspired resistance, and their presence proved largely counterproductive, as they drove citizens to support the communists for nationalist reasons. The Vietminh was, after all, the only prominent local actor with real domestic roots. The image of the Vietminh only improved when contrasted with the French, Bao Dai, and American anticommunists.[52]

U.S. nation-building goals were undermined by the surrogates Washington supported, and the adversaries Washington alienated. This broke with the experience from the Philippines and Germany, and it opened a pattern that would plague American efforts through the early twenty-first century. Instead of shifting positions and formulating new policies, American leaders stubbornly stuck to failing relationships, fearful of alternatives. Instead of seriously addressing whether the alignment of forces posed a real possibility for success, American leaders told themselves that they could "win" if they put in more treasure, more brains, and ultimately, more muscle. Many observers feared "falling dominoes" if the communists took full control of Vietnam, but the real cascade came from American Sisyphean efforts to push discredited actors on a populace that knew it had better options.

Entering the White House in the last months of the Korean War, President Dwight Eisenhower continued this self-defeating process. He rejected calls for direct American military (even nuclear) intervention in Vietnam, but he replaced the French forces defeated in the 1954 battle at Dien Bien Phu with increased American assistance to a corrupt and incompetent anticommunist regime. Following negotiations in Geneva, Ho Chi Minh's Democratic Republic of Vietnam gained control of North Vietnam; the anticommunist forces possessed nominal authority in South Vietnam, centered on the capital city of Saigon. In fact, Ho Chi Minh held more support in the South than any American surrogate. The Vietminh had worked for a decade to create deep roots in the North, as well as the South. Despite the superficial division of the peninsula, the communists benefited from unparalleled political activism and organization. The anticommunists had American support, but little to offer on the ground.[53]

Eisenhower escalated the American commitment to Ngo Dinh Diem, Bao Dai's handpicked prime minister in South Vietnam. Diem sought to modernize the country with little domestic legitimacy and little understanding of the needs of his people. Although he was talented and hardworking, Diem had shown poor political instincts throughout his career. He had spent much of the postwar period living in Catholic seminaries on the East Coast of the United States, isolated from the revolutionary events in Vietnam. Most significant, Diem was neither trained nor experienced—as Ho Chi Minh was—for the task of building a functioning state. He was more of a monkish aesthete and an ideological dogmatist than a pragmatic institution-builder. He lacked organizational skills, a compelling biography for Vietnamese citizens, and a persuasive local vision for a noncommunist state. Diem looked far more impressive to his initial American backers than to his own citizens. That was precisely his problem. Thanks to Washington's generous public support, that was also America's problem.[54]

Hostage to Incompetence

Eisenhower never liked Diem. The former commander of American forces in Europe during the Second World War recognized incompetence when he saw it. He understood that Diem's plans for land reform, economic growth, and military training looked good on paper, but they lacked effective leadership. In particular, the South Vietnamese ruler surrounded himself with family members and other sycophants who furthered his isolation from the population. Diem relied on personalist authority, refusing to build a competent administrative apparatus for the South. In contrast to the loyal cadres of Ho Chi Minh's Communist Party, America's ally was so distrusting of his own people that he resorted to extremes of micromanagment. He refused to empower people he could not control.[55]

Ngo Dinh Diem received extensive American military and economic support after 1954. He proved ineffective at building a functioning South Vietnamese nation-state. *Howard Sochurek, Time & Life Pictures, Getty Images*

J. Lawton Collins—the distinguished U.S. Army corps commander in Europe whom Eisenhower sent to advise Diem—reported to the president in 1955 that "the continuation of the present government under Diem was no longer supportable." Collins recounted how "Diem has lost his cabinet ministers one by one." As "an example of his lack of administrative capability," Collins explained, the South Vietnamese ruler was "signing personally all visas for entry into and exit from the country." This was no way to run a state that desperately needed pragmatic reforms, persuasive appeals to the public, and inspiring leadership. The whole of South Vietnam was far less than the sum of its mismanaged parts.[56]

When he was not signing visas, Diem preoccupied himself with other self-destructive acts that reflected his isolation and his growing paranoia. He terrorized dissenters who questioned his policies. His attacks on Buddhists were particularly offensive, denying them equal access to land, jobs, and government support. Diem felt he could trust Catholics, like himself, more than others. As a consequence, he stubbornly sought to grant Catholics favoritism in a largely Buddhist country. By the early 1960s, Buddhist monks took to the streets to demonstrate their frustration. One monk, Thich Quang Duc, went so far as to burn himself in public on 11 June 1963 as a protest against the government and its foreign supporters. Duc's self-immolation shocked viewers around the world. It gruesomely illustrated how the people of South Vietnam, including religious men of tolerance, despised Diem's rule. Buddhist protests mobilized thousands of observers, in Vietnam and abroad, to reject the American-supported South Vietnamese regime. Once again, Ho Chi Minh's communist state looked better by comparison.[57]

Greed accompanied prejudice. Diem developed an insatiable appetite for financial assistance from the United States. He and Eisenhower agreed that the United States should have a small military footprint in Vietnam, but the South Vietnamese leader felt he deserved almost unlimited access to American weapons, products, and, of course, cash. Diem often deployed the lavish resources from the United States to destroy his opponents and enrich his friends. He also allowed the influx of American money to create skyrocketing inflation, diminishing the modest savings of families throughout the country. A small cadre of Diem's supporters grew very wealthy; the rest of the population languished in poverty. These circumstances only reinforced the message of Ho Chi Minh's anticapitalist rhetoric.[58]

Conspicuous corruption and pervasive terror made the South Vietnamese state a dysfunctional dependency. The growing American lifeline kept the regime in power; it simultaneously undermined any chance for public acceptance. In pursuit of nation-building, the United States financed a figure who, at best, offered a distorted model of what Americans had in mind. At worst, Diem sent citizens running to the obvious alternative in the communist North. South Vietnam's anticommunist ruler was therefore America's chief surrogate and its chief liability. Collins repeatedly warned the White House that he saw "no alternative to the early replacement of Diem." He seemed unable to reform. If the United States did not remove him, Collins believed the communists would, with wide public support.[59]

This was the recurring problem for American nation-building in the Cold War. The anticommunists whom the United States sponsored did not have the support of their own people. More often than not in former colonial areas, the communists proved more effective at organizing, infiltrating, and mobilizing local society. The communists were frequently the most popular and effective nationalists. Americans had a very hard time accepting that indisputable fact.

President Eisenhower, like Secretary of State Marshall before him, recognized the problems with America's ally in Vietnam. He lamented the mutual dependence created between his government and Diem's, but he clung to the assumption that the United States needed a safe harbor between "chaos and communism." This was a core belief, central to the organization of American Cold War politics. By the late 1950s, Diem had used his support from Washington to make himself nearly indispensable. For all his problems, he was a reliable anticommunist with access to government power in Vietnam. Diem's efforts to murder other moderates, or send them into the arms of the communists, meant that he left the United States few alternative leaders to support. Without a better option, Eisenhower felt he could not abandon Diem, just as Obama felt he could not abandon Afghanistan's Hamid Karzai a half century later. Anything other than continued support for a flawed surrogate promised something worse—at least according to American assumptions.

In Vietnam and other parts of the "third world," American nation-building became a hostage to incompetent, corrupt, and unpopular local leaders. This was a consequence of an inherited interest in nation-building mixing with a rigid Cold War commitment to anticommunism. The result in countries like Vietnam—where communism had a serious hold on the nationalist imagination and the organizational infrastructure—was an unbridgeable contradiction.

Nation-building with illegitimate anticommunists as the chief local actors turned into disaster. The resulting nation was neither popular nor united. The resulting state was neither stable nor secure. Rigid and dogmatic tactics undermined the pragmatic and idealistic purposes of American activity in the first place.[60]

Historical Traps

The evidence of failed nation-building in Vietnam, despite ever-increasing commitments, finally convinced American policymakers to remove Diem in November 1963—long after he had eliminated any possibility for an improved successor. Less than eighteen months later, President Lyndon Johnson sent the first two American combat battalions to Vietnam, designed to save America's investment in the region from complete failure at the hands of the more effective communist forces. For the next ten years, American escalations—on the ground and in the air—would not change the basic reality: the United States could not build a viable nation-state in South Vietnam, or any other part of the region, without a legitimate and effective set of local collaborators. For all its economic and military might, the United States needed positive partners on the ground. Washington never nurtured the crucial relationships with the correct people, especially Ho Chi Minh and the communist-dominated Vietminh.[61]

Everything that Washington had done before the insertion of ground forces undermined positive partnerships. Everything Washington did after it deployed combat soldiers reinforced past damage. As Americans learned in the Confederate South, the Philippines, and Germany, U.S. military officers could act as effective nation-builders, but only when they persuaded local citizens to trust them. The history of the first two decades after the Second World War—the years before American combat forces entered Vietnam—reinforced distrust and recrimination between the representatives of the United States and the people of Vietnam. Accumulated anger, disillusion, and militancy crippled American nation-building efforts, even when a remarkable president, Lyndon Johnson, expended enormous treasure and energy for what he perceived as benevolent purposes. The United States had lost all credibility in Southeast Asia. The escalation of American military deployments in the 1960s and early 1970s only deepened the gap between American aims and local reactions.[62]

For all their devotion to what they viewed as a noble cause, Johnson and his fellow Americans were trying to build upon contaminated land—land where prior American policies had scattered the available soil for a more inclusive, united, and open society. In nation-building, as in foreign policy as a whole, you never get to start over. In nation-building, as in all human affairs, key moments of political transformation—usually after the conclusion of a major war—set the stage for future developments. Even the most powerful country in the world cannot remake history at will. Nation-building ultimately hinges on the ability to push and pull existing social trends in strategic ways. Change is incremental and it is dependent on past actions. Wholesale reversals of recent experience are usually impossible—even with all the bombs and B-52s in the American arsenal.

Only in negotiating a long and painful withdrawal of American forces, after 1968, did the United States finally engage the Vietnamese communists in serious political discussions. President Richard Nixon and his closest foreign policy aide, Henry Kissinger, were the first American leaders since the 1940s to recognize that they had no choice but to work as partners with the most popular and organized Vietnamese groups. The White House continued to deploy overwhelming destructive force in the region—including bombing raids that inflamed whole villages, and expanded ground operations that maimed citizens in neighboring Cambodia. At the same time, Nixon and Kissinger entered into marathon meetings with the communists. They ultimately abandoned the dysfunctional government of South Vietnam for a political settlement with Ho Chi Minh's successors.

The Vietnam War ended when the United States terminated its close relationship with its anticommunist surrogates. That was Nixon and Kissinger's key contribution.[63]

President Richard Nixon and his chief foreign policy assistant, Henry Kissinger, recognized that they had to work with the communist regime in North Vietnam. Here Kissinger shakes hands with Le Duc Tho, North Vietnam's main negotiator for the Paris Peace Accords of 1973. *Xuan Thuy, Le Duc Tho, and Henry Kissinger at the Paris Conference 1973, Keystone-France, Gamma Keystone Collection, Getty Images*

It had come far too late in the war. Following three decades of conflict and thousands of deaths, the United States returned to Franklin Roosevelt's policy of working with the local figures who had the best chance of governing Vietnamese society. It took thirty years of poor decision-making to return Americans to serious negotiations with the most credible nation-builders in Indochina—the communists. It took thirty years of rigid, dogmatic, and hubristic policy for Americans to relearn the old lesson that nation-building is cooperative, flexible, and far more supple than Cold War anticommunism. The tragedy of the Vietnam War taught Americans—or it should have taught them—that money, arms, and ideology were not the only tools necessary for achieving their foreign policy aims.

More than ever in the late twentieth century, the United States needed diplomacy, negotiation, and creative partnerships across societies. Despite the allure of morally clairvoyant chest-thumping leaders, Americans needed more cool, careful, and pragmatic judgment—more of the qualities displayed by Oliver Otis Howard, William Howard Taft, and Herbert Hoover. These were men who, in prior decades, showed that they knew how to forge productive relationships with antagonistic groups. They knew how to understand the demands of diverse societies and identify common points of interest. Most of all, these old, seasoned men of difficult times knew how to build sources of shared political power between former belligerents. In comparison to the flash of John F. Kennedy and Lyndon Johnson, Howard, Taft, and Hoover were somewhat dull. They were not eloquent or sexy. They were, however, ruthlessly strategic in guiding the hands of American power amidst very sensitive circumstances.

At his best moments, Henry Kissinger played this role in the 1970s. He negotiated political agreements with communist leaders in the Soviet Union, China, and Vietnam. At his worst, Kissinger succumbed to the easy self-righteousness and intoxicating hubris of America's enormous Cold War capabilities. He triggered more civilian destruction in Africa, Latin America, and Southeast Asia than many of his predecessors. Kissinger's bipolarity on these issues is what makes him such an enduring and controversial figure from the last years of the Vietnam War. He represents the best and the worst of American politics—the promise and the tragedy of American nation-building.[64]

No More Vietnams?

The lessons of America's failures in Vietnam were painful, but still partial in their effects on society. After the Vietnam War the United

States did not take military commitments to nation-building lightly. Communism had proven its potency as an alternative form of nation-building, and Americans recognized that their global appeal to former colonial peoples would not go unchallenged. The United States was indeed chastened by its defeat in Vietnam. Even a boisterous advocate of American power, President Ronald Reagan, was careful to avoid the appearance of "another Vietnam" in Lebanon, Libya, and other areas of distant conflict.[65]

The children of Madison and Hamilton, however, reaffirmed their faith in a world composed of sovereign, self-contained, and self-determining people—an American-led "society of states." That is why the end of the Cold War did not mark a strengthening of world government, through the United Nations, or a feared emergence of uncontrolled anarchy, as one prominent author predicted. Instead, Americans and their many allies around the world struggled to build nation-states that would anticipate, co-opt, and, if necessary, destroy the new communist-like movements—with focused ideologies, sophisticated organizations, and broad popular appeals—that had shown their potential in Vietnam. American actions against the Taliban and al Qaeda in Afghanistan at the dawn of the twenty-first century were just that: a renewed, and sometimes desperate, race to nurture a stable nation-state where other political actors had already implemented contrary plans.[66]

If the Vietnam War was an effort at nation-building after a communist revolution, the Afghanistan War was an attempt to fulfill similar aspirations after another kind of upheaval. Americans never abandoned their nation-building creed. Failure reinforced a determination to succeed.

Chapter 6

Reconstruction After September 11

The survival of liberty in our land increasingly depends on the success of liberty in other lands. The best hope for peace in our world is the expansion of freedom in all the world. America's vital interests and our deepest beliefs are now one. From the day of our Founding, we have proclaimed that every man and woman on this earth has rights, and dignity, and matchless value, because they bear the image of the Maker of Heaven and earth. Across the generations we have proclaimed the imperative of self-government, because no one is fit to be a master, and no one deserves to be a slave. Advancing these ideals is the mission that created our Nation. It is the honorable achievement of our fathers. Now it is the urgent requirement of our nation's security, and the calling of our time. So it is the policy of the United States to seek and support the growth of democratic movements and institutions in every nation and culture, with the ultimate goal of ending tyranny in our world.

President George W. Bush, January 2005[1]

The people of Afghanistan have endured violence for decades. They've been confronted with occupation—by the Soviet Union, and then by foreign Al Qaeda fighters who used Afghan land for their own purposes. So tonight, I want the Afghan people to understand—America seeks an end to this era of war and suffering. We have no interest in occupying your country. We will support efforts by the Afghan government to open the door to those Taliban who abandon violence and respect the human rights of their fellow citizens. And we will seek a partnership with Afghanistan grounded in mutual respect—to isolate those who destroy; to strengthen those who build; to hasten the day when our troops will leave; and to forge a lasting friendship in which America is your partner, and never your patron.

President Barack Obama, December 2009[2]

The most powerful states dominate international politics, but the small places in between define the fate of the world. That is the history of modern Poland, surrounded by Russia to the east and Germany to the west. Struggles for control of this poor north European lowland contributed to two world wars and the Cold War. The Korean Peninsula has a similar history. Conflicts over influence in this mountainous territory—surrounded by China, Russia, and Japan—have embroiled the countries of East Asia in wars, rivalries, and recriminations since the late nineteenth century. Location often matters more than wealth. Poor places often draw the most attention from the strongest actors. The most vulnerable societies frequently determine regional security and the global balance of power.

Afghanistan is the Poland or Korea of the Middle East. Its poverty, vulnerability, and location between empires have inspired recurring wars on its barren and rocky terrain. The landlocked country, about the size of Texas, sits astride Iran in the west, the Indian subcontinent in the east, and China, Russia, and the former Soviet states of Central Asia. This complex space marks the middle of major population movements across what one observer famously called the Eurasian "heartland"—the geographic pivot of power on the world's largest landmass. Afghanistan has never been a center of wealth, but it has long served as a transit route between east and west. It has had what one scholar calls "a positively magnetic attraction for conquerors."[3]

Going back to the eighth century, Afghanistan was a major site for clashes and connections between a rich Persian culture and an expanding Islamic religion. In subsequent centuries, Mongol invaders brought new forms of horse-borne warfare and organized political administration from the Asiatic steppe to Afghanistan. The Mongols conquered and ruled much of the region for more than two hundred years, mixing their own traditions with influences from Iran, India, and Islam. The Turks, cousins of the Mongols, did much the same for another four hundred years. The rise of modern European empires in the late eighteenth century brought British and Russian power to

211

former Mongol-Turkish lands. The Europeans were latecomers to the region, but they were attracted by the same circumstances that enticed their predecessors. The desert mountains between Persia and India offered promising soil for planting regional influence.[4]

More than most places, Afghanistan was a staging ground for going elsewhere. It was a transit society composed of nomadic peoples. It was defined by what it was near, and which foreigners entered its terrain en route to greater ambitions. These conditions have made Afghanistan a cockpit for conquest and other efforts at control by peoples trying to reach another destination. Foreigners have always longed for movement, not occupation, in this land. They have conceived of Afghanistan as a bridge, carrying them to wealth or, alternatively, conveying their enemies to their throats. For more than a millennium, countless groups have seized—or attempted to seize—Afghanistan in order to facilitate their broader regional goals.[5]

Contrary to common assumptions, foreigners—including Mongols, Persians, and various Islamic groups—have successfully controlled Afghanistan. They settled amidst the countryside; they built towns and roads; they also implanted new forms of government and religious practice. The ethnic and religious diversity of the modern country is an enduring legacy of repeated invasions. The long history of different groups living together—often side by side—is a testament to the acceptance of outside influences. For all the conflict in Afghanistan, ethnic and religious wars are quite rare.[6]

In the nineteenth century, British and Russian imperial forces became the most powerful foreign influences in the region. Like their predecessors, they maneuvered against one another to ensure transit through Afghanistan. They also postured to prevent their adversary from enjoying similar privileges. For Russia, control of Afghanistan was crucial to protect the czar's empire from attack on its southern flank. For Britain, control of Afghanistan was vital for the defense of India against land invasion. Neither country could allow the other to dominate this treacherous terrain.[7]

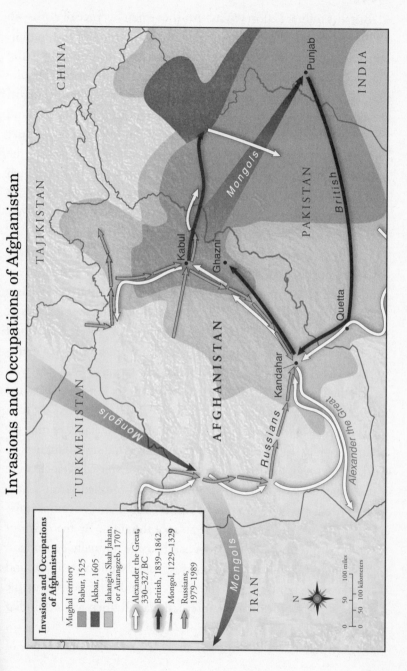

Invasions and Occupations of Afghanistan

Britain's military efforts to subdue the region by force of arms—in 1839, 1878, and 1919—produced disastrous casualties and humiliating retreats for imperial forces. Many recent histories emphasize that point without a proper understanding of the period. Despite their painful losses, the British successfully contained threats across the border they drew between Afghanistan and India—the Durand Line. The British dislodged Peshawar and the Northwest Frontier province from Afghanistan, making them additional buffers for the protection of India. London's efforts were costly, but they paid high strategic dividends. If given a chance to rewrite history, most British leaders would have made the same basic choices, although they probably would have used military force with greater caution.[8]

The Russians acted in similar ways. They expanded their boundary along the north of Afghanistan. St. Petersburg's forces seized Samarkand and Bukhara, increasing their strategic depth in the region. They continued to encroach on new territories through the last decades of the nineteenth century. Beyond their land grabs, the Russians and the British exerted continued influence through annual payments to tribal leaders, and frequent military assistance to warlords who served their interests. British and Russian power deeply penetrated nineteenth-century Afghanistan.[9]

The people of the region proved their stubborn defiance of military occupiers, but they also displayed their long-standing willingness to work with foreign influences at the same time. External alliances were a fundamental part of internal politics. The so-called Great Game around Afghanistan involved close contact and intensive compromise between British, Russian, and diverse local figures. By the dawn of the twentieth century, these actors had become mutually dependent; their ever-shifting alliances created surprising stability, built around common respect and understanding. For the diverse peoples of the region, political order amidst international rivalries was a familiar state of affairs.[10]

Afghanistan's development has always occurred in the shadow of foreign empires. Influence in and around the country has brought little wealth, and often great heartache, but it has determined the regional balance of power. The merchants who controlled the villages and towns on the trade routes also controlled access to the wealth of Persia, India, and much of China. The soldiers who controlled the mountain passes also controlled the movement of militaries. Afghanistan was the crossroad for exercising power across neighboring territories since before our modern era. It was—and remains—a vital strategic land base, a crucial regional choke point.

The 11 September 2001 terrorist attacks on New York, Washington, D.C., and rural Pennsylvania grew from this strategic geography. In the aftermath of the Cold War, Afghanistan had become a political vacuum. The retreat of Soviet and American power, accompanied by the diversion of Iranian and Indian influences, meant that the region became a magnet for other groups. In the absence of a functioning state, the country entered a period of prolonged civil war, aided by organizations in Pakistan, Saudi Arabia, and other nearby societies seeking a foothold between Iran and India. Most notorious, the Saudi-born heir to a large fortune, Osama bin Laden, allied his extremist brand of Islam and terroristic politics with a collection of militant clerics and warlords from around Afghanistan who called themselves the Taliban—the "students" of a new brand of repressive politics merged with fanatical displays of Muslim faith.[11]

The Taliban were the new occupiers of Afghanistan. Like their predecessors, they had roots inside the country but derived their capabilities from more powerful sponsors abroad. Osama bin Laden and his al Qaeda network of militant warriors were yet another set of mercenaries enticed by the possibilities of expansion from the strategic center of the Eurasian heartland. The Taliban and al Qaeda updated a long tradition of warfare focused on Afghanistan for larger regional, and in this case global, purposes. They used the country as a springboard to shape societies far beyond. Their references to earlier precedents for their aims were well founded.[12]

Most international observers, particularly in the United States, were not ready for this. They had abandoned Afghanistan, convinced that the new "global" geography of the twenty-first century bypassed foreign states—and domestic neighborhoods—mired in poverty, disease, and violence. Traditional borders seemed to matter less than ever for the circulation of wealth and capital. Traditional warfare seemed less important than ever for an integrated and interdependent world. An international class of educated professionals constituted what looked like a fast-moving, dominant cross-national network of high performers who leaped over increasingly isolated pockets of backwardness. Jet-setting between Shanghai and New York, New Delhi and London—the wealthy and powerful flew over places like Afghanistan.

Those who watched the planes from the Central Asian mountains prepared for flights of their own. Like their many predecessors, the Taliban and al Qaeda used the territory of Afghanistan to plan foreign attacks. They acquired weapons, recruited followers, set up training camps, and, most important, built an effective organization for their aims. They created a new Afghanistan-based international army. They defined success not by what they did for the people of Afghanistan, but how much destruction they brought to the region's greatest oppressors, in their eyes. Due to its wealth and reach, the United States was a top target for terror.

When al Qaeda struck on 11 September 2001, Americans learned that they could not fly over failed states. They witnessed how places with little intrinsic value to foreigners could nurture acts that changed the world. Most jolting, Americans recognized that they could no longer ignore festering seedbeds of violence, especially when local actors had access to territory, government institutions, and methods of distant delivery. If Afghanistan had long served as a regional point of transit for war-making groups, modern transportation and communications greatly expanded the reach of its most violent belligerents. With Taliban extremism and al Qaeda training camps throughout its territory,

Afghanistan had now become a crossroad between Middle East terror and American targets. Regional conflicts expanded into global threats.

After 9/11

How would Americans react to the shocking horror of hijacked planes, collapsing buildings, and threats of much worse? The bleakest nightmares about twenty-first-century Armageddon now seemed real. What kind of policy would the United States pursue in response to deadly attacks from distant and nontraditional adversaries? How could Americans make themselves feel secure again?

Many observers—including this author—asked those questions in the frightening hours after 11 September 2001. It is hard to re-create the uncertainty, anxiety, and disorientation of those days. "No one knew what might happen next," *New York Times* columnist Maureen Dowd explained. "Would there be a gas attack? Would the White House blow up? Would another plane crash into the Capitol?" Accustomed to frequent air travel, I vividly remember my nervousness about boarding another plane. The faces in airports revealed that I was hardly alone in these newfound anxieties about what had been a largely uneventful form of transportation.[13]

In the coming months the terror spread, shaking core assumptions about security and stability. Citizens across the country followed daily reports on the dispersion of deadly anthrax spores through the U.S. Postal Service. Hidden within innocuous letter-sized envelopes, the mysterious white powder killed five people. No one knew the source of these biological attacks at the time. Was it al Qaeda again? No one knew when the attacks would stop. Would they infect the entire country? Receiving mail became a heart-stopping endeavor. I remember carefully surveying every envelope for suspicious signs, and then obsessively washing my hands to remove potentially dangerous residue. Friends and colleagues did the same.

Unfortunately, the cycle of terror did not end with the anthrax. More violent and random incidents of murder occurred close to home. A year after the 11 September 2001 incidents, a delusional former soldier and a teenager he befriended began a spree of sniper attacks around Washington, D.C. They shot ordinary citizens from a distance with no clear cause or purpose. They chose their victims at random, and they identified themselves with extremists pledging to destroy American society. Ten men and women died as they pumped gas into their cars, exited family stores, or sat on a bench reading a book. Schools went into permanent lockdown, shoppers stayed away from malls, and drivers avoided filling their gas tanks near open areas. As far from Washington, D.C., as Madison, Wisconsin, police began patrolling open public spaces—football stadiums, playgrounds, and common eating areas—looking for potential copycat snipers. Daily life, even in the safest of neighborhoods, had turned deadly. Basic safety seemed to be slipping away.[14]

Public fear is a corrosive phenomenon, especially when experienced so close to home. It stimulates simplified images of a unified, hyperactive, brilliant, and all-powerful enemy. It inspires exaggerated feelings of peril and vulnerability. Most difficult, public fear builds on itself. Each incident confirms the worst; the nonoccurrence of trumpeted threats is discounted as mere luck or preparation by the enemy for something even more horrible. Citizens caught in a cycle of fear find it difficult to assess their circumstances, the constraints on their adversaries, and the opportunities for creative action. The fearful instinct is to lash out and seek immediate revenge.[15]

Cooler heads cannot quell public fear through argument, analysis, or even evidence. On the contrary, inflamed emotions demand conspicuous, often caricatured, acts of courage. To conquer fear the public must believe that it can scare its enemies even more, that it can intimidate the intimidators, that it can destroy challengers before they destroy us. This is why fear consistently inspires aggressive force in American history. This is why fear drives expansive wars with unreasonable expectations of rapid world transformation.[16]

Public fear clouds the careful judgment of costs and benefits that is crucial for effective policymaking. When enemies appear overwhelming and vulnerabilities seem ubiquitous, calls for caution and warnings against excess sound weak, ineffective, and cowardly. Big threats demand big responses. Treacherous enemies justify tough tactics. Scary events elicit firm statements of strength. These tendencies are magnified in a democracy, where leaders feel pressure in a time of crisis to show empathy with public demands for immediate action. Time and again, American presidents have responded to foreign threats—the Japanese attack on Pearl Harbor, Soviet expansionism after the Second World War, and, of course, the terrorist attacks of 11 September 2001—with rhetoric about total war for "unconditional surrender," pledges to "contain" communist advances, and promises to destroy terrorists and their "rogue" supporters. Extreme responses in extreme times are understandable, and perhaps unavoidable, but they are rarely wise or sustainable.[17]

In late 2001 Americans were caught in precisely this dynamic. Although the threats were exotic to traditional American observers, the mechanism and substance of policy deliberation were strikingly familiar. Citizens almost universally called for a strong and forceful response—"take off the gloves," "take no prisoners." The United States had enormous reservoirs of military capability that were unused at the time of the terrorist attacks. It had sophisticated information and surveillance technologies that were insufficiently deployed when the bad guys entered the country. The vast majority of Americans believed that the time had come to put the nation's most powerful resources onto the field of battle, finding and annihilating those who sponsored and supported the attacks on the nation. As in the past, Americans mobilized their strength to combat what appeared to be an existential threat to the state. This response echoed earlier generations who had fought the Civil War, the Second World War, and the Cold War.[18]

Like almost everyone else, President George W. Bush was shaken by these circumstances. His face showed the same horror, indignation, and stubborn determination displayed in the windows of homes across the country, covered with a collage of American flags cut from newspapers and posted for public view in the aftermath of the terrorist attacks. This conspicuous patriotism in the wake of tragedy conveyed a fleeting but powerful unity of purpose among Americans. This conspicuous patriotism also drove Americans to expect that they could reaffirm their security by bringing their collective might against evil-doers.[19]

"These acts of mass murder," President Bush announced on the night of the 11 September attacks, "were intended to frighten our nation into chaos and retreat. But they have failed. Our country is strong. A great people has been moved to defend a great nation." As the ruins of the destroyed buildings continued to burn and disoriented citizens struggled to make sense of the horrifying images replayed on their television screens, the president explained that this was now a "war against terrorism." As in the past, Americans and their friends around the world would "stand together to win." "We will make no distinction," Bush told millions of listeners, "between the terrorists who committed these acts and those who harbor them." The United States would do more than defend itself. It would destroy the evil-doers and it would change a corrupted world.[20]

Bush made this final point clear in his speech to a joint session of Congress on 20 September 2001. Focusing first on the perpetrators of the most recent attacks, the president explained: "Our war on terror begins with al Qaeda, but it does not end there. It will not end until every terrorist group of global reach has been found, stopped and defeated."

Our response involves far more than instant retaliation and isolated strikes. Americans should not expect one battle, but a lengthy campaign unlike any other we have ever seen. It may include dramatic strikes visible on TV and covert operations secret even in success. We will starve terrorists of funding, turn them one against another, drive them from place to place until there is no refuge or no rest. And we will pursue nations that provide aid or safe haven to terrorism. Every nation in every region now has a decision to make: Either you are with us or you are with the terrorists. From this day forward, any nation that continues to harbor or support terrorism will be regarded by the United States as a hostile regime.[21]

Fearful and indignant, the president had returned to a common, perhaps hyper-militaristic, articulation of the American nation-building creed. The threat to the United States did not come only from individuals, groups, or a particular region of the world. Nor did the threat emanate from an extremist ideology or degenerate social conditions. Bush argued that the fundamental problem was "failed states"—governments that "harbor or support terrorism," regimes that offer "refuge" to criminals who take advantage of good citizens and civilized societies. The problem of terrorism was, like communism and fascism before, a failure of countries to progress on the route to stable nation-states—the most effective protectors of "freedom and security," in Bush's words. The attacks on America were the result of absent political development abroad, and the president argued that the United States had to correct that.

Bush did not explain why certain societies had deviated from appropriate nation-state formation. He did, however, focus on Afghanistan as an example of the horrors and threats that arose when societies violated this model, when they rejected the modern society of states and its common expectations. Internal violence and repression, the president argued, became exported commodities by regimes that depended on these tactics for survival. Cruelty and conflict spread throughout unstable regions of the world as war-making leaders forced others to react to them in kind. Tortured and impoverished citizens could not live at peace with themselves and their neighbors. Instead, their experience of suffering spread around them.

The Taliban regime that ruled Afghanistan and allied with al Qaeda, Bush explained, "is not only repressing its own people, it is threatening people everywhere by sponsoring and sheltering and supplying terrorists. By aiding and abetting murder, the Taliban regime is committing murder." The president used language that called for the removal, or at least major transformation, of the Afghanistan government: "we condemn the Taliban regime. . . . They will hand over the terrorists or they will share in their fate." Bush demanded, without "negotiation or discussion," that the regime apprehend perpetrators of foreign violence, close "terrorist training camps," provide the United States access to these facilities, and offer basic protections to foreigners entering the country. Afghanistan had to stop acting like an international outlaw and begin to play by the accepted rules of conduct among nation-states. If the Taliban refused, which everyone expected it would, then Washington would force change through war.[22]

Bush's words were strong, but they were not new. He echoed Lincoln's belief after 1861 that the scourge of slavery in the Confederacy was incompatible with the preservation of the Union. He repeated McKinley's claim that the chaos of a degenerate Spanish Empire threatened grave harm to American security. Most obvious, he returned to Woodrow Wilson and Franklin Roosevelt, who had argued for total war against irredeemable regimes that undermined international order. Like Roosevelt and his Cold War successors, in particular, Bush contended that the world would be safe only when new nation-states replaced fascism, communism, and, now, Islamic extremism. The comforting shadow of this history motivated the president's missionary impulse amidst tragedy and fear: "This is a day," he exclaimed on the evening of 11 September, "when all Americans from every walk of life unite in our resolve for justice and peace. America has stood down enemies before, and we will do so this time."[23]

Bush expanded on this deep-rooted American rhetoric less than two weeks later:

> Some speak of an age of terror. I know there are struggles ahead and dangers to face. But this country will define our times, not be defined by them. As long as the United States of America is determined and strong, this will not be an age of terror. This will be an age of liberty here and across the world. . . . Our nation, this generation, will lift the dark threat of violence from our people and our future. We will rally the world to this cause by our efforts, by our courage. We will not tire, we will not falter and we will not fail.[24]

Lincoln and Roosevelt would have recognized these words. They would have understood the fear and ambition that inspired these remarks. They would have shared the impulse to destroy new threats to American society by spreading the model of American governance. Bush was never as sophisticated as Lincoln or Roosevelt—or McKinley for that matter—but he embraced the same nation-building creed in his analysis of threats to the United States and the expansive purposes of the country at moments of crisis. This profound but simple sensibility resonated for many Americans in 2001, as it did in 1861 and 1941.

Defeating the Taliban

In the hours and days after the shock of the World Trade Center's collapse, Americans reaffirmed their basic creed of building nations to replace chaos and disorder. Witnessing the destruction wrought by a failing Afghan state, the United States embarked, with little debate, on a war to kill the criminals who infested that regime. Americans had faith that their military efforts could contribute to the construction of a better nation-state in its place. They knew little about Afghanistan and what might replace the Taliban, but they expected the people of the region to embrace representative government, territorial unity, and popular sovereignty—especially after the domestic repression they had recently experienced.

The president encouraged this perception as American soldiers and bombs landed in Afghanistan to dislodge the Taliban's leadership. Speaking at the United States Military Academy on 1 June 2002, he described "an historic opportunity to preserve the peace." "We have our best chance since the rise of the nation state in the 17th century to build a world where the great powers compete in peace instead of prepare for war." Referring to American nation-building in Germany and other countries after the Second World War, he affirmed that "the tide of liberty is rising in many other nations." As in the past, Bush pledged that the United States would continue to "support and reward governments that make the right choices for their own people. In our development aid, in our diplomatic efforts, in our international broadcasting and in our educational assistance, the United States will promote moderation and tolerance and human rights. And we will defend the peace that makes all progress possible."[25]

These values centered on the creation of strong, stable, secure nation-states, beginning in Afghanistan. These promises depended on American efforts to support this process, not by imposition, but through a combination of local partnerships, long-term investments, and selective deployments of force. Bush and his closest advisors expected that Afghan citizens, liberated from oppressive rule, would embrace representative self-government in a single unified state. With American aid, Afghanistan would nurture new national leaders and institutions, according to Bush's vision. "America has no empire," the president explained. "We wish for others only what we wish for ourselves."[26]

This striking universalism envisioned American-style nation-states sprouting from the ashes of extremism in the Middle East and other regions. Bush fused the progressive assumptions of the American nation-building creed with a global urgency born of the recent attacks. "More and more civilized nations," Bush asserted, "find themselves on the same side, united by common dangers of terrorist violence and chaos."

Through most of history poverty was persistent and inescapable and almost universal. In the last few decades we've seen nations from Chile to South Korea build modern economies and freer societies, lifting millions of people out of despair and want. And there's no mystery to this achievement. The 20th century ended with a single surviving model of human progress based on nonnegotiable demands of human dignity, the rule of law, limits on the power of the state, respect for women and private property, and free speech, and equal justice and religious tolerance.[27]

Bush painted a picture that Americans wanted to see. It was the history they had told themselves for generations. The United States had a mission, born of its own domestic experience, to build stable and just political orders between the chaos of violent thugs and the empires of external oppressors. The Taliban and al Qaeda were the destructive consequences of uncontrolled anarchy. The Soviet occupation of Afghanistan, which preceded the Taliban, was a result of the expanding reach of empire that stunted the development of the state and contributed to continuing civil war. As Americans expected, neither anarchy nor empire allowed for stable political development in Afghanistan. As Americans anticipated, inadequate national governance gave power to the men with the guns, not the local reformers with the best ideas.

This analysis of Afghanistan and other "failed states" was not new, but it gained priority attention in the United States after 11 September 2001. Throughout the country observers focused on the problems of foreign development as they had not before—at least since the Vietnam War. The terrorist attacks made it clear that the absence of stable political order in distant societies, with little economic value to the United States, sent shocks far and wide. Failed states in far-away places threatened successful states close to home. With modern technology and communications, foreign turmoil that Americans had previously ignored now demanded immediate attention.[28]

Action came through a combination of military and political intervention. On 26 September 2001, two weeks after the terrorist attacks, CIA agents began to land in Afghanistan. U.S. Special Operations Forces soon followed. A ground-based American contingent of a few hundred soldiers and intelligence specialists attached itself to various warlord groups in the northeastern part of the country—the remnants of the anti-Taliban "Northern Alliance"—providing additional firepower, logistical support, and, of course, money. Americans dispensed millions of dollars in cash to buy assistance from local leaders. They also adapted with great agility to the challenges of the terrain: riding on horses, living among nomadic groups, and showing deference to local tribal and ethnic traditions.[29]

Inserted into unfamiliar circumstances, elite American soldiers had to transform themselves overnight from a clean-cut, highly disciplined, professional corps into bearded, dispersed, irregular mountain fighters. The transition was not easy. It was often comical in its precariousness. Near the northern city of Mazar-e-Sharif, American Special Forces joined the local warlord, Abdul Rashid Dostum:

> The terrain and conditions here were extraordinary: at elevations of up to 6,400 feet, movement was restricted to winding mountain trails in which sheer rock faces were sometimes separated from thousand-foot drops by no more than a three-foot width of rocky path. With no vehicles able to negotiate such trails, commandos hauling loads of over 40 pounds of equipment per man were given Afghan mountain ponies with wooden saddles and told to ride along with Dostum's troops. Luckily, the [American Special Forces] team commander assigned to Dostum had been a high school rodeo rider in Kansas, but

none of the other Americans had ever been on a horse before. Their knees in their chests, balancing heavy rucksacks on their backs, they were instructed by their commander to keep their downhill foot out of the stirrups and to lean uphill so if the pony lost its balance they would fall onto the trail as the pony went into the gorge.[30]

As far as we know, none of the pony-riding Americans fell fatally from their animals. They moved slowly and deliberately, observing and soon engaging Taliban forces in close combat. In many ways, the ground war in Afghanistan was a traditional series of battles between armed units struggling to mass force and outmaneuver their adversaries. Like the Americans who entered long-standing battlefields during the First and Second World Wars, the soldiers deployed in late 2001 tilted the balance of power because of the weapons, supplies, cash, and determined energy they brought to the fighting. Despite the distant terrain, the "face of battle" in Afghanistan was actually quite common.[31]

After 11 September 2001 American Special Forces worked with Afghan warlords, including Abdul Rashid Dostum, to overthrow the Taliban. In this photo from March 2002, Dostum and Afghanistan's interim government leader, Hamid Karzai, celebrate the traditional Afghan new year. *Hoang Dinh Nam, Getty Images*

227

American soldiers adjusted to the traditional nature of horse-borne fighting, and they married it to the most modern elements of high-technology combat. The United States supported and supplemented its ground capabilities with the unprecedented speed, flexibility, and accuracy of its airpower. On 7 October 2001 U.S. aircraft launched from Diego Garcia, countries around the Persian Gulf, and carriers in the Arabian Sea began pummeling Taliban positions in Afghanistan. While on horseback, American ground forces logged into their laptops, sending up-to-date targeting information to the planes overhead.

B-1, B-2, and B-52 bombers—the workhorses of the American air arsenal—dropped their bombs, guided with precision navigation technology, on specified locations. They flew approximately two hundred missions per day, and they hit as many targets with these flights as they did with three thousand or more daily missions in the First Persian Gulf War, just a decade earlier. American bombs were lethal, they were ubiquitous, and they frequently struck enemy forces, without warning, in difficult-to-reach caves and valleys. "These carefully targeted actions," the president announced, "are designed to disrupt the use of Afghanistan as a terrorist base of operations and to attack the military capability of the Taliban regime." "Our military action, he continued, "is also designed to clear the way for sustained, comprehensive and relentless operations to drive them out and bring them to justice."[32]

In the first weeks of combat, the United States deployed ten thousand bombs and missiles in Afghanistan. These strikes—termed "Operation Enduring Freedom" by the U.S. military—involved a vast web of aircraft and coordinating personnel, but very few Americans on the ground. The military campaign aimed to overthrow the Taliban and empower an alternative political system, dominated by figures with local legitimacy and new ties to the United States. The military campaign was also a new form of close ground–air force coordination with modern communications and precision guidance. The United States would extend its foreign reach and increase its lethality, while avoiding the perils of an intensive occupation. Firepower and accuracy would substitute for large deployments of soldiers.

A heavy boot with a "light footprint"—that combination of overwhelming airpower and limited ground intrusion—would, American policymakers hoped, allow more opportunities for the citizens of Afghanistan to assert their independence as Washington's allies. That was, of course, the lesson of the Vietnam War. For a generation of military and political figures who came of age in the shadow of America's failed efforts in Southeast Asia, and the domestic acrimony that accompanied those foreign policy failures, new wars required clear limits on the commitment of U.S. soldiers abroad. The Bush administration began the "War on Terror" with no draft, no calls for sacrifice at home, and, most conspicuous, no plans for long-term occupation of Afghanistan or any other country. The goal was to defeat the Taliban, empower a new regime, and build a stable nation-state from a distance. Partnerships with local anti-Taliban forces would cover for absent Americans in freed towns and villages.[33]

This was a revolution in warfare to dislodge a dug-in regime distant from American shores. This was also an ambitious effort to seed a new Afghanistan—independent, united, and allied with the United States. The American planes dropped food, equipment, and other assistance for the anti-Taliban groups. The president pledged that the "oppressed people of Afghanistan will know the generosity of America and our allies." The bombs from the air would help create openings for liberation on the ground. The tools for reconstruction would accompany the weapons of destruction.[34]

In late 2001 this plan looked brilliant. Operation Enduring Freedom produced a large number of devastating hits on Taliban and al Qaeda targets, and it created very few civilian casualties—less than four hundred confirmed deaths in three months of continuous bombing. Most remarkable, the United States lost only five aircraft in this intense period, without the death of a single American airman. Washington brought extraordinary power against its enemies with an efficiency no one had seen before. American planes hit enemy targets consistently and with very few collateral costs. Citizens of the United States and Afghanistan could contemplate a quick transition from Taliban rule to something much better.[35]

The euphoria was palpable in both societies by the end of 2001. If the attacks of 11 September created a cycle of fear, the apparent success of American military operations produced a collective feeling of relief. Here was the evidence that the United States could defeat its enemies. Here was the evidence that the American nation-building creed still offered a viable roadmap from repression to reform.

Citizens of Kabul cheered Northern Alliance fighters on November 13, 2001. Working with American Special Forces, anti-Taliban militias liberated the Afghan capital, opening a period of hope and possibility.
Scott Peterson, Getty Images

The Taliban fled the capital city of Kabul on the night of 12 November 2001. When a very small group of Americans entered the former enemy stronghold the next day, along with a much larger contingent of anti-Taliban Afghan soldiers, the residents greeted them with a joy unseen since Allied troops liberated Nazi-occupied Paris in August 1944. The popular reaction showed a sincere desire for good government, reform, and increased Western influence. Urban Afghan citizens looked like their American counterparts in their exuberant assertions of personal freedom, their embrace of foreign visitors, and their demand for representative political voice. For all the superficiality in these images, I remember how deeply moving they were, especially among fearful Americans looking for a vindication of their basic ideals.

This was not a delusion. Diverse observers saw similar things in liberated Kabul. The Pakistani newspaper *Dawn* reported that in defiance of Taliban prohibitions on music, people played patriotic songs and displayed public joy for the overthrow of their oppressors. They carried signs proclaiming "Death to Taliban," "Death to Mullah Omar," and even "Death to Pakistan." London's *Guardian* newspaper—a critic of Washington's war efforts—reported that children in Kabul chanted "Long Live America!" Television news around the world broadcast videos of women removing their forced coverings, couples dancing in the streets, and young people smiling at foreign visitors—an absent phenomenon in the dismal days of Taliban rule. The city and its citizens had apparently "awakened" from a long nightmare. Many viewers far from Afghanistan felt a similar charge of optimism.[36]

Nation-Building Begun

Afghans from various ethnic and regional groups saw an opportunity for a new future in their country. The decades of violence and civil war since the Soviet invasion of 1979, followed by the emergence of the Taliban in the 1990s, motivated many citizens to crave a rest from the madness. During these decades, millions of Afghans had fled their rural homes for temporary refuge in urban communities, and eventual exile in Pakistan, Iran, and other foreign lands. With the defeat of the Taliban in late 2001, they began to return in large numbers—as many as three million refugees came home after the beginning of American military operations. These long-suffering Afghans had spent years living abroad, running foreign businesses, and working with international aid groups. They were cosmopolitans of circumstance, still connected to their community roots, but also familiar with the possibilities of national and international institutions.[37]

In many cases, global relief organizations had saved their lives. The returning refugees brought their international experiences back to their country, fused with a determination to end the violence that had forced them to flee. This mix of the international and the local encouraged efforts at constructing a functioning, secure, and peaceful government in Afghanistan. To many, a "normal" nation-state looked like the most promising protector of local communities. What other set of institutions could address the problems in the country? What other regime could contain domestic and regional violence? What other models did the returning Afghans have? They observed effective nation-states abroad, and they recognized their own suffering in their decades of statelessness.

Despite their enduring differences, the people of Afghanistan had a broadly shared purpose after the defeat of the Taliban: to make their war-torn society into a stable nation-state, benefiting from American and other foreign support. Anthropologist Thomas Barfield, who spent more than a decade studying rural Afghan communities, observed that many local groups—at least in 2001—viewed the United States as a potential ally, not an invader. They also looked to Washington as a positive contributor to a united, independent Afghan governing system. As Barfield explains, and Afghans recognized, the United States was neither prepared nor willing to govern the region. There simply were not enough Americans in Afghanistan. Instead, Washington planned to help the Afghans rule themselves on terms compatible with the wishes of the people in the region, and American interests as well. That was the kind of deal-making politics that pragmatic and war-weary Afghans could understand and embrace. It certainly improved upon the violent exploitation they had felt for so long at the hands of foreign invaders and domestic strongmen.[38]

The model of governance that seemed possible in late 2001 approximated the experience of the region in the middle years of the Cold War, especially 1964 to 1973—a decade of great possibilities, in retrospect. During this period, Afghanistan was a stable, predictable, even progressive place. It had a constitutional government that included a national legislature, a professional administrative class, and protected rights for citizens, religions, and ethnic groups. It had an expanding educational system (including a somewhat "radical" university in Kabul), major infrastructure development projects, and growing international appeal as a destination for tourists, particularly young adventure-seekers. Annual foreign aid from the Soviet Union and the United States—both sides in the Cold War—surpassed the country's regular budget, creating a mix of international dependence and domestic capital liquidity that allowed for economic growth, despite continued impoverishment across the country. In the early 1970s the future looked bright for Afghanistan. It appeared to be advancing ahead of its Central Asian neighbors.[39]

Louis Dupree, one of the most experienced observers of Afghanistan, described the country's "economic vigor and diversity" at the time. He extolled the emergence after 1964 of "noncorrupt officials" and a population of taxpayers who appeared to feel "safe" in their relations with citizens of different ethnic backgrounds. Although Afghanistan still had serious problems of poverty, internal conflict, and corruption, it stood out among its neighbors for its progress toward stable statehood in the middle Cold War. Dupree admitted that the country's future was "far from clear," but he expressed confidence in its steady improvement. Many other observers shared this cautious optimism.[40]

New acts of violence, however, quickly took Afghanistan in a disastrous direction, with effects that lasted through the rise of the Taliban.

Two coups in 1973 and 1978, followed by the Soviet invasion in 1979 and the mujahideen resistance, upended regional stability. King Zahir Shah, heir to the dynasty that had ruled the country since 1929, stood atop the Afghan political hierarchy before his forced ouster by an ambitious cousin, Daud Khan, and then the communists. The king served as a unifying symbol for the Afghan people, a recognized representative abroad, and, most important, a respected broker between regions, tribes, and families. Zahir Shah was the nationwide boss who, like his urban counterparts in the United States, dispensed favors and privileges to different claimants. He bought friends. He negotiated compromises between groups in conflict. He punished enemies, often by calling upon friendly groups to act on his behalf. Zahir Shah's regime was not democratic, nor particularly modern, but it worked to hold the country together with some degree of comity and cohesion. Citizens who remembered those years had good reason to look for their return after the removal of the Taliban, and the arrival of promised foreign assistance.[41]

King Zahir Shah was a respected broker between regions, tribes, and families during a period of relative calm in Afghanistan before 1973. Here he is pictured in Germany negotiating for development assistance.
Popperfoto, Getty Images

This was the motivation behind the conference of Afghan notables assembled under United Nations auspices in Bonn, Germany, from 27 November to 5 December 2001. In a series of meetings the four dominant anti-Taliban groups—the Tajiks and Uzbeks from northern Afghanistan (now in control of Kabul), the Afghan émigrés allied to Iran, the Pashtuns surrounding the exiled King Zahir Shah, and the Pashtuns with strong ties to Pakistan—worked to create a shared government for Afghanistan. Their goal was to initiate a political process that would produce cooperation and stability in their war-torn country, and security against the return of the Taliban. James Dobbins, the American diplomat who led Washington's delegation to the conference, recounts that the atmosphere among the participants approximated an "extended family reunion." Dobbins contrasts the amity of the Afghans with the mutual hatred of the former Yugoslav factions that the ambassador had addressed in prior years. Unlike the Serbs, Croats, and Bosnians, who looked back upon generations of conflict, the anti-Taliban groups assembled in Bonn "recalled earlier eras," according to Dobbins, "as times of ethnic harmony and national unity." Afghanistan had a useful history that local and international leaders could invoke for nation-building. In the eyes of its own citizens, this was not a country doomed to stateless violence.[42]

The negotiations in Bonn were remarkably successful. The diverse group of Afghan elders who signed the final agreement at the conference pledged "to end the tragic conflict in Afghanistan and promote national reconciliation, lasting peace, stability and respect for human rights in the country." They embraced a vision for "the independence, national sovereignty and territorial integrity" of Afghanistan.[43]

The Bonn Agreement was the clearest evidence of a shared commitment to a united, peaceful, and representative future among a single Afghan people, under the protection of a functioning government. The agreement served as an initial constitution for a modern nation-state in Afghanistan. It provided a mandate for foreign countries, particularly the United States, to help the impoverished citizens of the region rebuild their society. This document was unthinkable before late 2001. It was a hopeful and recognizable consequence of the Taliban's defeat.[44]

Despite an obvious jockeying for influence, the different anti-Taliban groups agreed on three things. First, they affirmed the existence of a single Afghan state with limited but real powers to maintain countrywide stability. The provisions for security dominated the final document. They stipulated the creation of an Afghan national security force, trained and supported by the international community. They also included a recognition that the basic infrastructure of the country, especially the roads and tunnels, required central management. The Afghan state envisioned in Bonn was a protector of basic order, like its predecessor in the early 1970s.

Second, the conference attendees pledged to cooperate in managing the large expected infusions of foreign aid. The new government would receive the money from the donors and it would provide external accountability. Within Afghanistan, it would distribute aid to regional organizations, print currency, and float loans. The new government would become the central banker for Afghanistan. The new Supreme Court of Afghanistan would adjudicate disputes over law, property, and contract. These provisions represented a return to the 1964 constitution, and efforts to build modern economic and legal institutions in the country.

Third, and perhaps most important, the rival groups in Bonn embraced a coalition of leaders who would share power. This was the most difficult part of the negotiations. Each group demanded greater representation in the government. In the end, the delegates found agreement around a rough balance of power that also matched with long-standing traditions. Uzbeks and Tajiks occupied the key posts in the military and foreign affairs. Iranian-allied Pashtuns continued to dominate internal administration. Within this carefully calibrated framework, the Afghan groups chose a southern Pashtun, Hamid Karzai, as head of state—initially chairman of the Interim Administration of Afghanistan.

This was precisely the pattern of the prior century, before the coup against Zahir Shah in 1973. Like the king, Karzai would base his legitimacy on a regime composed of leaders from the various regions and ethnicities around the country. He would arbitrate between the groups. He would help to forge compromises. Most of all, Karzai would gain nationwide credibility from his role as a trusted elder, supported by all the major domestic constituencies and the most important international actors as well. A Pashtun, Karzai represented the most numerous group in Afghanistan, and the one with an enduring tradition of countrywide authority. Like his Pashtun predecessors, especially Zahir Shah, he would self-consciously tie his rule to the consent of the other stakeholders. Karzai's regime was a hierarchic coalition government, traditional to Afghanistan.[45]

Afghanistan's interim government leader, Hamid Karzai, and U.S. secretary of state Colin Powell gave a joint press conference in Kabul on 17 January 2002. Powell pledged America's long-term commitment to the country and Karzai.
Paula Bronstein, Getty Images

Living in exile since his overthrow, King Zahir Shah had a vital role to play in this process. Due to his age, his distance from contemporary Afghanistan, and his own hesitance to resume rule, the king did not join the new government. He granted it his blessing, affirming that it represented a unified collection of Afghan groups. He also opened the meeting of the Afghan tribal leaders in 2002 (the "Emergency" Loya Jirga) that lent the new government wide public support and confirmed Karzai's position as head of state. In early 2004 a second Loya Jirga met to approve a formal constitution. In October of that year a countrywide election—with little evidence of cheating—elected Karzai president of the nation. Thanks to the cooperation among the Afghan factions, including the king, James Dobbins recounts that "all the benchmarks laid out in the Bonn Agreement were met more or less on schedule."[46]

The notoriously divided people of the region were committed to nation-building on terms that matched local and international priorities. They clearly sought stability rather than war, effective governance rather than violent anarchy. The United States enabled this process and it offered crucial guidance, along with other countries and the United Nations. The key decisions were made by courageous Afghans inspired by the opportunity opened for their society in late 2001.

Nation-Building Aborted

The initial successes in Afghanistan encouraged a self-defeating strategic posture. This was a prime example of "victory disease," particularly among fearful and overconfident Americans. The rapid defeat of the Taliban and the smooth creation of a new regime led many observers to expect more for less in the near future. Despite the expert warnings about the fractious, violent, and xenophobic qualities of Afghan society, the United States had worked effectively with groups in the country to transform the government and create a new unified, representative political process. Despite the difficulties of conducting military operations in distant and forbidding terrain, a small American force had shown that it could seed local transformations in Washington's interests. It seemed so easy—too easy.[47]

At a time when terrorism raised the stakes for foreign policy in faraway places, Operation Enduring Freedom and its immediate aftermath affirmed the deepest hopes of Americans: the power of the United States could correct threatening dynamics in failed states. The United States could defeat enemies and create constructive solutions. On 11 September 2001 the terrorists showed how rigid, ineffective, and unimaginative the world's only superpower had become. Overthrowing the Taliban in a few short months, American policymakers recovered an image of courage, creativity, and even invincibility. The United States did not capture the criminals, but that did not matter. It had changed their surroundings. It had closed their hole in the international "society of states."

Secretary of Defense Donald Rumsfeld became a celebrity figure for his blunt advocacy of what he described as a rediscovered American flexibility in war, now married to the most precise and lethal modern technology. On "the plains of Afghanistan," Rumsfeld wrote, "the nineteenth century met the twenty-first century." The United States and its allies combined capabilities "from the most advanced (such as laser-guided weapons) to the antique (40 year-old B-52s updated with modern electronics) to the most rudimentary (a man with a gun on a horse)." Strategic "transformation" for the secretary of defense meant a sophisticated return to basics—replacing the single-enemy obsessions and excessive deployments of the Cold War with unique combinations of resources for maximum effect. A "more entrepreneurial approach" to force and change would return Americans to what they always did best: political reform, at home and abroad.[48]

In its best traditions, according to Rumsfeld, the United States did not build massive occupation armies. Nor, in this historical interpretation, did Washington waste resources on expensive efforts to direct the daily practices of foreign societies. Those were the behaviors of empires, not nation-builders. Instead of occupation and direction abroad, the secretary of defense argued that the United States was best suited to undertake targeted interventions, empowering positive local forces and dismantling their detractors. Washington would redirect political processes, but then it would let local figures make the decisions, build the institutions, and organize the investments. The United States would act as seed investor with early commitments and limited long-term obligations. The United States would initiate deep change from a careful distance.[49]

This strategy promised grand achievements at bargain costs. It offered the possibility of global influence and security without the burdens of empire. Most of all, it predicted that the world would become more like the United States as citizens in other societies made choices encouraged and modeled, but not imposed, by Washington. What could be more American? What could resonate more deeply with the American nation-building creed?

The promise of change on the cheap had a devastating effect on foreign policy. It justified an underinvestment of resources in Afghanistan. Rumsfeld and others in the Bush administration had a strong bias to reduce government interference in local decisions, best left to the market in their estimation. In addition, they believed that the United States had undermined its purposes when it became bogged down in the reconstruction of communities. This interpretation applied to poor regions at home and sites of violence abroad—America's inner cities and foreign countries like Vietnam. For Bush, Rumsfeld, and their closest advisors, the United States had to use its power more frequently against evil, but it also had to reject local efforts to tie down Washington's capabilities. Rumsfeld advocated decisive, far-reaching, and self-limiting military interventions.[50]

The American military, according to National Security Advisor Condoleezza Rice, would fight and win wars. It would then leave the rebuilding to allies on the ground—supported by the United States, but also expected to raise their own resources for a sustainable political future. Nation-building, in this context, would approximate child-rearing: the American parents would protect the child nation from destructive influences and they would finance the rudimentary foundations for modern adulthood (statehood). The new nation-state would then have to look within, organize its talents, and establish a future for itself. When the president invoked the examples of American nation-building in Germany and Japan after the Second World War, this was precisely the model he had in mind. Bush and his advisors were "neoconservatives" because they believed, as Rumsfeld promised, in a more forceful American example tied to a stingier civilian pocketbook. The United States would enable suffering peoples to rule themselves, but they would have to pay their own bills.[51]

The quick defeat of the Taliban reinforced this neoconservative interpretation and encouraged its application in Afghanistan. In late 2001, as the post-Taliban government emerged from the negotiations in Bonn, the Bush administration made it clear that it intended to maintain a light footprint in the region. The U.S. State Department, the United Nations, and much of the international community expected that the United States would deploy soldiers as peacekeepers throughout Afghanistan, but the Department of Defense and the White House rejected this option. "We don't want to repeat the Soviets' mistakes," Rumsfeld explained. "There's nothing to be gained by blundering around those mountains and gorges with armor battalions chasing a lightly armed enemy."[52]

If the United States did not undertake this security role, other allies would not do so either. Policymakers in Washington understood that very well. Bush administration officials had spent their early months in office lambasting their friends, particularly in Europe, for what they criticized as a self-defeating aversion to the use of force against threats. Washington's efforts to reduce its post-Taliban commitments in Afghanistan would only justify more of the same from other powerful societies. The United States led the early war, and then it led the retreat.[53]

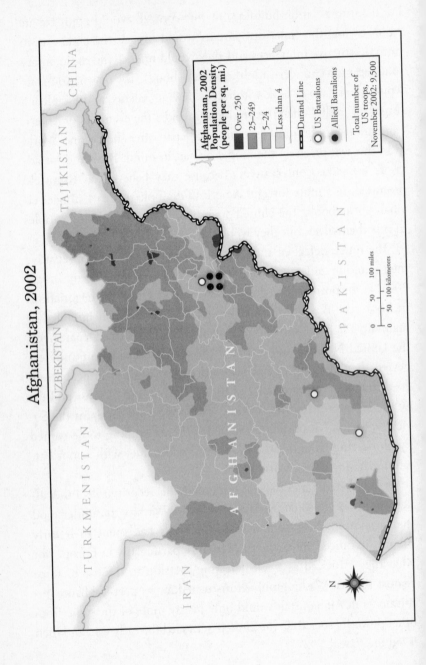

Afghanistan, 2002

It deployed only eight thousand additional troops to Afghanistan in 2002. One scholar has pointed out that American troop commitments in the country were smaller, in relation to the size of the Afghan population, than in any other major U.S. reconstruction effort since the Second World War. In Germany, for example, Washington deployed 89.3 soldiers for every 1,000 inhabitants. In Afghanistan, the United States and other international contributors stationed only 1.6 soldiers for every 1,000 inhabitants. Neoconservative nation-building left an unbridgeable gap between the rhetoric of political reform and the reality of absent manpower.[54]

Rooting out insurgents, including al Qaeda, and maintaining stability would have to fall on the shoulders of the new government's military and police units. The problem was that the Afghan military and police existed only on paper. Karzai's regime did not have the time, the resources, or the expertise to create cohesive security forces during its first months in power. If anything, the chaos of the early days encouraged plundering and corruption, not coherent long-term planning. A light American footprint opened a power vacuum that armed militias—warlords, drug-traffickers, Taliban loyalists, and al Qaeda operatives—quickly filled.

The Bush administration's self-confidence and neoconservative ideology led policymakers to deny this obvious reality, even when it was presented plainly to them. They rejected the history of extensive American force commitments in other nation-building cases, from the reconstruction of the American South to the occupation of postwar Germany. They ignored the evidence that political transitions require long-term assistance from external sources to nurture inclusive institutions, invest in productive industries, apprehend threatening figures, and educate young citizens. This was the history of the Marshall Plan that the Bush administration cited. It was the opposite of what the invading Soviet armies had undertaken in their efforts to dominate the region. Rumsfeld's invocation of the Soviet example as a warning against deep American investments in Afghanistan was a profound misreading of how nation-building really works.[55]

Without security, foreign donors turned away from Afghanistan. International pledges made to Karzai's government in the aftermath of the Bonn negotiations failed to materialize fully. Subsequent efforts to procure additional funding for infrastructure, industry, and education met resistance from wealthy countries that were hesitant to enter a violent and unpredictable environment. During 2002 and 2003 the Afghan government received an average of only $60 in foreign assistance per citizen. This was less than half the per capita aid allocation for citizens in postwar Germany, adjusted for inflation. It was far less than the subsidies sent to other countries in transition: Haiti, Mozambique, East Timor, and the Solomon Islands, among others.[56]

Inadequate aid to Afghanistan only increased the incentives for corruption among government leaders. They could not buy off all of the major groups, and they feared for their longevity in office. It made sense to hoard resources and invest them in self-protection, not broad social needs. In addition, the paltry international contributions to the country sent a discouraging message to citizens: the United States and its allies were not directly committed to the nation-building goals they articulated for Afghanistan. They had abandoned the country after the Soviet withdrawal in 1989. It looked like they would do the same again. Under these circumstances, Afghan men and women had little reason to take risks for a new political future. They had little incentive to abandon the warlords and Taliban figures who promised local protection and economic sustenance. An underfinanced Afghan nation-state devolved quickly into a collection of warring groups.

Foreign arms and assistance do not ensure successful nation-building. As the neoconservatives argued, they can encourage resistance, corruption, and dictatorship. In Afghanistan—as in the Philippines, Germany, and Vietnam—local leaders had to bear the most difficult burdens of building new institutions, nurturing new partnerships, and encouraging cooperation among citizens. The United States and its allies could only assist this process, they could not drive it. Political change had to come from within, supported at key points from without.

The tragedy of Afghanistan is that the local leaders initially assembled in Bonn were ready to work together. They had shown a commitment to compromise, partnership, and even collective sacrifice. They had created a new government. They had promoted an Afghan national identity and a vision of a modern state, dating to the decades before the Soviet invasion. Rebuilding Afghanistan in 2002 was a massive undertaking, with very uncertain results, but many of the key actors in the country appeared ready and willing. The American nation-building creed had found a people as enthusiastic as any other to embrace its political vision and adjust it to their local traditions.

The United States was the first to defect. Although American leaders continued to pursue a modern nation-state in Afghanistan, their ideology and the circumstances of their victory over the Taliban led them to diminish the crucial tools for long-term success: investments in security, constructive partnerships, and institution-building. American leaders did not support a Freedmen's Bureau for Afghanistan, they did not create another Philippine Commission, and they did not finance a Marshall Plan, despite their rhetorical gestures in that direction. The Bush administration's light footprint meant that Americans exerted little effort to seize the political opportunities available after the fall of the Taliban.

Nation-building was possible in Afghanistan, but Washington failed to act. The combination of fear and hubris after the 11 September terrorist attacks encouraged an outward search for enemies and an inward focus on avoiding expensive alliances. The United States destroyed, but it did not rebuild.[57]

Iraq

The United States also failed to set priorities. Successful nation-building in a country always requires commitment and focus. It cannot succeed as one of many projects. It must have a primary claim on the attention, resources, and energy of leaders. This was the case in the American South after the Civil War. The same was true for the Philippines in the early twentieth century and especially Germany after the Second World War. Vietnam received focused attention in 1945 and during the 1960s, but it suffered from distracted American priorities during the crucial intervening years. Nation-building is a full-time endeavor. You cannot do it far from home and part-time.

In Afghanistan the United States worked less than part-time. By 2003 the country that provided sanctuary and training for the terrorists who attacked the United States had become an afterthought in the "Global War on Terrorism." Historians will puzzle over that observation. Why did Washington divert its resources from the place that produced the enemies it sought to defeat? Why did American attention shift from denying Osama bin Laden sanctuary to overthrowing Saddam Hussein?

Never before had the United States begun a major nation-building endeavor, only to start a new war and another nation-building project at the same time. In the past, Washington had concentrated its efforts in a few places and limited new commitments. Most of all, it had tried to avoid new wars as it worked to deliver on the political vision of prior conflicts. Afghanistan was different because it was, from the very start, a first step for the Bush administration toward a broader effort at rapid global transformation. Nation-building had become world reform. The irony was that these neoconservative aspirations were matched to a faith in the most constrained allocations of American resources. The United States would work to end "tyranny in our world," according to President Bush, by hopping quickly from one site to another, not digging deeply into the soil of a particular society. For all the traditionalist rhetoric of the neoconservatives, this was an Internet model of nation-building—everywhere and nowhere at the same time.

Bush used the metaphor of fire to explain how American influence would spread, with little investment in infrastructure or institutions: "because we have acted in the great liberating tradition of this nation, tens of millions have achieved their freedom. And as hope kindles hope, millions more will find it. By our efforts, we have lit a fire as well—a fire in the minds of men. It warms those who feel its power, it burns those who fight its progress, and one day this untamed fire of freedom will reach the darkest corners of our world."[58]

Soon after its intervention in Afghanistan, the United States began to plan for the invasion of Iraq. Liberating the people of that suffering society and overthrowing the dictatorship of Saddam Hussein promised, according to President Bush's logic, to spread the fire of freedom throughout the region. The United States would immolate the evil regimes—the Taliban, Saddam Hussein, and others—that repressed modern nation-state development. This quick and violent process would have a purifying effect, opening space for the good citizens of each society to rise up and rebuild themselves, inspired by the American model. Vice President Dick Cheney, Deputy Secretary of Defense Paul Wolfowitz, and other influential administration officials expected Iraq to be easier than Afghanistan. It had an odious dictator, an educated citizenry, and natural oil wealth. It looked ready for liberation and nation-state development.[59]

Bush articulated these expectations, allegedly realized in Afghanistan, with some of the most utopian nation-building rhetoric heard in American history. "Eventually," the president explained, "the call of freedom comes to every mind and every soul. We do not accept the existence of permanent tyranny because we do not accept the possibility of permanent slavery. Liberty will come to those who love it."

Bush promised to liberate the oppressed, and he had faith that they could do the rest with American encouragement: "All who live in tyranny and hopelessness can know: the United States will not ignore your oppression, or excuse your oppressors. When you stand for your liberty, we will stand with you."[60]

In late March 2003 American soldiers overthrew Saddam Hussein's regime with ease, as Cheney and Wolfowitz predicted, but they immediately found that the people of Iraq did not greet them as liberators. There was no replay in Baghdad of the jubilation displayed in Kabul sixteen months earlier. Instead, the capital of Iraq and other cities quickly devolved into chaos and violence. A variety of insurgent groups emerged along ethnic and religious lines to fight for the resources formerly controlled by Saddam Hussein's government, and to settle old scores for mistreatment under the defeated regime.

After the overthrow of Saddam Hussein, the capital of Iraq and other cities devolved into chaos and violence that produced scenes like the one pictured here.
Spencer Platt, Getty Images

Saddam's government had enforced order by pitting antagonistic groups against one another. It had not established enduring traditions of cooperation. The removal of political controls, in a conflict-ridden society replete with weapons, elicited group militarization and combat. Young American soldiers found themselves caught between warring parties. The circumstances were, in fact, much more divided and dangerous than Afghanistan after the Taliban. Despite American expectations, liberation in Iraq encouraged tendencies that challenged nation-state development.[61]

Even in this tumultuous environment, there were many Iraqis who greeted the American soldiers with hopes for partnership. Charles Tripp, a distinguished scholar of Iraqi society, recounts: "in 2003 there were those who saw the collapse of the old regime as a golden opportunity to recapture some of what Iraq might have been."

> They sought to build organizations to give a voice to the voiceless—all those who had been written out of the narrative of Iraqi history by the strident commands of the Ba'thist vanguard and its instruments of repression. The array of new media, the possibilities offered for NGO (nongovernmental organization) and trade union activities, as well as the novel freedom to communicate and debate, were avidly seized upon, bringing a host of new and original Iraqi voices to the fore. However, they faced a hard struggle trying to carve out a secure space in which to enjoy these freedoms.[62]

The United States never secured political space for the Iraqi advocates of reform. Washington relied on a strategy of high expectations with minimal commitments—an extension of the policies pursued in Afghanistan. American and coalition (mostly British) forces deployed in Iraq numbered less than 200,000, in a country with a population of 25 million people. The foreign soldiers were trained to destroy the enemy, but they were poorly prepared for governing the society, even temporarily. They did not speak the language, understand the customs, recognize the security needs of the population, or plan for economic sustenance after Saddam's fall. American military forces were intrepid in battle, but ineffectual when widely dispersed on city streets and along village roadsides. They became sitting ducks for citizens who resented their presence.[63]

Jay Garner and L. Paul Bremer, the two successive civilian officials sent by the president to manage the occupation of Iraq, had neither the resources nor the skills to build a new political order. Garner sought to reestablish basic government services and distribute humanitarian assistance, but he failed to attract effective partners on the ground. Bremer took a more centralized approach, seeking to build a government around his office. His centralizing efforts, however, alienated an already suspicious population.[64]

Bremer made the monumental error of purging the new Iraqi government of all figures who had collaborated with Saddam Hussein. He also disbanded the former Iraqi military and security services. These two orders deprived hundreds of thousands of citizens of their jobs. Bremer's orders also denied the United States access to the most skilled, experienced, and effective people. Instead of winning over midlevel officials, Bremer alienated the most capable Iraqis. Instead of cultivating a cooperative image of the United States, he made enemies of those who lost their positions under his orders. Instead of focusing on basic problem-solving—distributing food, generating electricity, and ensuring public safety—Bremer chose to make a strong and rigid moral statement. Bremer's haste contradicted the experience of American cooperation with established elites in the post–Civil War South, the Philippines, and Germany.[65]

By 2004 American forces in Iraq confronted an antagonistic population that visibly resented the combination of American military imposition and political ineffectiveness. Armed insurgent groups organized around clerics—often supported by al Qaeda, Syria, or Iran—began attacking foreign soldiers. In July 2004 alone, 54 Americans died in action in Iraq, 552 were wounded. In August another 66 Americans died, 895 were wounded. This was a shattering summer for soldiers, policymakers, and citizens watching from the United States. After more than a year, American nation-building efforts were going backward. Iraq grew increasingly chaotic, violent, and deadly. It became nearly impossible to establish government services, protect transportation, or maintain civilian security. Potential local allies feared that any cooperation with the United States would elicit murderous reprisals. Insurgents against American power came to dominate daily activities in Iraq. Similar dynamics also began to appear in Afghanistan.[66]

The United States had stretched itself too thin in both countries, it had failed to support productive nation-building processes, and it had emboldened more enemies than when the Iraq War began. Global nation-building on the cheap had proven counterproductive. American expectations were too high and American commitments were too low. The results were devastating in Afghanistan, Iraq, and elsewhere. By 2006 the neoconservative vision had inflamed a nightmare of guerrilla wars.[67]

A Nation-Building Surge?

American leaders did not know what to do next. The prospect of failure in Iraq and Afghanistan raised numerous difficulties. First, there would be the obvious political fallout at home and abroad from the destruction without obvious benefit. The opponents of American power would be vindicated; the supporters of an internationally active United States would have trouble making their case. George W. Bush, in particular, would bear the historical burden of defeat, like his predecessor during the Vietnam War. Bush did not want to be another Lyndon Johnson.

The second and most significant difficulty centered on what to do next, especially if the United States withdrew all its forces from both war zones. Even the most vocal critics of American policy could not promise more stability and security without foreign soldiers. In Afghanistan, the international community had turned its back on the region after 1989, and the horrible results were evident with the rise of the Taliban, the expansion of al Qaeda, and the terrorist attacks of 11 September 2001. No one wanted to repeat that history. In Iraq, the destruction of Saddam Hussein's regime unleashed a civil war that promised to infect nearby societies if ignored by powerful international actors. Many observers might have wished that the United States had not intervened in the first place, especially in Iraq, but it was not possible to turn back the clock. As the insurgencies escalated, policymakers had no good options.

In his second inaugural address, President George W. Bush advocated a broad nation-building agenda. *Douglas Graham, Roll Call, Getty Images*

Critics, commentators, and even "experts" frequently lose sight of this point. Policymakers often confront problems without a solution. They often face challenges they know they cannot master. Even the most skilled leader is still a human being struggling with complex social and economic changes he or she cannot control. Even the most creative thinker is constrained by his or her own particular experiences in a world filled with almost infinite possibilities. To condemn the shortcomings of policy is easy, but misleading. All policies—especially those designed to change societies—fail to meet expectations. This is especially true for powerful, ambitious countries like the United States. The more you can do, the more you are expected to achieve, despite the incredible difficulties. Nation-building as the world's only superpower means that dissatisfaction is unavoidable, but alternatives are almost impossible. No one wants the United States to abandon its efforts to improve the world, and look inward at itself alone. No one wants the United States to build a traditional empire of forceful repression. In the twenty-first century, as in earlier periods, nation-building falls somewhere in between. After all the violence and controversy, the question in Iraq and Afghanistan remained not whether to nation-build, but how.[68]

The Bush administration followed the pattern set by Harry Truman in Germany and Lyndon Johnson in Vietnam. Confronted with failure, it doubled down. Abandoning the cost-cutting efforts of Donald Rumsfeld and the neoconservatives, the president made major new investments of soldiers, money, and time in both countries. He sent thirty thousand additional troops to Iraq, deployed largely in Baghdad to provide security in the capital. He promised more aid for the economy, more assistance with institution-building, and, most important, more flexibility in negotiating deals with diverse groups. Bush sent an iconoclastic commander, General David Petraeus, to the region with a strong commitment of close, continual, and concerted attention from the White House. As he had not before, the president pledged direct American protection for Iraqi citizens, partnering closely with them as they tried to build a new political order.[69]

The "surge" in Iraq was a return to more traditional American nation-building. Petraeus's orders to his soldiers made this clear.

Instead of targeting enemies and leaving the rest to the Iraqis, the United States would focus on assisting citizens in their efforts to rebuild. Instead of isolating themselves from the population, American soldiers would mingle closely with ordinary Iraqis, nurturing relationships for mutual benefit. Instead of creating a light footprint, the United States would show a long-term commitment to the country, not as a permanent ruler, but as a visiting partner. Petraeus articulated these points with the brevity and punch often lacking in policy documents:

1. Secure and serve the population.
2. Live among the people.
3. Hold areas that have been secured.
4. Pursue the enemy relentlessly.
5. Generate unity of effort.
6. Promote reconciliation.
7. Defeat the network, not just the attack.
8. Foster Iraqi legitimacy.
9. Employ all assets to isolate and defeat the terrorists and insurgents.
10. Employ money as a weapon system.
11. Fight for intelligence.
12. Walk.
13. Understand the neighborhood.
14. Build relationships.
15. Look for sustainable solutions.
16. Maintain continuity and tempo through transitions.
17. Manage expectations.
18. Be first with the truth.
19. Fight the information war relentlessly.
20. Live our values.
21. Exercise initiative.
22. Prepare for and exploit opportunities.
23. Learn and adapt.[70]

Petraeus's points were the distilled wisdom of American nation-building over two centuries. The general did not necessarily recognize that, but he had studied the failures of the last four years, and he had arrived at many of the same insights as Oliver Otis Howard, William Howard Taft, and Herbert Hoover. Petraeus's reflections were more historically grounded than anything recommended by his predecessors in Vietnam or Iraq and Afghanistan before 2007. He understood that nation-building started with security and civilian relationships. He recognized that the military had to take the lead not in blowing things up, but in constructing partnerships, institutions, and other forms of trust. Most of all, Petraeus internalized the hardest lesson: success comes slowly, through constant adaptation, adjustment, and flexible negotiation. The United States had to work with some of the insurgent groups, co-opt them within a new governing structure, and make them stakeholders in a unified nation with a functioning state. The goal was not American-style democracy, at least not for a long time. The more realistic aim was to create representative, inclusive, and effective Iraqi institutions.

As in the American South, the Philippines, and Germany, nation-building remained a very difficult process. Violence declined precipitously after the surge in Iraq, but sectarian conflict remained ripe. Local groups that allied with the new Petraeus strategy, particularly the "Sunni Awakening," often seemed intent on grabbing power for themselves, rather than contributing to an inclusive political process. When American combat forces drew down in Iraq during the summer of 2010, elections failed to produce a unified government or a reconciliation process for groups at war since Saddam Hussein's overthrow. Almost fifty thousand American soldiers remained in Iraq to ensure security, and the United States continued to spend billions of dollars each month in the country. Conditions in Iraq had improved dramatically from the first years of the American occupation, and also from the time of Saddam Hussein's rule, but the country's emergence as a stable, secure, and legitimate nation-state remained deeply uncertain.[71]

General David Petraeus led the American "surge" in Iraq. He
later applied the lessons of that experience to Afghanistan.
Chris Hondros, Getty Images

In Afghanistan the United States was slower to adjust. Leaders
of the Taliban and al Qaeda found sanctuary in Pakistan after the
American invasion. They began to return to Afghanistan in 2005.
They took advantage of the very thin American and NATO military
presence, as well as the poor training of Afghan national forces, to
reestablish links with armed militias. Pakistani sympathizers—some
associated with the government's Inter-Services Intelligence Agency
(ISI)—encouraged this violent process. The Taliban and al Qaeda
also began to intimidate local citizens and reconstruct their authority, especially in the Pashtun areas in the south of the country, near
Kandahar. The American failure to fill the security vacuum in Afghanistan after 2001 left a wide opening for extremist elements to
exploit.[72]

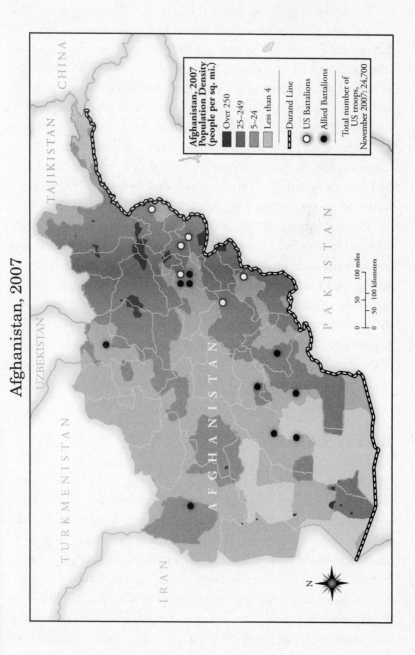

Afghanistan, 2007

The weakness and corruption of Hamid Karzai's government made it incapable of resisting Taliban and al Qaeda incursions. American forces were also too few in number and poorly prepared for counter-insurgency operations against battle-hardened and politically astute enemies. One Afghan resident described the situation very well in the summer of 2005: "In the daytime, this [American-supported] government is coming to us, and in the nighttime the Taliban are coming to us. We are stuck in the middle." Under these conditions many Afghan citizens refrained from working with the Karzai regime. Many men and women joined the Taliban because they looked like the more effective force. Intimidation and efficacy are powerful persuaders.[73]

This was exactly the dynamic predicted by the Australian counterinsurgency expert David Kilcullen. Caught between an ineffective government with foreign support, and a growing insurgency with strong local roots, many Afghan citizens became "accidental guerrillas." They sided with the groups they knew best—those who seemed most predictable, those who could credibly reward supporters and kill opponents. Despite the evidence of progress in Iraq after the surge, in 2008 President Bush handed a spiraling Afghan crisis to his successor. It felt like Vietnam in the 1960s to those who could remember.[74]

Back to the 1960s?

Afghanistan immediately became Obama's war. Like a prior Democrat four decades earlier, the new president entered the White House with an ambitious agenda for domestic reform, but also a lingering foreign conflict that he could not easily end. Thanks to the signs of recent success in Iraq, Obama could withdraw soldiers and treasure from that war. In the case of Afghanistan, he confronted an immediate crisis that challenged American nation-building investments throughout the region. The return of the Taliban also threatened to undermine order in neighboring Pakistan, destabilize that country's nuclear arsenal, and reignite terrorism near and far. Afghanistan was the strategic pivot for many areas that Americans cared deeply about. History seemed to be repeating itself.

Like Lyndon Johnson in the 1960s, Barack Obama in 2009 needed to salvage American goals in a distant country for the sake of fortifying public confidence in his presidency. If he allowed the Taliban to reestablish power, he would appear weak and traitorous to American aims. If a major terrorist attack on American soil followed the return of the Taliban, his entire presidential agenda would evaporate. Like Johnson in Vietnam, the fate of Obama's presidency would be determined in Afghanistan. He could not simply withdraw, even if he wanted to. The pressure to nation-build in the face of growing threats was too strong to resist.[75]

After a long and acrimonious internal review, on 1 December 2009 the president announced his new strategy. It called for another surge, combined with a regional diplomatic offensive. The United States and its NATO allies would enlarge their military forces in Afghanistan from fewer than 65,000 at the start of Obama's presidency to almost 150,000 by the middle of 2010. American troop deployments would increase from approximately 32,000 in January 2009 to more than 90,000 eighteen months later. This was the Petraeus strategy from Iraq, applied to Afghanistan. Reversing the Bush administration's initial diversion of talent and resources from Kabul to Baghdad, Petraeus assumed command for all American forces in the broader region (United States Central Command). He then moved into direct leadership of American troops in Afghanistan—the same position he had held in Iraq. Obama made defeat of the Taliban and reconstruction of political order his clear priority.[76]

Washington increased its aid to the region, including Pakistan, and it pushed Afghanistan's neighbor to interdict and destroy Taliban sympathizers. Richard Holbrooke, an experienced negotiator in war-torn regions (including Vietnam and the former Yugoslavia), took the lead as the president's special envoy for this purpose. The U.S. departments of Defense and State, and other civilian agencies, also deployed more personnel to Afghanistan with skills to help reconstruction efforts. Newly arrived American officials did not bring grand plans for modernizing the country. Instead, they worked locally—as engineers, farmers, teachers, and advisors—to address basic problems and build a sustainable foundation for coordinated national efforts. During Obama's first fifteen months in office the number of these diplomats on the ground more than doubled, deployed in all parts of Afghanistan.[77]

President Barack Obama greets cadets after announcing his Afghanistan policy at the United States Military Academy at West Point,
1 December 2009.
Roger L. Wollenberg, Getty Images

Despite frequent criticisms of Hamid Karzai's corruption, Obama pledged to work closely with the Afghan leader. The president hoped to encourage Karzai to build more effective governing institutions and attract local groups that had become disaffected from the regime. Recognizing the importance of negotiations with diverse figures (not just a Ngo Dinh Diem or a Hamid Karzai), Obama advocated cooperation with neighboring Iran and even elements of the Taliban who appeared willing to join a national government. "We will support efforts by the Afghan government," the president announced, "to open the door to those Taliban who abandon violence and respect the human rights of their fellow citizens."[78]

Like a good Chicago party boss, the president sought to combine sticks with carrots—in this case aerial drone attacks with targeted bribes. The United States would help Karzai destroy or buy off his opponents. The United States would emphasize security, inclusion, and development at the local level—beyond the capital city of Kabul. The United States would also nurture a web of relationships throughout Afghanistan to support and discipline the national government. This was not a vision of democracy. It was a vision of a functioning nation-state that would protect order, deliver goods to citizens, and encourage broad participation. Obama hoped for stable self-governance in Afghanistan. That would be a victory, and it would allow for a withdrawal of American soldiers.

Whether intentional or not, this model of nation-building returned to the promising years between 1964 and 1973 in Afghan history. This was a useful history for saving the region in the twenty-first century. During that decade, King Zahir Shah played precisely the role Americans envisioned for Karzai. He brokered deals and punished defectors. He channeled foreign assistance and maintained stability. Most of all, the king built a national government around promises of mutual benefit for local groups that wanted safety, resources, and respect for their traditions. The Afghan nation-state of the 1960s was a mosaic united by common institutions and an effective figurehead. It resembled the "machine politics" of many large twentieth-century American cities—including Chicago. Obama and his advisors wanted Karzai, like Zahir Shah, to play the role of national boss, bringing different groups together for collective self-interest. The United States would provide Karzai with the resources and the police to make that possible.[79]

U.S. Marine captain Eric Meador speaks with an Afghan village
leader after helping to clear his village of Taliban fighters in 2009.
Joe Raedle, Getty Images

All of these nation-building commitments in Afghanistan were
promising, but they showed few immediate results. By all measures—insurgent attacks, assassinations of government officials,
civilian deaths, and troop fatalities—Afghanistan became a much
more violent and chaotic place in 2009. American aerial drone
strikes showed some success in targeting Taliban and al Qaeda figures, but the heavier American footprint on the ground did not increase daily security. American aid did not produce improved living
conditions. Most frustrating, American support for Hamid Karzai
and his Pakistani counterpart, Asif Ali Zardari, only seemed to encourage more corruption. Karzai and Zardari—like Ngo Dinh Diem
decades earlier—exploited Washington's dependence on their rule.
Nation-building in Afghanistan made the United States a hostage to
deeply flawed figures.[80]

The president recognized this problem. It clearly troubled him. In response, the White House worked to expand its relationships in the region and enforce deadlines on its allies. Unlike Lyndon Johnson, Barack Obama would not continue to escalate American commitments with no end in sight. He would not allow local figures to continue demanding more arms and assistance without evidence that they were doing their part too. Obama wanted a partnership in nation-building, not an American endowment for incompetence, corruption, and double-dealing. This was a logical position, and it led the president to announce in December 2009: "After 18 months, our troops will begin to come home. These are the resources that we need to seize the initiative, while building the Afghan capacity that can allow for a responsible transition of our forces out of Afghanistan." "This effort," Obama continued, "must be based on performance. The days of providing a blank check are over."

> And going forward, we will be clear about what we expect from those who receive our assistance. We'll support Afghan ministries, governors, and local leaders that combat corruption and deliver for the people. We expect those who are ineffective or corrupt to be held accountable. And we will also focus our assistance in areas—such as agriculture—that can make an immediate impact in the lives of the Afghan people.[81]

Obama said the correct things about nation-building. The United States had to make a broad and inclusive investment. It needed partnerships on the ground and throughout the region. The United States also needed to work with a variety of difficult, even despicable, figures. The goal was stability, unity, and cooperation within a functioning set of state institutions. The Afghan people would have to make the difficult sacrifices, but the United States would provide the space and the resources for that process.

A timetable for American commitments made sense, but eighteen months was unrealistic. Two hundred years of experience with nation-building had shown that, even under the most propitious circumstances, this endeavor requires careful and continuous work across generations. Effective nation-building calls for intensive action and leadership at early transitional moments; it then needs sustained attention and assistance over many years. That was the history of the American founding, Reconstruction after the Civil War, the Philippines in the early twentieth century, and postwar Germany. That was also the history of Ho Chi Minh's activities in Vietnam. Nation-building cannot begin with an "exit strategy."

Both George W. Bush and Barack Obama made that same mistake in Afghanistan. The citizens of the region, aware of how Americans have abandoned them before, will invest in real partnerships only when they believe that the United States is committed to help for years and decades, not days and months. If Americans are not prepared to make that kind of commitment in Afghanistan, or any other site for nation-building, then they should simply withdraw.

Choices

The horrible terrorist attacks of 11 September 2001 strengthened the attraction of the American nation-building creed. Amidst the smoldering ruins of the World Trade Center and the Pentagon, Americans were confirmed in their faith that a violent and chaotic world needed the United States to help erect peaceful, stable, and modern nation-states. Madison's and Jefferson's vision of a "society of states" was the goal for the "Global War on Terrorism." It brought American soldiers and treasure to Afghanistan, Iraq, and many other societies.

The problem was not *what* Americans were trying to do, but *where* and *how* they were trying to do it. Nation-building was possible (and remains possible) in Afghanistan and Iraq if stability, unity, and representativeness—not democracy—are the defining features. Nation-building was sustainable (and remains sustainable) if Americans are willing to speak frankly about the costs, the sacrifices, and the long-term commitments. These issues should not be taken lightly, nor elided with simple phrases or false deadlines. Honest conversation characterized the American debate about postwar Germany; it was absent from much of the debate about postwar Vietnam. It has also remained rare in discussions about Afghanistan and Iraq.

The American nation-building creed does not determine outcomes. It encourages hard choices. To support nation-building far from home, Americans must decide where, if anywhere, they are willing to invest themselves—bodies and resources—for multiple election cycles. They must prioritize places and they must create consensus, at home and abroad. President Obama has started to do some of this in Afghanistan, but he has remained too hesitant and too torn between strategic priorities and partisan disputes. In the coming years, he and the American people will have to choose whether Afghanistan, or some other country, will be the pivot for a more peaceful "society of states" amidst the extremism and suffering that threaten global stability. American citizens will make the crucial choices. Their choices will look forward, but they will draw on a deep past.

The Future of Nation-Building

The affair of the establishment of a government is a very difficult under-taking for foreign powers to act in as principals; *though as* auxiliaries and mediators, *it has been not at all unusual, and may be a measure full of policy and humanity, and true dignity.*

Edmund Burke, 1793[1]

N ation-building is not new. It is not a transitory topic either. Nation-building is central to the history of American politics and society. From the founding, Americans have been nation-builders. From the founding, Americans have worked at home and abroad to spread a model of united peoples, organized in representative governments, with strong attachments to territory. That is the American creed. That is the history Americans have replayed from the aftermath of the Revolution to the war in Afghanistan. A society of independent, similar, and cooperative states—that is the consistent American vision of peace and justice, especially in times of extreme threat. Americans seek security and prosperity through efforts at creating political congruence amidst cultural diversity.

This vision of a "society of states" is idealistic and realistic, naive and self-serving. It has promoted American profit, as other authors have argued at length. It has also contributed to stability, good governance, and growth in places like the American South and postwar Germany. Many people have embraced the promise of nation-building. Many others have criticized, resisted, and ignored American efforts. The history of nation-building is filled with conflicts and contradictions. It is a history that defies easy categorization.[2]

The long record of nation-building is, in fact, quite mixed. It contains enough hopes and frustrations to inspire both additional efforts and popular discontents. The complex consequences of intervention encourage a recurring cycle of improvements and inadequacies. Nation-building never succeeds sufficiently to convince its critics, nor does it fail enough to put off its promoters. The never-ending controversies over nation-building are what make Americans who they are.

Since the days of George Washington, the United States has contributed to the spread of the nation-state as the most accepted form of political organization on the planet. The genius of this project comes from its encouragement of local autonomy without anarchy, and effective authority without empire. Nation-building is an effort to nurture behavioral patterns that balance freedom and order, independence and cooperation. Although Americans frequently push this process along, they have long believed that it is an organic phenomenon—the product of natural human desires and needs. Americans see their own history in their repeated nation-building efforts. They see their own ideals and experiences in their endeavors to remake the world.

Nation-building is a form of federalism that grew out of the pioneering political work of George Washington, James Madison, Alexander Hamilton, and their founding generation. It seeks to create nested levels of authority, with specific institutions exerting power in different territories. The "government of the whole," according to federalism, should be the sum of separate parts, each protecting its own interests as it contributes to a larger set of shared goals. The different representative units, not the center, should drive change. Cooperation should come from negotiation and compromise among different units; it should not be imposed by a single figure or government.[3]

Federalism encourages diversity and difference. It presumes that pluralism will prevent tyranny by any single group. It expects that coalitions of different political actors can form and re-form to check one another, and to balance competing claims. Political actors, in this context, adjust and adapt, and they coordinate to address common challenges and opportunities. The organized diversity of federalism promises greater freedom and efficacy than the rigidity of a centralized empire, or the chaos of unconnected actors. The goal of federalism is to provide a political framework for independent cooperation, what later generations might define as flexible connectivity. In some ways, federalism does for politics what the Internet has done for communications. Order comes from more, not less, independence.[4]

Any system of independent cooperation requires some basic agreement on infrastructure. Personal computers on the Internet have to recognize one another, and they have to communicate in a language they can all understand. The same is true for a society of states. Their continued separateness and diversity requires coordinating institutions that facilitate exchange without imposing false uniformity. A single "world government" for either the Internet or global politics would destroy diversity, flexibility, and local responsiveness. Cooperation through institutional congruence works much better. Similarities among political organizations enable communication, negotiation, and trust. Order built around coordination of this kind promises continued complexity, with some basic rules and routines that everyone recognizes. It promises regularity with continued space for spontaneity and surprise.

Political authority in a federalist framework is clear and complex. It is defined by a common set of institutions. The rest is left to the independent states to decide. For federalism to work, power must be divided but functional; it must encourage more creative action, not less. Independent cooperation ultimately demands basic agreement on *who* can speak for *whom*, and what are the terms of negotiation.

The units—or "unions" in George Washington's terms—make the system, but the system must have some consensus on what designates some units as legitimate and others as not. Otherwise, independent cooperation breaks down into chaos. The federalist genius is to see the unity in diversity. The federalist genius is to see that nation-states are the common machines that can connect and empower. Nation-building is a form of wiring for a more interactive, diverse, and stable world.

Nation-states—or something like them—are necessary because the world is not flat. The violence, inequality, and disorganization of different societies encourage war, destruction, and suffering. Cooperation is not natural between peoples, even when the incentives are quite clear. Although nation-building does not remove the animosities that antagonize groups and individuals, it can provide an institutional architecture that shifts the balance of power toward mutual interests rather than narrow self-regard. Nation-building can support the basic order that allows societies to assess their needs and capabilities, and draw on a wider range of possibilities. It can encourage long-term investments in progress, rather than short-term survival. Most of all, nation-building has the potential to bring legitimate figures from different societies together to negotiate deals that serve a large and diverse number of people, not just a well-placed few. Nation-states do not flatten the world, but they help to create a common survey for navigating a complex terrain.[5]

For better and for worse, the United States has a special role to play in this nation-building process. To some extent, Americans invented it. They have also done more than any other society to spread a system of nation-states during the last two hundred years. Despite the economic difficulties of the early twenty-first century, the United States continues to possess many of the necessary resources—military, political, cultural, and financial—to deliver on the federal vision of independent global organization. The United States also has the most to lose if this vision is destroyed. The terrorist attacks of 11 September 2001 made that clear. Having benefited enormously from the movement of peoples, goods, and capital that accompanied the rise of the nation-state, Americans can sustain their interests—and the interests of their allies—only if they strengthen the society of nation-states for the future. The United States needs stronger nation-states at home and abroad.

This is the most promising investment for limited American resources. It is the most likely program for encouraging broad international support. Many people in the Middle East and other regions resent America's nation-building role, but they see value in its success, especially if Washington acts with wisdom rather than impulse alone. Stable, prosperous, and peaceful nation-states in regions racked by violence would serve the interests of many divided groups. United, representative, well-managed governing institutions would give many more people local voice than the extremist and dictatorial politics that presently dominate countries like Lebanon, Iran, Saudi Arabia, and especially Pakistan. Serious nation-building promises to reform America's enemies and its friends, as well as the United States itself.

The process is aimed at political inclusiveness, not the destruction of a particular threat. For this reason, nation-building has deep international legitimacy—more than any other contemporary system of political organization. In conjunction with other countries and institutions, including the European Union and the United Nations, the United States must continue to nurture foreign and domestic stakeholders. It must continue to build a diverse, independent, and organized society of states. There are no better alternatives.

This is a generational project that dates back to the eighteenth century and forward into the twenty-first. It has produced a long historical record that this book has analyzed, in part. Every case is unique. Each effort at nation-building would have benefited from closer attention to the specificities of circumstances. Each effort needed more time, more resources, more focus. The commitments to nation-building were always too little, and sometimes too late. That, of course, is the necessary limitation of human politics. Our wants and goals always exceed our capabilities and our resolve. Americans, in particular, want it all—and they want it fast and cheap.

From one case of nation-building to another, history does not repeat itself, but it does rhyme. As previewed in the introductory chapter, five major themes cut across the two hundred years and the vast landscape covered in this book. Each of these themes is a common insight about nation-building. Each of these themes is a potential lesson for wiser policy in the future. These are the 5 Ps of nation-building, and politics in general.

Partners

Nation-building always requires partners. It cannot succeed without a diverse collection of contributors within and across societies. The challenges of building new political institutions are too monumental for any single power to act alone. The openings for innovation and change are too complex for any single set of policymakers to comprehend. The adjustments and reconsiderations that are crucial in every case are possible only when there is a dynamic connection between local and international voices—people on the ground and those in distant government offices. Nation-building, in this sense, is more about relationships than raw power.

From the American South to Afghanistan, the key relationship-builders were transitional figures. They were individuals who inhabited multiple worlds at once. They had connections to elite policymakers, but they were not presidents, prime ministers, or kings. They maintained connections to local communities, often through birth, residence, or profession. They also circulated between societies. The transitional figures were firmly rooted in the United States, but personally familiar with life in foreign countries. They served as the diplomats who managed the interpersonal and cross-cultural connections that make partnership possible. This kind of "classic diplomacy" is often neglected—even disparaged—but it is the lifeblood of effective policy.

The transitional diplomats of this book—Oliver Otis Howard, William Howard Taft, Herbert Hoover, and to some extent David Petraeus—were skilled at negotiating differences between peoples and societies. They recognized their dependence on diverse and unequal groups. They appreciated the limits of their power. Most important, the transitional diplomats saw themselves as mediators and joiners. They emphasized negotiations, compromises, and partnerships. They used force to ensure basic security, they dispensed money to gain access and influence, but they built working connections above all. Howard's support for free slaves, Taft's collaborations with Filipino figures, Hoover's cooperation with postwar Germans, and Petraeus's appeal to various Iraqi and Afghan factions—these efforts made nation-building possible.

Relationships rise and fall on the work of those navigating between societies. Where the United States has had skilled transitional diplomats—in the post–Civil War South, the Philippines, and, above all, Germany—it has produced positive results. Where the United States has neglected diplomacy—especially in Vietnam—it has fallen into disaster. Afghanistan remains an open case. Early American efforts at partnership in the region were promising, but then abandoned by Washington. Renewed American diplomacy in Afghanistan—including negotiations with some elements of the Taliban—offers hope after too many years of misguided unilateralism. From the Revolution to the war in Afghanistan, Americans have always needed partners for their aspiration to construct a peaceful society of states.

This might be the most important historical insight. Americans credit themselves with accomplishing great deeds, but their successes have come when they have avoided dominance and intimidation. Muscle-flexing rarely encourages trust and cooperation. The United States is most effective when it is one among many powers, when it emphasizes its commitment to local independence instead of empire, and when it allows others to take responsibility for political change. Too often since the Second World War, a well-intentioned but impatient United States has taken on too much, acted too aggressively, and alienated too many people. Nation-building requires the opposite. Americans must focus and prioritize their goals, they must act cooperatively, and they must give as many people as possible ownership in policy. Nation-building requires the humility of partnerships, not the arrogance of bullying.

Edmund Burke, the great British political thinker of the late eighteenth century and a contemporary of George Washington, made this point better than anyone else. Observing the American and French revolutions, Burke recognized that people can change the workings of society. Their actions are most effective and sustainable when, according to Burke, they act "as auxiliaries and mediators," not "as principals." Contrasting the American and French experiences, Burke foresaw the power of new partnerships designed around common goals and affirmations of continued difference. That was the American federalist vision, embodied in the nation-state.[6]

Burke also recognized the dangers of excessive zeal, overwhelming force, and supreme self-confidence—embodied in the violence of the French Revolution. Positive political change required ambition disciplined by humility, power tempered by partnerships. From Burke's time to the present, the United States is most effective when it uses its capabilities to act as auxiliary and mediator, not as principal or imposer. Leadership, above all, depends on the quality and diversity of one's relationships. Eloquence, money, and muscle are overrated. Connections matter most.[7]

Process

Nation-building is a process. It is a creative, frustrating, and unpredictable process. The same is true for politics in general. Human societies do not follow formulas. They do not adhere to rational expectations. What worked to elicit positive change in one setting will not work in another. Effective policymaking is necessarily iterative.

Through trial and error, leaders learn how to get more done. Through trial and error, citizens learn how to get more for themselves. There are no silver bullet solutions for major problems. There are only processes for bringing people together to learn and respond. Success comes—on a small scale—through a willingness to fail, to reassess, and to try again. That is the messy process of politics in the modern world.

The American experience with nation-building exemplifies this complexity. From the founding to the Afghanistan War, the history of the United States has involved trial-and-error efforts to spread a vision of political order. Americans have never known how to do this, and they have never produced fully satisfactory results. They have frequently underestimated the difficulties involved with initiating social change, but they have quickly confronted the realities of distrust, misperception, and resistance. Americans have learned the limits of their capabilities in each effort, although they have often forgotten that lesson in later engagements. As American power has grown, citizens have come to expect more global influence with less cost. This exaggerated expectation has produced repeated disappointment, often with tragic consequences.[8]

The desire to build effective and humane nation-states explains initial American aims, but how those aims are imagined and implemented must change in every case. The goals of American actions must continually evolve. One cannot write the history backward from a set of chosen ends we hope to attain. A society of states is the preferred American destination, but the roads that best match the terrain will transform the exact contours of each journey. There is, in fact, no final "end state," no final "victory." Instead, nation-building is a process that continues to reshape and redefine itself. The American government's role will also shift in each case, as it has from our own Reconstruction to similar efforts in the Philippines, Germany, Vietnam, Iraq, and Afghanistan.

American aims are best served when citizens resist the temptation to assume they have all the answers, and accept that policy improvements emerge from extended interactions between different groups. The process of nation-building therefore rejects claims to consistency, moral clarity, and essential "truths." These exist in theory, but not in practice. If one tries to guide nation-building with rigid values, then one will never adjust to the complexities of another society. This was the case for the United States in Vietnam, where American dogmatism prohibited cooperation with the most credible, but communist, leader of the country: Ho Chi Minh. More open trial-and-error processes in the American South, the Philippines, and Germany produced better results—allowing Oliver Otis Howard, William Howard Taft, Herbert Hoover, and others to learn, adapt, and adjust. Embracing an open process of political transformation allows much more freedom for intelligent action than repeated assertions of preexisting beliefs and prejudices. Process-thinking is crucial for flexibility and adjustment.

Seeing nation-building as a process means accepting uncertainty and indeterminate outcomes. As Carl von Clausewitz famously said of war, once the effort begins we cannot know how it will end. That is what Clausewitz called the "fog" of war. The same is true for nation-building. Like war, citizens must know why they are committing themselves, and they must have confidence that they can achieve some of their aims. They also must understand that the course of events will take unpredictable twists and turns. The more ready and willing Americans are to adjust and adapt, the more they will accomplish. The more ready and willing Americans are to reassess and rethink their own actions, the more effectively they will navigate the unknown. Patience and resolve are crucial, but they are not excuses for stubbornness and self-justification. Seeing nation-building as a process should encourage citizens to test their assumptions, examine their actions, and ask what they can do better. Political processes produce policy improvements only when they involve rigorous self-criticism.[9]

Leaders have a crucial role to play, as they do in every case examined in this book. Figures from George Washington to Barack Obama are most effective when they work to manage what they recognize as a complex political process. For all their power, presidents cannot make change happen. For all their eloquence, they cannot persuade people to transform their behavior. Presidents have the ability, however, to encourage a wise trial-and-error process for policy improvement. For this to happen, they must do three things.

First, presidents must appoint skilled transitional diplomats to investigate the area of targeted action and report openly about challenges and opportunities. There should be no wishful thinking. Americans must enter unfamiliar societies with open eyes. When Americans have done this, especially in postwar Germany, they have acted most effectively.

Second, presidents must encourage debate, in public and in private. Nation-building is too complex for anyone to understand it fully. The American nation-building creed is supple and subject to many interpretations in different times and places. Debate helps to clarify goals, interests, capabilities, and limits. Debate helps to build consensus, if managed well by a skilled figure, like Franklin Roosevelt. Most of all, debate shows non-Americans the range of opinions in the United States, and the earnest efforts of Americans to find a path to political order between empire and anarchy. Americans as a whole do not march gleefully into war and they do not selfishly close themselves off to the rest of the world. Americans debate, search, and sometimes fight for political reforms that will benefit multiple societies. That must be clear in all moments of attempted nation-building.

Third, and perhaps most important, presidents must educate their citizens. This does not mean condescending speeches about the need to buck up against foreign threats. Those cries for toughness actually encourage weakness—they pander to public fear, not acquired wisdom. Instead, presidents must play the role of historians, informing citizens of what we have seen in this book: nation-building is a long-term process, it does not produce quick and clear results, and it works best when American expectations are modest. Citizens in a powerful society need reminding of their limits and the imperative to set priorities. Nation-building can contribute to positive processes of change, but Americans must understand and embrace the difficulties. They did this throughout the Cold War. They can do it again, if leaders really lead.[10]

Problem-Solving

Leadership starts small. It begins with addressing basic problems. From the eighteenth century to the present, American nation-building efforts have worked best when they emphasized projects with immediate payoff for local people. After the Civil War, that meant food, shelter, and basic education in the South. In the Philippines, the United States concentrated on a combination of education and policing to empower local communities and repress insurgents. American activities in postwar Germany were most effective when they focused on feeding a starving population, rebuilding basic infrastructure, and promising economic opportunity. Public trust during a period of occupation emerges from the provision of basic public needs. Popular government is government that serves its people.

The United States did not support this kind of government in Vietnam, Afghanistan, or Iraq. American forces did not secure local populations from attack, they did not ensure access to basic services, and they did not offer economic opportunity. If anything, they did precisely the opposite as they excluded loyalists of the Communist Party, the Taliban, and Saddam Hussein's regime from gainful employment. Purging the old guard placed moral clarity above

277

problem-solving. It denied new governments the ability to draw on experienced administrators, buy off local elites, and regulate possible troublemakers. Better than anyone else, members of the prior regime understand the problems confronting the population, and they know how to address those problems. Nation-building works only when it draws on that knowledge, experience, and networking.

Problem-solving, then, is about connections with the recent past. The credibility of a new regime emerges only from its ability to build on its immediate predecessor. Even after war, political change is incremental. The history of American nation-building proves this point. It has worked best where it has forged unity and representativeness through measures that bring people together for mutual security, food distribution, and education. It has worked poorly where plans for "counterinsurgency" and "modernization" diverted American attention from basic public services to broader anticommunist and capitalist development agendas. Those plans had little local credibility because they could not feed the citizens they claimed to save. Those plans inspired widespread resistance because they did not connect with the immediate priorities of people. Nation-states are built on security, stomachs, and schools. They are made by giving citizens more of what they need.

The American figures who understood this dynamic best were the men who had experience managing large organizations with public responsibility. General Oliver Otis Howard learned from his years in the Union Army, occupying densely populated Confederate territories. William Howard Taft came of age in the urban politics of Cincinnati and the local courts. Herbert Hoover was a leading figure in American business and the dynamic secretary of commerce for the United States before his presidency. All three men understood the power of small deeds, the importance of basic services, and the need to please customers. All three men recognized this was a process of negotiation, compromise, and partnership—often with skilled but scandalous figures. All three men created a foundation for American nation-building through their understanding of local needs, and their acumen in identifying useful people and resources.

Howard, Taft, and Hoover did not solve problems fully, and they did not please all groups. They had many limitations. Nonetheless, they made a credible case in the American South, the Philippines, and Germany that the United States government could help. They made the lives of many citizens better than before. Americans must do the same in Afghanistan today. Nation-building is a big project that begins small.

Purpose

Small beginnings must serve larger purposes. Citizens need to see the value in what they are doing. They must recognize a clear connection between daily activities and long-term goals. They must feel like they are moving forward toward something bigger and better.

This attention to purpose seems obvious, but it is often the first casualty of conflict. The perceived need to justify prior actions quickly distracts leaders from why they began those actions in the first place. Once you spend large sums of money on a project, you must show "success" even if it undermines the deeper purpose of the project. Once you begin negotiating, you must reach "agreement," even if it contradicts the initial goals of the negotiations. Once you start a war, you must "win," even if it destroys the society you sought to save by taking up arms.

This is the cruel irony of the human condition, repeated throughout history. We are all captives of the most recent controversial decision. We are all driven to defend our choices, even when they are destructive to our goals and values. Distraction from purpose is common in policymaking, and it is a recipe for unsatisfying results—even in the case of "victory."

Politics incentivizes self-justification, rather than attention to purpose. Every leader wants to appear strong, decisive, and infallible. Every leader wants to avoid the accusation that he or she wasted money, time, or lives on a flawed endeavor. The death of soldiers in battle inspires especially strong incentives for self-justification. Once citizens have died because a president sent them to war, it becomes very difficult for the leader to question that decision. Instead of asking if we are fighting the appropriate enemy in the correct way, policymakers often ask how they can redeem their prior deployments of force. How can they justify the past losses of life? How can they make sure that the recent deaths did not occur in vain? The smallest hint of hesitation sounds like disrespect for the dead.

These questions are hardwired into a political system that values human life and penalizes the misguided deployment of citizens to battle. Avoiding condemnation for needless or abandoned sacrifice is a powerful influence on every policymaker. As a consequence, the dynamics of nation-building encourage a divergence between strategy and purpose. A strategy of counterinsurgency warfare locks leaders into doing more of the same. A strategy of overwhelming force also becomes self-reinforcing. To prove in Vietnam, Afghanistan, and Iraq that they made the right decisions at the start of each conflict, American presidents felt compelled to escalate rather than rethink. To prove that they were not abandoning the sacrifices of those who had followed their earlier calls to war, American presidents prolonged failing policies, hoping they could find success with more effort—not new policies. If only they tried harder, they hoped they could turn setback to success. If only they sucked it up, they believed they could outlast their enemies.

For Lyndon Johnson, George W. Bush, and Barack Obama it was preferable to do more of the same, rather than shift direction. This is the pattern of action they had followed throughout their careers. This is how they had made it to the top of American society—by displays of toughness and determination, not mistake or redirection. From that vantage point, it was easier to send more soldiers to die than to question basic strategy.

Leaders must resist self-justification. That is the true nature of political courage—the willingness to question past decisions, accept responsibility for deadly mistakes, and pursue risky alternatives. Leaders must recognize failure, adjust, and try again. They must replace stubborn self-justifications with creative reforms. Above all, they must remember that the American creed motivates citizens to build a peaceful society of nation-states. That purpose, rather than the exoneration of past activities, must guide policy. That purpose, rather than an avoidance of criticism, must drive every decision. Americans should act to build a society of nation-states. They should not nation-build to justify recent actions.

This sounds easy, but it is the hardest part of leadership, especially when so much is expected of powerful American presidents. The pressures of governance make it very difficult to remain focused on purpose rather than short-term political needs. The history of the last two centuries shows how destructive a diversion from purpose can become. If the United States deploys its citizens and treasure to justify its prior deployments, it can never build nation-states.

Americans had the most success—in the early years after the Civil War and the decade after the Second World War—when they remembered why they fought. United States policies served the clear purpose of building peaceful nation-states to replace war-torn societies. Americans had the least success—in Vietnam, Afghanistan, and Iraq—when they forgot why they fought. United States policies diverted in Afghanistan from the destruction of the terrorists and the reconstruction of the region to an incoherent mix of wider wars, premature declarations of victory, and underfunded programs. After 2002, American leaders acted to justify these poor choices, rather than serve the goals of war in the first place. Bush, and to some extent Obama, spoke the language of America's nation-building purpose (which they believed), but they pursued policies that served short-term needs. They followed the political path of least resistance, not the trajectory of strategic purpose.

Why are Americans fighting in Afghanistan? How will American policies in Afghanistan contribute to nation-building? How will nation-building in Afghanistan create a safer and more stable world? These are the questions that President Obama still has not answered to the satisfaction of American and non-American citizens. He must answer these questions if the United States is to succeed in Afghanistan. Policy and purpose must connect. If they do, nation-building is a promising path to a peaceful society of states. If policy and purpose continue to diverge, then present actions predict continued frustration and failure. Nation-building requires a disciplined focus on purpose.

People

Nation-building is all about people. Ordinary men and women make decisions about war, they forge partnerships to rebuild societies, and they deal with the consequences. Ordinary men and women struggle to balance irreconcilable demands and find better options among bad alternatives. Nation-building is an endeavor driven by a combination of human frailty and imagination, repeated disappointment but continued hope. Large forces do not move history. Human beings move history.

This book begins and ends with the difficult decisions people must make. Should Americans invest their lives and treasure in building nations from failed states? Should local citizens invest their future in programs directed, in part, by people far away? The history of nation-building does not promote easy answers. It does not provide a road map for the future. What the history of nation-building offers is a powerful reminder that human beings are a work in progress. At its best, nation-building begins with that insight and it seeks to create political conditions that enhance organized self-rule with security and stability. At their best, Americans deploy their resources at home and abroad to encourage good government. That is the American dream, shared by many other peoples and cultures.

The history of American efforts to remake the world is neither imperialistic nor altruistic. It is something in between. Americans have consistently sought to escape the repressive elements of empire and the chaotic qualities of a disorderly world. Americans have pursued nation-building—with very mixed results—because they believe a society of united, representative, and territorially sovereign states best serves the interests of diverse peoples. Americans believe that good government is good for everyone.

The struggle is not about what we want. The American nation-building creed remains compelling, especially in times of crisis. The struggle is to figure out *how* we can implement that creed amidst new challenges. Our opportunity is to remind ourselves *why* we do what we do, and think carefully about what that means today. Our future requires the courage of our convictions and the willingness to make them work in a very complex world. Americans are a nation-building people in search of creative nation-builders at home and abroad.

Notes

Introduction

1. George Washington's Farewell Address, 1796, http://avalon.law.yale .edu/18th_century/washing.asp (accessed 11 January 2010). Emphasis added. James Madison and Alexander Hamilton wrote much of the text for Washington's Farewell Address. See Felix Gilbert, *To the Farewell Address: Ideas of Early American Foreign Policy* (Princeton: Princeton University Press, 1961).

2. Speech by President Barack Obama, United States Military Academy at West Point, New York, 1 December 2009. Available at: http://www.whitehouse .gov/the-press-office/remarks-president-address-nation-way-forward-afghan istan-and-pakistan (accessed 13 September 2010). Emphasis added.

3. One of the few exceptions to the eighteenth-century conventional wisdom about the infeasibility of republican government in a vast territory was Charles de Secondat, Baron de Montesquieu. His treatise, *The Spirit of the Laws,* published in French in 1748, had enormous influence on James Madison, Alexander Hamilton, Thomas Jefferson, George Washington, and other early Americans. See *The Spirit of the Laws* (Cambridge: Cambridge University Press, 1989). See also Jack P. Greene, *The Intellectual Construction of America: Exceptionalism and Identity from 1492 to 1800* (Chapel Hill: University of North Carolina Press, 1993); J. G. A. Pocock, *The Machiavellian Moment: Florentine Political Thought and the Atlantic Republican Tradition* (Princeton: Princeton University Press, 1975), esp. 506–52.

4. On the exceptionalism of early-American ideas and institutions for governance, see Gordon S. Wood, *The Radicalism of the American Revolution* (New York: Alfred A. Knopf, 1992), esp. 229–369; Jack N. Rakove, *Original Meanings: Politics and Ideas in the Making of the Constitution* (New York: Alfred A. Knopf, 1996), esp. 35–93; Greene, *The Intellectual Construction*

of America, esp. 200–9. On the many alternatives to the nation-state before the nineteenth century, and their replacement, see Charles Tilly, *Coercion, Capital, and European States, AD 990–1990* (Malden, Mass.: Blackwell, 1990); Ernest Gellner, *Nations and Nationalism* (Ithaca: Cornell University Press, 1983); John A. Hall, "Nation-States in History," in T. V. Paul, G. John Ikenberry, and John A. Hall, eds., *The Nation-State in Question* (Princeton: Princeton University Press, 2003), 1–28; Hendrik Spruyt, *The Sovereign State and Its Competitors* (Princeton: Princeton University Press, 1994); Benedict Anderson, *Imagined Communities: Reflections on the Origin and Spread of Nationalism* (London: Verso, 1991); Anthony D. Smith, *The Ethnic Origins of Nations* (Malden, Mass.: Blackwell, 1986); Stephen D. Krasner, *Sovereignty: Organized Hypocrisy* (Princeton: Princeton University Press, 1999); Friedrich Kratochwil, "Of Systems and Boundaries, Reflections on the Formation of the State System" *World Politics* 39 (October 1986): 27–52.

5. On the participatory nature of American politics, see Wood, *The Radicalism of the American Revolution*, esp. 271–369; Sean Wilentz, *The Rise of American Democracy: Jefferson to Lincoln* (New York: W. W. Norton, 2005); Michael Kazin, *The Populist Persuasion: An American History* (New York: Basic Books, 1995).

6. See the very suggestive scholarship on "world society": John W. Meyer, John Boli, George M. Thomas, and Francisco O. Ramirez, "World Society and the Nation-State," *American Journal of Sociology* 103 (July 1997): 144–81; John W. Meyer, "Globalization: Sources and Effects on National States and Societies," *International Sociology* 15 (June 2000): 233–48. This work draws on insights about "international society," especially: Hedley Bull, *The Anarchical Society: A Study of Order in World Politics* (New York: Columbia University Press, 1977).

7. See Meyer, Boli, Thomas, and Ramirez, "World Society and the Nation-State," 144–81.

8. On the continuing importance of nation-states in the context of proliferating nongovernmental and intergovernmental organizations, see Akira Iriye, *Global Community: The Role of International Organizations in the Making*

of the Contemporary World (Berkeley: University of California Press, 2002); Jeremi Suri, "Non-Governmental Organizations and Non-State Actors," in Patrick Finney, ed., *Palgrave Advances in International History* (New York: Palgrave, 2005), 223–46.

9. On this point, authors with very different politics agree: see Walter Russell Mead, *Special Providence: American Foreign Policy and How It Changed the World* (New York: Routledge, 2002); Robert Kagan, *Dangerous Nation: America's Foreign Policy from Its Earliest Days to the Dawn of the Twentieth Century* (New York: Alfred A. Knopf, 2006).

10. See Meyer, "Globalization"; Paul Kennedy, *The Parliament of Man: The Past, Present, and Future of the United Nations* (New York: Random House, 2006); Strobe Talbott, *The Great Experiment: The Story of Ancient Empires, Modern States, and the Quest for a Global Nation* (New York: Simon & Schuster, 2008).

11. See Spruyt, *The Sovereign State and Its Competitors*; Alexander Wendt, "Anarchy Is What States Make of It: The Social Construction of Power Politics," *International Organization* 46 (Spring 1992): 391–426.

12. Speech by President Barack Obama, United States Military Academy at West Point, New York, 1 December 2009.

13. Ibid.

Chapter 1: The American Nation-Building Creed

1. James Madison, Federalist 10, originally published 22 November 1787, reprinted at http://www.constitution.org/fed/federa10.htm (accessed 3 January 2010). Emphasis added.

2. Alexander Hamilton, Federalist 78, originally published 14 June 1788, reprinted at http://www.constitution.org/fed/federa78.htm (accessed 3 January 2010). Emphasis added.

3. Oh, it is monstrous, monstrous!

   Methought the billows spoke, and told me of it,

   The winds did sing it to me, and the thunder.

   See William Shakespeare, *The Tempest*, Act 3, Scene 3, lines 80, 95–97.

4. Shakespeare quoted in ibid., line 102. In his erudite examination of empires since 1400, historian John Darwin writes: "This is not to say that no limits exist to America's power. But, on almost any criterion, this now transcends the limits of empire that we have observed in force since the early fifteenth century. Those writers who have likened America's 'hegemonic' status to that of Victorian Britain betray a staggering ignorance of the history of both. Whether this power will be used to make the world safer, or to sharpen its conflicts by ill-managed interventions, is a different question entirely. No prediction is safe." John Darwin, *After Tamerlane: The Rise and Fall of Global Empires, 1400–2000* (New York: Bloomsbury, 2008), 485.

5. See, among many others, Joyce Appleby, *Inheriting the Revolution: The First Generation of Americans* (Cambridge: Belknap Press of Harvard University Press, 2000); Pauline Maier, *American Scripture: Making the Declaration of Independence* (New York: Alfred A. Knopf, 1997); Jack N. Rakove, *Original Meanings: Politics and Ideas in the Making of the Constitution* (New York: Alfred A. Knopf, 1996); Bernard Bailyn, *The Ideological Origins of the American Revolution* (Cambridge: Harvard University Press, 1967); Bernard Bailyn, *The Origins of American Politics* (New York: Random House, 1967); Felix Gilbert, *To the Farewell Address: Ideas of Early American Foreign Policy* (Princeton: Princeton University Press, 1961).

6. See the video recording of President George W. Bush's "Bullhorn Address to Ground Zero Rescue Workers," 14 September 2001, http://www.americanrhetoric.com/speeches/gwbush911groundzerobullhorn.htm (accessed 8 January 2010); President Bush's speech to a Joint Session of Congress, 20 September 2001, http://archives.cnn.com/2001/US/09/20/gen.bush.transcript (accessed 8 January 2010).

7. Thomas Paine, "The Crisis," 23 December 1776, http://www.ushistory.org/PAINE/crisis/c-01.htm (accessed 8 January 2010). For an excellent discussion of Thomas Paine's enduring influence on American politics, see Harvey J. Kaye, *Thomas Paine and the Promise of America* (New York: Hill & Wang, 2005).

8. Two influential works of history that point to an eighteenth- and nineteenth-century analogue for the American-led "War on Terror" after 2001 are: Rob-

ert Kagan, *Dangerous Nation: America's Place in the World from Its Earliest Days to the Dawn of the Twentieth Century* (New York: Alfred A. Knopf, 2006); John Lewis Gaddis, *Surprise, Security, and the American Experience* (Cambridge: Harvard University Press, 2004).

9. Kagan, *Dangerous Nation*, 64.

10. President George W. Bush's Second Inaugural Address, 20 January 2005, http://www.bartleby.com/124/pres67.html (accessed 8 January 2010).

11. Melvyn P. Leffler, "9/11 and American Foreign Policy," *Diplomatic History* 29 (Summer 2005): 396. See also Jeremi Suri, "American Attitudes Toward Revolution," in Alexander DeConde, Richard Dean Burns, and Fredrik Logevall, eds., *Encyclopedia of American Foreign Policy*, 2nd ed. (New York: Charles Scribner's Sons, 2002), 425–42.

12. See Gordon S. Wood, *The Radicalism of the American Revolution* (New York: Alfred A. Knopf, 1991), esp. 229–369; Rakove, *Original Meanings*, esp. 339–65.

13. The seminal book on the creation of popular sovereignty as political practice in revolutionary and post-revolutionary America remains Edmund Morgan, *Inventing the People: The Rise of Popular Sovereignty in England and America* (New York: W. W. Norton, 1988). See also J. S. Maloy, *The Colonial American Origins of Modern Democratic Thought* (Cambridge: Cambridge University Press, 2008); Wood, *The Radicalism of the American Revolution*, esp. 169–89; Peter S. Onuf, *Jefferson's Empire: The Language of American Nationhood* (Charlottesville: University of Virginia Press, 2000), esp. 1–79.

14. Edmund Morgan puts this very well: "even before the [Constitutional] [c]onvention met, Madison recognized that it could achieve the objectives he had in mind for it only by appealing to a popular sovereignty not hitherto fully recognized, to the people of the United States as a whole. . . . To that end he envisioned a genuine national government, resting for its authority, not on the state governments and not even on the peoples of the several states considered separately, but on an American people, a people who constituted a separate and superior entity, capable of conveying to a national government an authority that would necessarily impinge on the authority of the state governments." Morgan, *Inventing the People*, 267. See also Douglas Bradburn,

The Citizenship Revolution: Politics and the Creation of the American Union, 1774–1804 (Charlottesville: University of Virginia Press, 2009), esp. 19–60.

15. Hamilton, Federalist 78; Rakove, *Original Meanings*, esp. 105–7. John Murrin employs a powerful metaphor to explain the significance of the U.S. Constitution as a foundational but evolving source of state power and national identity: "Americans had erected their constitutional roof before they put up the national walls. . . . The Constitution alone could not do the job, but the job could not be done at all without it. The Constitution was to the nation a more successful version of what the Halfway Covenant had once been to the Puritans, a way of buying time. Under the shade of this lofty frame of government, the shared sacrifices of the Revolutionary war could become interstate and intergenerational memories that bound people together in new ways." John M. Murrin, "A Roof Without Walls: The Delimma of American National Identity," in Richard Beeman, Stephen Botein, and Edward C. Carter II, eds., *Beyond Confederation: Origins of the Constitution and American National Identity* (Chapel Hill: University of North Carolina Press, 1987), 347.

16. J. S. Maloy's recent book is particularly insightful on the more inclusive, representative, and accountable alternatives to the U.S. Constitution available at the time: *The Colonial American Origins of Modern Democratic Thought*, esp. 1–23. See also the classic: Merrill Jensen, *The Articles of Confederation: An Interpretation of the Social-Constitutional History of the American Revolution, 1774–1781* (Madison: University of Wisconsin Press, 1940).

17. Wood, *The Radicalism of the American Revolution*, 232.

18. Ibid., 363–64.

19. Thomas Jefferson, *Notes on the State of Virginia*, originally written in 1781–82, published by Jefferson in 1787, reprinted in Merrill D. Peterson, ed., *Thomas Jefferson Writings* (New York: Library of America, 1984), esp. 218–32; Thomas Jefferson to James Madison, 30 January 1787, in Peterson, ed., *Thomas Jefferson Writings*, 882. See also Anthony F. C. Wallace, *Jefferson and the Indians: The Tragic Fate of the First Americans* (Cambridge: Belknap Press of Harvard University Press, 1999); Lawrence S. Kaplan, *Jefferson and France* (New Haven: Yale University Press, 1967).

20. On this often neglected point, see George C. Herring, *From Colony to Su-*

perpower: U.S. Foreign Relations Since 1776 (New York: Oxford University Press, 2008), 56–133; Bradford Perkins, *The Cambridge History of American Foreign Relations*, Vol. 1, *The Creation of a Republican Empire, 1776–1865* (Cambridge: Cambridge University Press, 1993); Bradford Perkins, *Prologue to War: England and the United States, 1805–1812* (Berkeley: University of California Press, 1961).

21. George Washington's Farewell Address, 1796, http://avalon.law.yale .edu/18th_century/washing.asp (accessed 11 January 2010). See the classic analysis of Washington's Farewell Address, and its fundamental internationalism, in Gilbert, *To the Farewell Address*, esp. 3–18, 115–36. Among other things, Gilbert shows the influence of Madison and especially Hamilton on the writing of Washington's Farewell Address.

22. See the accounts of Western filibusterers in the nineteenth century who moved into territories outside the control of the United States, and then demanded protection from the federal government as "Americans." Robert E. May, *Manifest Destiny's Underworld: Filibustering in Antebellum America* (Chapel Hill: University of North Carolina Press, 2002); Sam W. Haynes and Christopher Morris, eds., *Manifest Destiny and Empire: American Antebellum Expansionism* (College Station: Texas A&M University Press, 1997). The classic work on the subject remains Frederick Merk, *Manifest Destiny and Mission in American History: A Reinterpretation* (New York: Alfred A. Knopf, 1963).

23. Napoleon counted on the fracturing and further European colonization of North America when he sold the Louisiana territories to the United States. He planned to retake these territories, and others in the Western Hemisphere, after he had completed his conquest of the European continent. See Alexander DeConde, *The Affair of Louisiana* (New York: Scribner, 1976); James E. Lewis, Jr., *The Louisiana Purchase: Jefferson's Noble Bargain?* (Chapel Hill: University of North Carolina Press, 2003).

24. James Madison, "Vices of the Political System of the United States," April 1787, http://www.constitution.org/jm/17870400_vices.htm (accessed 11 January 2010).

25. Ibid.

26. Ibid. Perhaps the emergence of the European Union in the late twentieth century is an example of successful Union in Europe as well, influenced by the earlier experience of the United States. See Anthony Pagden, ed., *The Idea of Europe: From Antiquity to the European Union* (New York: Cambridge University Press, 2002); Geir Lundestad, *"Empire" by Integration: The United States and European Integration, 1945–1997* (New York: Oxford University Press, 1998); William I. Hitchcock, *The Struggle for Europe: The Turbulent History of a Divided Continent, 1945–2002* (New York: Doubleday, 2003).

27. George Washington's Farewell Address, 1796. Italics added.

28. Ibid.

29. Article VI of the Northwest Ordinance of 1787 prohibited slavery in the new states of Ohio, Illinois, Indiana, Michigan, and Wisconsin, but this article later attracted intense debate. Many Southerners contested its legitimacy and enforcement. The question of slavery in other new states became increasingly controversial in subsequent decades, contributing to the Civil War. See Peter S. Onuf, *Statehood and Union: A History of the Northwest Ordinance* (Bloomington: Indiana University Press, 1987), 109–32; Paul Finkelman, "Slavery and the Northwest Ordinance: A Study in Ambiguity," *Journal of the Early Republic* 6 (Winter 1986): 343–70.

30. Onuf, *Statehood and Union*, 108. Italics in original.

31. See ibid., esp. 44–87; Peter S. Onuf, "New State Equality: The Ambiguous History of a Constitutional Principle," *Publius* 18 (Autumn 1988): 53–69; Reginald Horsman, "The Northwest Ordinance and the Shaping of an Expanding Republic," *Wisconsin Magazine of History* 73 (Autumn 1989): 21–32; R. Douglas Hurt, "Historians and the Northwest Ordinance," *Western Historical Quarterly* 20 (August 1989): 261–80.

32. Historians have, curiously, given minimal attention to the meaning of "Union" for the early thinkers about American politics and foreign policy. For some notable and valuable exceptions, see David Hendrickson, *Peace Pact: The Lost World of the American Founding* (Lawrence: University Press of Kansas, 2003), esp. 14–23, 211–60; David Hendrickson, *Union, Nation, or Empire: The American Debate over International Relations, 1789–1941* (Lawrence: University Press of Kansas, 2009), esp. 6–12; Peter S. Onuf, *The Origins*

of the Federal Republic: Jurisdictional Controversies in the United States, 1775–1787 (Philadelphia: University of Pennsylvania Press, 1983), esp. 149–72; Daniel Deudney, "The Philadelphia System: Sovereignty, Arms Control, and Balance of Power in the American States-Union, Circa 1787–1861," *International Organization* 49 (Spring 1995): 191–228; Rogan Kersh, *Dreams of a More Perfect Union* (Ithaca: Cornell University Press, 2001), 23–57, 104–52. On the modern definition of "national security" and its twentieth-century echoes of late-eighteenth-century thought, see Aaron L. Friedberg, *In the Shadow of the Garrison State: America's Anti-Statism and Its Cold War Grand Strategy* (Princeton: Princeton University Press, 2000); Michael J. Hogan, *A Cross of Iron: Harry S. Truman and the Origins of the National Security State, 1945–1954* (New York: Cambridge University Press, 1998).

33. See Hendrickson, *Peace Pact*, 14–23.

34. Appleby, *Inheriting the Revolution*, 263, 266. For the phrase "Unionist Paradigm," see Hendrickson, *Peace Pact*, 14–23. See also Steven Hahn, *A Nation Under Our Feet: Black Political Struggles in the Rural South from Slavery to the Great Migration* (Cambridge: Belknap Press of Harvard University Press, 2003), esp. 62–115; Ira Berlin, Barbara J. Fields, Steven F. Miller, Joseph P. Reidy, and Leslie S. Rowland, *Slaves No More: Three Essays on Emancipation and the Civil War* (New York: Cambridge University Press, 1992).

35. See Russell Weigley, *The American Way of War: A History of United States Military Strategy and Policy* (New York: Macmillan, 1973); Robert A. Divine, *Perpetual War for Perpetual Peace* (College Station: Texas A&M University Press, 2000); Walter A. McDougall, *Promised Land, Crusader State: The American Encounter with the World Since 1776* (New York: Houghton Mifflin, 1997).

36. See Hendrickson, *Union, Nation, or Empire*, 6–12.

37. Immanuel Kant, "Perpetual Peace: A Philosophical Sketch" (1795), available at: http://www.mtholyoke.edu/acad/intrel/kant/kant1.htm (accessed 15 January 2010). For an excellent discussion of Kant's essay and its deeper vision, see James Bohman and Matthias Lutz-Bachman, eds., *Perpetual Peace: Essays on Kant's Cosmopolitan Ideal* (Cambridge: MIT Press, 1997). For an excellent discussion of the role that Kant and other thinkers played in imagining a new framework for international peace and cooperation at the end of the

eighteenth century, see Michael Howard, *The Invention of Peace: Reflections on War and International Order* (New Haven: Yale University Press, 2000), esp. 33–60.

38. Thomas Jefferson's Second Inaugural Address (4 March 1805), in Peterson, ed., *Thomas Jefferson Writings*, 518.

39. This argument draws on Hendrickson, *Union, Nation, or Empire*. This argument also echoes many of the claims from G. John Ikenberry and other liberal internationalists in the early twenty-first century. See Ikenberry, *After Victory: Institutions, Strategic Restraint, and the Rebuilding of Order After Major Wars* (Princeton: Princeton University Press, 2001); G. John Ikenberry, Thomas J. Knock, Anne-Marie Slaughter, and Tony Smith, *The Crisis of American Foreign Policy: Wilsonianism in the Twenty-first Century* (Princeton: Princeton University Press, 2009). For a sampling of Kennan's and Kissinger's critiques, see George F. Kennan, *American Diplomacy, 1900–1950* (Chicago: University of Chicago Press, 1951); Henry Kissinger, *Diplomacy* (New York: Simon & Schuster, 1994).

40. See Anders Stephanson, *Kennan and the Art of Foreign Policy* (Cambridge: Harvard University Press, 1989); David Mayers, *George Kennan and the Dilemmas of U.S. Foreign Policy* (New York: Oxford University Press, 1988); Jeremi Suri, *Henry Kissinger and the American Century* (Cambridge: Belknap Press of Harvard University Press, 2007), esp. 138–96.

41. Akira Iriye, *Global Community: The Role of International Organizations in the Making of the Contemporary World* (Berkeley: University of California Press, 2002).

42. For the seminal theoretical work on international society and the society of states, see Hedley Bull, *The Anarchical Society: A Study of Order in World Politics*, 2nd ed. (New York: Columbia University Press, 1995; originally published, 1977), esp. 3–50. See also Hedley Bull and Adam Watson, eds., *The Expansion of International Society* (Oxford: Clarendon Press, 1984); John Rawls, *The Law of Peoples* (Cambridge: Harvard University Press, 1999).

43. Hendrickson, *Union, Nation, or Empire*, 6–12. On "self-similarity across scale" and other related concepts from complexity theory, see, among others,

John H. Holland, *Hidden Order: How Adaptation Builds Complexity* (New York: Perseus, 1995); Melanie Mitchell, *Complexity: A Guided Tour* (New York: Oxford University Press, 2009).

44. For some of the best histories of U.S. modernization, development, and nation-building efforts, see David Ekbladh, *The Great American Mission: Modernization and the Construction of an American World Order* (Princeton: Princeton University Press, 2009); Odd Arne Westad, *The Global Cold War: Third World Interventions and the Making of Our Times* (Cambridge: Cambridge University Press, 2005); Nils Gilman, *Mandarins of the Future: Modernization Theory in Cold War America* (Baltimore: Johns Hopkins University Press, 2004); Michael E. Latham, *Modernization as Ideology: American Social Science and "Nation-Building" in the Kennedy Era* (Chapel Hill: University of North Carolina Press, 2000).

45. On the internal transformations accompanying external policy aims, especially in the aftermath of the Civil War and the Second World War, see James McPherson, *Abraham Lincoln and the Second American Revolution* (New York: Oxford University Press, 1991); Hogan, *A Cross of Iron.*

46. On the efforts by American revolutionaries to break with the conservative forces of political tradition in the British Empire, see Wood, *Radicalism of the American Revolution,* 11–92; Morgan, *Inventing the People,* 94–121.

47. On the cultivation of regional expertise and its connection to policy in the United States, especially after the Second World War, see Suri, *Henry Kissinger and the American Century,* 92–137; David C. Engerman, *Know Your Enemy: The Rise and Fall of America's Soviet Experts* (New York: Oxford University Press, 2009); Bruce Cumings, *Parallax Visions: Making Sense of American–East Asian Relations at the End of the Century* (Durham: Duke University Press, 1999), 173–204. The literature on democratization and democratic theory is enormous. For discussions of democracy that emphasize its diverse forms and applications, see Charles Tilly, *Democracy* (New York: Cambridge University Press, 2007); Larry Diamond, *The Spirit of Democracy: The Struggle to Build Free Societies Throughout the World* (New York: Henry Holt, 2008); Robert Dahl, *On Democracy* (New Haven: Yale University Press, 2000).

48. On this point, see the thoughtful introduction and annotations in Jack N. Rakove, *The Annotated U.S. Constitution and Declaration of Independence* (Cambridge: Belknap Press of Harvard University Press, 2009).

49. On the problems of hastily organized elections in conflict-torn societies, see Fareed Zakaria, *The Future of Freedom: Illiberal Democracy at Home and Abroad* (New York: W. W. Norton, 2003).

50. See Chalmers Johnson, *Blowback: The Costs and Consequences of American Empire* (New York: Henry Holt, 2000); Tim Weiner, *Legacy of Ashes: The History of the CIA* (New York: Random House, 2007).

51. See Ahmed Rashid, *Descent into Chaos: The United States and the Failure of Nation Building in Pakistan, Afghanistan, and Central Asia* (New York: Viking, 2008); Robert Lacey, *Inside the Kingdom: Kings, Clerics, Modernists, Terrorists, and the Struggle for Saudi Arabia* (New York: Viking, 2009).

52. See Peter L. Bergen, *Holy War, Inc.: Inside the Secret World of Osama Bin Laden* (New York: Free Press, 2002); Bruce Hoffman, *Inside Terrorism* (New York: Columbia University Press, 2006); Lawrence Wright, *The Looming Tower: Al Qaeda and the Road to 9/11* (New York: Vintage, 2006).

53. This argument echoes the classic account of international war and peace by A. J. P. Taylor: *The Struggle for Mastery in Europe, 1848–1918* (Oxford: Oxford University Press, 1954).

54. Frank Ninkovich traces this argument about powerful interdependent nation-states and the growing potential for global violence back to the early twentieth century. See *Modernity and Power: A History of the Domino Theory in the Twentieth Century* (Chicago: University of Chicago Press, 1994).

55. For some of the seminal books on business and cultural expansion, see William Appleman Williams, *The Tragedy of American Diplomacy*, 50th anniversary edition (New York: W. W. Norton, 2009); Akira Iriye, *The Cambridge History of American Foreign Relations*, Vol. 3, *The Globalizing of America, 1913–1945* (New York: Cambridge University Press, 1995); Emily S. Rosenberg, *Spreading the American Dream: American Economic and Cultural Expansion, 1890–1945* (New York: Hill & Wang, 1982); David Reynolds, *One World Divisible: A Global History Since 1945* (New York: W. W. Norton, 2001); Cumings, *Parallax Visions.*

Chapter 2: Reconstruction After Civil War

1. Abraham Lincoln's Last Public Address, 11 April 1865, available at: http://showcase.netins.net/web/creative/lincoln/speeches/last.htm (accessed 12 February 2010).

2. Frederick Douglass, "Reconstruction," *Atlantic Monthly* 18 (December 1866): 764.

3. See James M. McPherson, *Abraham Lincoln and the Second American Revolution* (New York: Oxford University Press, 1991); Charles and Mary Beard, *The Rise of American Civilization* (New York: Macmillan, 1927), Chapter 28.

4. Steven Hahn, *A Nation Under Our Feet: Black Political Struggles in the Rural South from Slavery to the Great Migration* (Cambridge: Belknap Press of Harvard University Press, 2003), 215. See also Eric Foner, *Reconstruction: America's Unfinished Revolution, 1863–1877* (New York: Harper & Row, 1988), 77–119.

5. See Hahn, *A Nation Under Our Feet*, 265–313; Foner, *Reconstruction*, 119–23, 425–59.

6. See Wayne Andrews, ed., *The Autobiography of Carl Schurz* (New York: Charles Scribner's, 1961), 316–28. For the broader influence of the Civil War and Reconstruction on German political and social thought, see Andrew Zimmerman, *Alabama in Africa: Booker T. Washington, the German Empire, and the Globalization of the New South* (Princeton: Princeton University Press, 2010), 66–111.

7. William Stanley Hoole, ed., *Reconstruction in West Alabama: The Memoirs of John L. Hunnicutt* (Tuscaloosa: Confederate Publishing Company, 1959), 39–40, 44. Hunnicutt's memoir is a very difficult and disturbing read. He glorifies personal violence against freed slaves and their sympathizers. He seems to take sadistic pleasure in the pain he inflicts on his perceived enemies. Hunnicutt's memoir shows how profoundly difficult it was to convert the citizens of the former Confederacy into democratic participants in a post–Civil War Union.

8. Quoted in Foner, *Reconstruction*, 123. See also Dan T. Carter, "The Anatomy of Fear: The Christmas Day Insurrection Scare of 1865," *Journal of Southern History* 42 (August 1976): 345–64.

9. Quoted in Dan T. Carter, *When the War Was Over: The Failure of Self-Reconstruction in the South, 1865–1867* (Baton Rouge: Louisiana State University Press, 1985), 34.

10. See Drew Gilpin Faust, *This Republic of Suffering: Death and the American Civil War* (New York: Random House, 2008).

11. Carter, *When the War Was Over*, 36–39.

12. Ibid.

13. See Hahn, *A Nation Under Our Feet*, 265–313.

14. W. E. B. Du Bois, "Reconstruction and Its Benefits," *American Historical Review* 15 (July 1910): 781–99. Du Bois originally read this paper at the annual American Historical Association meeting in December 1909. W. E. B. Du Bois, *Black Reconstruction* (New York: Harcourt, Brace, 1935); Kenneth M. Stampp, *The Era of Reconstruction, 1865–1877* (New York: Alfred A. Knopf, 1966), 214; Foner, *Reconstruction*, 603.

15. My argument here builds on the rich social science literature on state-building since the late Middle Ages. I see the history of nation-building as part of a broader world historical process that scholars can trace to the rise of capitalism, mass warfare, and public media. My argument, however, emphasizes contingency to a greater degree than most prior scholars. I also place greater emphasis on the role of the United States as a model and a powerful actor, for better and for worse. See, among others, Thomas N. Bisson, *The Crisis of the Twelfth Century: Power, Lordship, and the Origins of European Government* (Princeton: Princeton University Press, 2009); Hendrik Spruyt, *The Sovereign State and Its Competitors* (Princeton: Princeton University Press, 1994); Charles Tilly, *Coercion, Capital, and European States: AD 990–1992* (Malden, Mass.: Blackwell, 1990); Ernest Gellner, *Nations and Nationalism* (Ithaca: Cornell University Press, 1983); Anthony D. Smith, *The Ethnic Origins of Nations* (Malden, Mass.: Blackwell, 1986); Benedict Anderson, *Imagined Communities* (London: Verso, 1983).

16. On the efforts to create a separate Confederate nation-state in the mid-nineteenth century, see John Majewski, *Modernizing a Slave Economy: The Economic Vision of the Confederate Nation* (Chapel Hill: University of North Carolina Press, 2009).

17. Quotations from Count S. Stakelberg, "Tolstoi Holds Lincoln World's Greatest Hero," *New York World* (7 February 1909), available at: http://www.loa.org/images/pdf/Tolstoy_on_Lincoln.pdf (accessed 8 March 2010). This extraordinary article is also cited in Doris Kearns Goodwin, *A Team of Rivals: The Political Genius of Abraham Lincoln* (New York: Simon & Schuster, 2005). For more examples of Lincoln's enduring influence as a statesman and nation-builder, see Harold Holzer, ed., *The Lincoln Anthology: Great Writers on His Life and Legacy from 1860 to Now* (New York: Library of America, 2008).

18. See, among others, Frederick Cooper, Thomas C. Holt, and Rebecca J. Scott, *Beyond Slavery: Explorations of Race, Labor, and Citizenship in Postemancipation Societies* (Chapel Hill: University of North Carolina Press, 2000); Rebecca J. Scott, *Degrees of Freedom: Louisiana and Cuba After Slavery* (Cambridge: Belknap Press of Harvard University Press, 2005); Thomas C. Holt, *The Problem of Freedom: Race, Labor, and Politics in Jamaica and Britain, 1832–1938* (Baltimore: Johns Hopkins University Press, 1992); Peter Kolchin, *Unfree Labor: American Slavery and Russian Serfdom* (Cambridge: Belknap Press of Harvard University Press, 1987).

19. The seminal work on this topic remains: Eric Foner, *Free Soil, Free Labor, Free Men: The Ideology of the Republican Party Before the Civil War* (New York: Oxford University Press, 1970).

20. Writing in May 1865, Secretary of the Navy Gideon Welles criticized Stanton and his supporters for "radical" and "arbitrary" efforts to deploy federal power for the enforcement of "negro suffrage" in the South. Welles believed that full citizenship for freed slaves would transform social and political life in the South, without constitutional precedent. That was precisely the reason that Stanton and others supported this policy. *Diary of Gideon Welles*, Vol. 2 (Boston: Houghton Mifflin, 1909), 301–3.

21. Quotations from Harold Schwartz, *Samuel Gridley Howe: Social Reformer, 1801–1876* (Cambridge: Harvard University Press, 1956), 260–61.

22. As discussed later in this chapter, the Freedmen's Inquiry Commission constructed the intellectual and institutional foundation for the creation of the Freedmen's Bureau in 1865, officially the Bureau of Refugees, Freedmen, and Abandoned Lands. Although the Freedmen's Inquiry Commission and

the Freedmen's Bureau have attracted extensive attention from scholars, no one has examined them in the context of the longer history of U.S. nation-building at home and abroad. For some of the best works on the Freedmen's Bureau, see John Cox and LaWanda Cox, "General O. O. Howard and the 'Misrepresented Bureau,'" *Journal of Southern History* 19 (November 1953): 427–56; George R. Bentley, *A History of the Freedmen's Bureau* (Philadelphia: University of Pennsylvania Press, 1955); James E. Sefton, *The United States Army and Reconstruction, 1865–1877* (Baton Rouge: Louisiana State University Press, 1967); William S. McFeely, *Yankee Stepfather: General O. O. Howard and the Freedmen* (New Haven: Yale University Press, 1968); Howard A. White, *The Freedmen's Bureau in Louisiana* (Baton Rouge: Louisiana State University Press, 1970); Donald G. Nieman, *To Set the Law in Motion: The Freedmen's Bureau and the Legal Rights of Blacks, 1865–1868* (Milwood, N.Y.: KTO, 1979); Foner, *Reconstruction*, esp. 142–75; Paul A. Cimbala, *Under the Guardianship of the Nation: The Freedmen's Bureau and the Reconstruction of Georgia, 1865–1870* (Athens: University of Georgia Press, 1997); Paul A. Cimbala, *The Freedmen's Bureau: Reconstructing the American South After the Civil War* (Malabar, Fla.: Krieger, 2005).

23. See Bentley, *A History of the Freedmen's Bureau*, 25–29.

24. Report to the Secretary of War, 22 June 1864, U.S. Senate, 38th Congress, 1st Session, Executive Document 53, including Preliminary Report Touching the Condition and Management of Emancipated Refugees Made to the Secretary of War by the American Freedmen's Inquiry Commission, 30 June 1863, available in the Wisconsin Historical Society Library, Madison, Wisconsin.

25. Ibid., 3, 20.

26. Senator Charles Sumner's Speech in Defense of Establishing a Freedmen's Bureau 13 June 1864, reprinted in Cimbala, *The Freedmen's Bureau*, 112.

27. Quoted in Bentley, *A History of the Freedmen's Bureau*, 38.

28. Bentley, *A History of the Freedmen's Bureau*, 38–39.

29. Congressional Act Creating the Freedmen's Bureau, 3 March 1865, reprinted in Cimbala, *The Freedmen's Bureau*, 114–16. Also available at: http://www.history.umd.edu/Freedmen/fbact.htm (accessed 27 April 2010).

30. Ibid.

31. Quoted in Cox and Cox, "O. O. Howard and the 'Misrepresented Bureau,'" 432.

32. Sherman quoted in Oliver Otis Howard's memoir: *Autobiography of Oliver Otis Howard*, Vol. 2 (New York: Baker & Taylor, 1907), 209–10.

33. Ibid., 208.

34. On the Union Army's efforts to mix force and restraint for the purpose of remaking the South, see Mark Grimsley, *The Hard Hand of War: Union Military Policy Toward Southern Civilians, 1861–65* (New York: Cambridge University Press, 1995).

35. White, *The Freedmen's Bureau in Louisiana*, 84.

36. *Autobiography of Oliver Otis Howard*, 220.

37. See Foner, *Reconstruction*, 153–70; White, *The Freedmen's Bureau in Louisiana*, 101–33; Hahn, *A Nation Under Our Feet*, 163–264.

38. See Carl F. Kaestle, *Pillars of the Republic: Common Schools and American Society, 1780–1860* (New York: Hill & Wang, 1983), esp. 182–225; William J. Reese, *America's Public Schools: From the Common School to "No Child Left Behind"* (Baltimore: Johns Hopkins University Press, 2005), esp. 10–78.

39. Bureau of Refugees and Freedmen, Report of the Assistant Commissioner for Alabama, 1866, available in the Wisconsin Historical Society Library, Madison, Wisconsin.

40. See Jacqueline Jones, *Soldiers of Light and Love: Northern Teachers and Georgia Blacks, 1865–1873* (Chapel Hill: University of North Carolina Press, 1980), esp. 14–48, 140–66.

41. Quoted in James D. Anderson, *The Education of Blacks in the South, 1860–1935* (Chapel Hill: University of North Carolina Press, 1988), 15.

42. Jacqueline Jones analyzes many of the tensions that arose between Northern educators who traveled south and freed slave communities seeking to control their own education. See Jones, *Soldiers of Light and Love*, 49–108. See also Anderson, *The Education of Blacks in the South*, 4–78; White, *The Freedmen's Bureau in Louisiana*, 166–200.

43. Alvord quoted in Anderson, *The Education of Blacks in the South*, 15; Bureau of Refugees and Freedmen, Report of the Assistant Commissioner for Alabama, 1866.

44. See Anderson, *The Education of Blacks in the South*, 4–78; Jones, *Soldiers of Light and Love*, 191–208; Reese, *America's Public Schools*, 70–78.

45. See W. E. B. Du Bois's famous essay "The Talented Tenth," originally published in September 1903, available at: http://teachingamericanhistory.org/library/index.asp?document=174 (accessed 1 November 2010). For Booker T. Washington's account of the Tuskegee Institute and its emphasis on industrial education, see his autobiography: *Up from Slavery* (New York: Doubleday, 1901). See also Zimmerman, *Alabama in Africa*, 20–65.

46. Quotation from Bureau of Refugees and Freedmen, Report of the Assistant Commissioner for Alabama, 1866.

Chapter 3: Reconstruction After Empire

1. Excerpt from Rudyard Kipling's infamous poem, "The White Man's Burden," originally published in *McClure's Magazine*, February 1899. The full poem is available at: http://www.fordham.edu/halsall/mod/kipling.html (accessed 30 June 2010).

2. Elihu Root, secretary of war to President William McKinley, 24 January 1901, in *Reports of the Taft Philippine Commission* (Washington, D.C.: U.S. Government Printing Office, 1901), 7.

3. See Brian McAllister Linn, *The Echo of Battle: The Army's Way of War* (Cambridge: Harvard University Press, 2007), esp. 68–115, quotation on 94. Despite Alfred Thayer Mahan's tireless efforts to prepare the United States for forward warfare in Asia, Russell Weigley notes the inadequacy of American planning and preparations. See *The American Way of War: A History of United States Military Strategy and Policy* (New York: Macmillan, 1973), 167–91.

4. See Lawrence Gelfand, "Toward a Merit System for the American Diplomatic Service, 1900–1930," *Irish Studies in International Affairs* 2 (1988): 49–63; Robert D. Schulzinger, *The Making of the Diplomatic Mind: The Training, Outlook, and Style of United States Foreign Service Officers, 1908–1931* (Middletown, Conn.: Wesleyan University Press, 1975). The spoils system for U.S. government appointments dated back to the presidency of Andrew Jackson, and even earlier in some cases.

5. See Frank Ninkovich, *The United States and Imperialism* (Malden, Mass.: Blackwell, 2001), esp. 200–246; Frank Ninkovich, *Global Dawn: The Cultural Foundation of American Internationalism, 1865–1890* (Cambridge: Harvard University Press, 2009).

6. See Alan Dawley, *Changing the World: American Progressives in War and Revolution* (Princeton: Princeton University Press, 2003); Daniel T. Rodgers, *Atlantic Crossings: Social Politics in a Progressive Age* (Cambridge: Belknap Press of Harvard University Press, 1998); James T. Kloppenberg, *Uncertain Victory: Social Democracy and Progressivism in European and American Thought, 1870–1920* (New York: Oxford University Press, 1986).

7. The literature on this period is enormous. For a start, see William Appleman Williams, *The Tragedy of American Diplomacy*, 50th anniversary edition (New York: W. W. Norton, 2009), esp. 18–57; Walter LaFeber, *The New Empire: An Interpretation of American Expansion, 1860–1898*, 35th anniversary edition (Ithaca: Cornell University Press, 1998); Emily S. Rosenberg, *Spreading the American Dream: American Economic and Cultural Expansion, 1890–1945* (New York: Hill & Wang, 1982), esp. 3–62; Kristin Hoganson, *Fighting for American Manhood: How Gender Politics Provoked the Spanish-American and Philippine-American Wars* (New Haven: Yale University Press, 1998); Jackson Lears, *Rebirth of a Nation: The Making of Modern America, 1877–1920* (New York: HarperCollins, 2009).

8. This is how Frank Ninkovich defines the emergence of a "modern" American foreign policy in the early twentieth century, especially during Woodrow Wilson's presidency. Ninkovich focuses on two motives for American policymaking at the time: the political-economic challenges based on deeper global interdependence and the hope for an American-led alternative to empire through the spread of liberal-capitalist nation-state structures. See Frank Ninkovich, *Modernity and Power: A History of the Domino Theory in the Twentieth Century* (Chicago: University of Chicago Press, 1994); Frank Ninkovich, *The Wilsonian Century: U.S. Foreign Policy Since 1900* (Chicago: University of Chicago Press, 2001).

9. Kipling, "The White Man's Burden."

10. For a superb essay on Kipling's disillusion, ambivalence, and frequent skepticism about "civilization," see Irving Howe, "Editor's Introduction," in Irving

Howe, ed., *The Portable Kipling* (New York: Penguin, 1982), ix–xxxix. See also Rudyard Kipling, *Kim* (New York: Penguin, 1987; originally published, 1901); Peter Hopkirk, *The Quest for Kim* (Ann Arbor: University of Michigan Press, 1999); David Gilmour, *The Long Recessional: The Imperial Life of Rudyard Kipling* (New York: Farrar, Straus and Giroux, 2002).

11. For a thoughtful account of U.S. efforts in Asia during the decades after the Civil War, and the various failures, see Bruce Cumings, *Dominion from Sea to Sea: Pacific Ascendancy and American Power* (New Haven: Yale University Press, 2009), 83–89.

12. These were all arguments made forcefully by anti-imperialists at the time. See Robert L. Beisner, *Twelve Against Empire: The Anti-Imperialists, 1898–1900* (New York: McGraw-Hill, 1968).

13. See, among others, Thomas A. Bailey, "Dewey and the Germans at Manila Bay," *American Historical Review* 45 (October 1939): 59–81; Paul M. Kennedy, *The Samoan Tangle: A Study in Anglo-German-American Relations, 1878–1900* (Dublin: Irish University Press, 1974); Thomas J. McCormick, *China Market: America's Quest for Informal Empire, 1893–1901* (Chicago: Quadrangle, 1967); Friedrich Katz, *The Secret War in Mexico: Europe, the United States, and the Mexican Revolution* (Chicago: University of Chicago Press, 1981).

14. For the classic interpretation of the Open Door, see Williams, *The Tragedy of American Diplomacy*, 27–57. See also Kenton J. Clymer, *John Hay: The Gentleman as Diplomat* (Ann Arbor: University of Michigan Press, 1975).

15. See, among others, Lewis L. Gould, *The Spanish-American War and President McKinley* (Lawrence: University Press of Kansas, 1982); David F. Trask, *The War with Spain in 1898* (New York: Free Press, 1981); Ernest R. May, *Imperial Democracy: The Emergence of America as a Great Power* (New York: Harcourt Brace, 1961).

16. These assumptions ran through McKinley's justifications for the war against Spain and subsequent American actions in Cuba and the Philippines. See, for example, McKinley's Second Inaugural Address, 4 March 1901. Closing his speech with a long reflection on American purposes in the Philippines, McKinley explained: "I shall continue the efforts already begun until order

shall be restored throughout the islands, and as fast as conditions permit will establish local governments, in the formation of which the full co-operation of the people has been already invited, and when established will encourage the people to administer them. The settled purpose, long ago proclaimed, to afford the inhabitants of the islands self-government as fast as they were ready for it will be pursued with earnestness and fidelity. . . . Order under civil institutions will come as soon as those who now break the peace shall keep it. Force will not be needed or used when those who make war against us shall make it no more. May it end without further bloodshed, and there be ushered in the reign of peace to be made permanent by a government of liberty under law!" McKinley's Second Inaugural Address is available at: http://avalon.law.yale.edu/19th_century/mckin2.asp (accessed 26 July 2010).

17. Elihu Root, *Reports of the Taft Philippine Commission*, 7.

18. William Howard Taft to H. W. and Horace D. Taft, 28 January 1900, quoted in Henry F. Pringle, *The Life and Times of William Howard Taft*, Vol. 1 (Hamden, Conn.: Archon, 1964; originally published, 1939), 160.

19. President William McKinley's Proclamation on the Philippines, 21 December 1898, available at: http://www.msc.edu.ph/centennial/benevolent.html (accessed 12 July 2010).

20. See Creighton Stuart Miller, *Benevolent Assimilation: The American Conquest of the Philippines, 1899–1903*, 4th ed. (New Haven: Yale University Press, 1984). On American racism toward Filipinos, and its influence on policy, see Paul A. Kramer, *The Blood of Government: Race, Empire, the United States, and the Philippines* (Chapel Hill: University of North Carolina Press, 2006), esp. 87–158.

21. William Howard Taft to Elihu Root, 14 July 1900, Reel 463, Series 8, William Howard Taft Papers, Microfilm Collection, Wisconsin Historical Society Library, Madison, Wisconsin [hereafter Taft Papers].

22. See Brian McAllister Linn, *The Philippine War, 1899–1902* (Lawrence: University Press of Kansas, 2000), 185–224; David J. Silbey, *A War of Frontier and Empire: The Philippine-American War, 1899–1902* (New York: Hill & Wang, 2007), 126–206.

23. William Howard Taft to Elihu Root, 14 July 1900, Reel 463, Series 8, Taft Papers; William Howard Taft to Helen H. Taft, 8 July 1900, Reel 24, Series 2, Taft Papers.

24. William Howard Taft to Annie G. Roelker, 10 July 1900, Reel 31, Series 3, Taft Papers.

25. Pringle, *Life and Times of William Howard Taft*, 179–80.

26. Rene R. Escalante, *The Bearer of Pax Americana: The Philippine Career of William H. Taft, 1900–1903* (Quezon City: New Day, 2007), 257.

27. On this point, see ibid., esp. 254–64; Kramer, *The Blood of Government*, esp. 159–227.

28. The concept of civil society has drawn extensive scholarly attention in the last two decades. The seminal work, especially as civil society relates to modern nation-building, is Jürgen Habermas, *The Structural Transformation of the Public Sphere: An Inquiry into a Category of Bourgeois Society*, trans., Thomas Burger (Cambridge: MIT Press, 1989; originally published in German, 1969). See also Michael Edwards, *Civil Society* (Cambridge, U.K.: Polity, 2004).

29. Jacob Burckhardt, *The Civilization of the Renaissance in Italy* (New York: Dover, 2010).

30. William Howard Taft, "Inaugural Address as Civil Governor of the Philippines," Manila, 4 July 1901, in William Howard Taft, *Present Day Problems: A Collection of Addresses Delivered on Various Occasions* (Freeport, N.Y.: Books for Libraries Press, 1908; reprinted 1967), 3–4.

31. During the 1850s and 1860s William Magear Tweed, known as "Boss Tweed," ran the Democratic Party machine (Tammany Hall) in New York City. He distributed favors to ethnic groups, business figures, and other powerful people in order to secure his own power and enormous wealth. Tweed's corruption and accumulated enemies led to his ignominious downfall in 1871. Nonetheless, Tweed's consensus politics contributed to what one scholar identifies as the modern New York City—with its centralized government, transportation, and social services. See Seymour J. Mandelbaum, *Boss Tweed's New York*, expanded edition (Chicago: Ivan R. Dee, 1990).

32. See Alfred W. McCoy, " 'An Anarchy of Families': The Historiography of State and Family in the Philippines," in Alfred W. McCoy, ed., *An Anarchy of Families: State and Family in the Philippines* (Madison: University of Wisconsin Press, 1993), 1–32; Michael Cullinane, *Ilustrado Politics: Filipino Elite Responses to American Rule, 1898–1908* (Quezon City: Ateneo de Manila University Press, 2003).

33. Report of the United States Philippine Commission, 30 November 1900, in *Reports of the Taft Philippine Commission* (Washington, D.C.: U.S. Government Printing Office, 1901), 20–21.

34. Ibid., 21; Civil Service Act, Act 5 of the U.S. Philippine Commission, reprinted in ibid., 247–52.

35. See Glenn Anthony May, *Social Engineering in the Philippines: The Aims, Execution, and Impact of American Colonial Policy, 1900–1913* (Westport, Conn.: Greenwood, 1980), 24–32; Ruby R. Paredes, "Ilustrado Legacy: The Pardo de Taveras of Manila," in McCoy, ed., *An Anarchy of Families*, 347–427; Kramer, *The Blood of Government*, 181–82, 205–6.

36. May, *Social Engineering in the Philippines*, 24–32.

37. See Frank Hindman Golay, *Face of Empire: United States–Philippine Relations, 1898–1946* (Madison: University of Wisconsin Press, 1998), 76–77.

38. See Linn, *The Philippine War*, esp. 255–76; Silbey, *A War of Frontier and Empire*, 173–81.

39. See Alfred W. McCoy, *Policing America's Empire: The United States, the Philippines, and the Rise of the Surveillance State* (Madison: University of Wisconsin Press, 2009), esp. 3–56, 94–97.

40. On this point, see Julian Go, "Chains of Empire, Projects of State: Political Education and U.S. Colonial Rule in Puerto Rico and the Philippines," *Comparative Studies in Society and History* 42 (April 2000): 333–62.

41. See McCoy, *Policing America's Empire*, 59–93.

42. Ibid., 530–35.

43. Joseph Ralston Hayden described this process in the mid-twentieth century as "education for nationhood" in the Philippines. See his excellent chapters in *The Philippines: A Study in National Development* (New York: Macmillan, 1942), 463–580.

44. May, *Social Engineering in the Philippines*, 78–79; Fred W. Atkinson, *The Philippine Islands* (Boston: Ginn, 1905), 381–83.

45. See William J. Reese, *America's Public Schools: From the Common School to "No Child Left Behind"* (Baltimore: Johns Hopkins University Press, 2005), 79–117.

46. On this point, see Lewis E. Gleeck, Jr., *American Institutions in the Philippines* (Manila: Historical Conservation Society, 1976), 40–49, 272–82; May, *Social Engineering in the Philippines*, 82–83.

47. Atkinson quoted in May, *Social Engineering in the Philippines*, 84. Act 3 of the U.S. Philippine Commission, reprinted in *Reports of the Taft Philippine Commission*, 246. On urban education reformers in the early twentieth century, see Reese, *America's Public Schools*, 118–48.

48. See May, *Social Engineering in the Philippines*, 81–84; Acts 11 and 15 of the U.S. Philippine Commission, reprinted in *Reports of the Taft Philippine Commission*, 257–58, 263.

49. Act 74 of the Philippine Commission, quoted in May, *Social Engineering in the Philippines*, 82.

50. Gleeck, *American Institutions in the Philippines*, 41.

51. Quoted in Hayden *The Philippines*, 515–16.

52. Hayden, *The Philippines*, 516.

53. May, *Social Engineering in the Philippines*, 89–93; Glenn Anthony May, "The Business of Education in the Colonial Philippines, 1909–30," in Alfred W. McCoy and Francisco Scarano, eds., *Colonial Crucible: Empire in the Making of the Modern American State* (Madison: University of Wisconsin Press, 2009), 151–62.

54. Pardo de Tavera quoted in May, *Social Engineering in the Philippines*, 84.

55. Atkinson, *The Philippine Islands*, 392.

56. Ibid., 395–97.

57. Arthur Griffiths, unpublished essay, "Philippine Independence—Why?", Arthur L. Griffiths Papers, Sterling Memorial Library, Manuscripts and Archives, Yale University, Manuscript Group Number 1352, available on microfilm: Memorial Library, University of Wisconsin–Madison [hereafter Griffiths Papers].

58. Ibid.; Arthur Griffiths, "Wild Days in the Philippines," unpublished memoir, written during 1943–44, in Griffiths Papers. The last two quotes in this paragraph come from pages 483–84 of "Wild Days in the Philippines."

59. Griffiths, "Wild Days in the Philippines," 482, 484.

60. Ibid., 769.

61. Ibid., 768.

62. Ibid., 499, 511, 768–69.

63. Ibid., 770, 773–74.

64. On this point, see Gleeck, *American Institutions in the Philippines*, 282–321.

65. See Kramer, *The Blood of Government*, esp. 347–431.

66. This is the theme of Stanley Karnow, *In Our Image: America's Empire in the Philippines* (New York: Random House, 1989).

Chapter 4: Reconstruction After Fascism

1. Political Advisor for Germany (Robert Murphy) to Secretary of State James Byrnes, 6 January 1947, Foreign Relations of the United States [hereafter FRUS], 1947, Vol. 2, 845.

2. Digest of a Meeting, Former President Herbert Hoover, Allen Dulles presiding, Council on Foreign Relations, 7 April 1947, Council on Foreign Relations Records, MC 104, Box 441, Seeley Mudd Manuscript Library, Princeton University, Princeton, New Jersey.

3. *New York Times*, 18 May 1947, E5; Dolph Simons, *Germany and Austria in May–June, 1947* (Lawrence, Kans.: The Journal-World, 1947), 12. See also Lewis H. Brown, *A Report on Germany* (New York: Farrar, Straus, 1947).

4. Simons, *Germany and Austria in May–June, 1947*, 12; United States Military Governor for Germany (Lucius Clay) to Secretary of State George Marshall, 2 May 1947, FRUS, 1947, Vol. 2, 915–18; Acting Political Advisor for Germany (Heath) to Secretary of State George Marshall, 3 April 1947, FRUS, 1947, Vol. 2, 1144; quotation from "What Would You Do?," *Time*, 17 March 1947.

5. Political Advisor for Germany (Robert Murphy) to Secretary of State George Marshall, 11 May 1947, FRUS, 1947, Vol. 2, 867–68.

6. Ibid., 867–68.

7. See Acting Political Advisor for Germany (Heath) to Secretary of State George Marshall, 15 March 1947; Acting Political Advisor for Germany (Heath) to Secretary of State George Marshall, 14 April 1947, FRUS, 1947, Vol. 2, 856–58, 863–64. The connection between capitalism and the rise of fascism in Germany and other countries remains deeply contested. Business interests do not appear to have been any more likely than nonbusiness interests to support the Nazi Party. Communist Party activists were the most consistent antifascists, at least until the Nazi-Soviet Non-Aggression Pact of 1939, but they supported many of the most militaristic and murderous policies of the period. The literature on all of these topics is enormous. For a start, see Peter Hayes, *Industry and Ideology: IG Farben in the Nazi Era*, new ed. (New York: Cambridge University Press, 2001); Richard J. Evans, *The Coming of the Third Reich* (New York: Penguin, 2003), Ian Kershaw, *Hitler, the Germans, and the Final Solution* (New Haven: Yale University Press, 2008).

8. Memorandum by Mr. George F. Kennan to Mr. Carmel Offie, 10 May 1946; Chargé in the Soviet Union (George Kennan) to Secretary of State James Byrnes, 6 March 1946, FRUS, 1946, Vol. 5, 555, 518.

9. See John Lewis Gaddis, *Strategies of Containment: A Critical Appraisal of American National Security Policy During the Cold War*, rev. ed. (New York: Oxford University Press, 2005), 24–86; Melvyn P. Leffler, *A Preponderance of Power: National Security, the Truman Administration, and the Cold War* (Stanford: Stanford University Press, 1992), esp. 100–46; Robert L. Beisner, *Dean Acheson: A Life in the Cold War* (New York: Oxford University Press, 2006), 48–65.

10. Political Advisor for Germany (Robert Murphy) to Secretary of State James Byrnes, 6 January 1947, FRUS, 1947, Vol. 2, 845. See also Gaddis, *Strategies of Containment*, 24–86; Leffler, *A Preponderance of Power*, esp. 147–219; Beisner, *Dean Acheson*, 69–79.

11. On this point, I share some of Robert Kagan's views about the necessary mix of idealism and realism in American foreign policy, but I place much more emphasis on the role of political negotiation. Kagan overemphasizes, I believe, the role of military force. See Robert Kagan, *The Return of History and the End of Dreams* (New York: Alfred A. Knopf, 2008).

12. See, among others, Leffler, *A Preponderance of Power*, esp. 157–81; Alan S. Milward, *The Reconstruction of Western Europe, 1945–1951* (Berkeley: University of California Press, 1984); Michael Hogan, *The Marshall Plan: America, Britain, and the Reconstruction of Western Europe, 1947–1952* (New York: Cambridge University Press, 1987); Carolyn Woods Eisenberg, *Drawing the Line: The American Decision to Divide Germany, 1944–1949* (New York: Cambridge University Press, 1996); Arnold A. Offner, *Another Such Victory: President Truman and the Cold War, 1945–1953* (Stanford: Stanford University Press, 2002); Charles Maier with Günter Bischof, eds., *The Marshall Plan and Germany: West German Development with the Framework of the European Recovery Program* (New York: Berg, 1991); Greg Behrman, *The Most Noble Adventure* (New York: Free Press, 2007).

13. On the emergence of institutions for "transitional diplomacy" in the United States, including think tanks and postwar universities, see Jeremi Suri, "Hamilton Fish Armstrong, the 'American Establishment,' and Cosmopolitan Nationalism," *Princeton University Library Chronicle* 63 (Spring 2002): 438–65; Jeremi Suri, *Henry Kissinger and the American Century* (Cambridge: Belknap Press of Harvard University Press, 2007), esp. 92–137.

14. See, for example, Peter M. Haas, "Epistemic Communities and International Policy Coordination," *International Organization* 46 (Winter 1992): 1–35.

15. For the records of the remarkable Council on Foreign Relations' "Study Group on the Problem of Germany" in late 1946 and early 1947—including group deliberations and efforts at influencing policy—see Council on Foreign Relations Records, MC 104, Box 138, Seeley Mudd Manuscript Library, Princeton University, Princeton, New Jersey.

16. Digest of a Meeting, Former President Herbert Hoover, Allen Dulles presiding, Council on Foreign Relations, 7 April 1947, Council on Foreign Relations Records, MC 104, Box 441, Seeley Mudd Manuscript Library, Princeton University.

17. On this point, see Suri, *Henry Kissinger and the American Century*, 52–91.

18. Ibid., 16–91.

19. For the influence of transatlantic ideas about "Western civilization" in the postwar years, see, among others, Hans-Peter Schwarz, *Die Ära Adenauer:*

Gründerjahre der Republik, 1949–1957 (Stuttgart: Deutsche Verlags-Anstalt, 1981); Geir Lundestad, *The United States and Western Europe Since 1945: From "Empire" by Invitation to Transatlantic Drift* (Oxford: Oxford University Press, 2003), William I. Hitchcock, *The Struggle for Europe: The Turbulent History of a Divided Continent, 1945 to the Present* (New York: Doubleday, 2003).

20. Franklin Roosevelt, Quarantine Speech, Chicago, Illinois, 5 October 1937, available at: http://millercenter.org/scripps/archive/speeches/detail/3310 (accessed 1 June 2010).

21. See John Milton Cooper, Jr., *Breaking the Heart of the World: Woodrow Wilson and the Fight for the League of Nations* (New York: Cambridge University Press, 2001); David Reynolds, *The Creation of the Anglo-American Alliance, 1937–1941: A Study in Competitive Cooperation* (Chapel Hill: University of North Carolina Press, 1982); John Moser, *Twisting the Lion's Tail: American Anglophobia Between the World Wars* (New York: New York University Press, 1998).

22. See Reynolds, *The Creation of the Anglo-American Alliance*; Robert Dallek, *Franklin D. Roosevelt and American Foreign Policy, 1932–1945* (New York: Oxford University Press, 1979); Warren F. Kimball, *The Juggler: Franklin Roosevelt as Wartime Statesman* (Princeton: Princeton University Press, 1994); Elizabeth Borgwardt, *A New Deal for the World: America's Vision for Human Rights* (Cambridge: Harvard University Press, 2005).

23. See Wilfried Mausbach, *Zwischen Morgenthau und Marshall: Das wirtschaftspolitische Deutschlandkonzept der USA, 1944–1947* (Düsseldorf: Droste Verlag, 1996), 41–80, 90–109; William I. Hitchcock, *The Bitter Road to Freedom: A New History of the Liberation of Europe* (New York: Free Press, 2008), 125–365.

24. See David Reynolds, *Rich Relations: The American Occupation of Britain, 1942–1945* (New York: Random House, 1995); Hitchcock, *The Bitter Road to Freedom*, 125–365; Suri, *Henry Kissinger and the American Century*, 52–91; John W. Dower, *Embracing Defeat: Japan in the Wake of World War II* (New York: W. W. Norton, 1999).

25. Patrick Thaddeus Jackson describes the ways in which many Americans defined Germany as an uncivilized "other" at the end of the Second World War. He shows how key postwar West German figures, particularly Kurt Schum-

acher and Konrad Adenauer, allied with Winston Churchill and George Kennan to redefine Germany as a central part of a Christian, anticommunist, capitalist "Western civilization." See Jackson, *Civilizing the Enemy: German Reconstruction and the Invention of the West* (Ann Arbor: University of Michigan Press, 2006), 112–48.

26. See Hitchcock, *The Bitter Road to Freedom*, esp. 367–73; Thomas Alan Schwartz, *America's Germany: John J. McCloy and the Federal Republic of Germany* (Cambridge: Harvard University Press, 1991).

27. For an excellent discussion of how civilizational rhetoric redefined policy, particularly in postwar Germany, see Jackson, *Civilizing the Enemy*, 13–45, 243–53.

28. See Mausbach, *Zwischen Morgenthau und Marshall*, 117–23.

29. For the contrast between the cosmopolitan internationalism of the early twentieth century and the hyper-nationalism of the mid-twentieth century, see Daniel T. Rodgers, *Atlantic Crossings: Social Politics in a Progressive Age* (Cambridge: Belknap Press of Harvard University Press, 1998); James T. Kloppenberg, *Uncertain Victory: Social Democracy and Progressivism in European and American Thought, 1870–1920* (New York: Oxford University Press, 1986); Alan Dawley, *Changing the World: American Progressives in War and Revolution* (Princeton: Princeton University Press, 2003); Frank Ninkovich, *Global Dawn: The Cultural Foundation of American Internationalism, 1865–1890* (Cambridge: Harvard University Press, 2009).

30. See Herbert Hoover, *An American Epic*, Vol. 4 (Chicago: Henry Regnery, 1964), 105–67.

31. See Leffler, *A Preponderance of Power*, 100–64; Michael J. Hogan, *A Cross of Iron: Harry S. Truman and the Origins of the National Security State, 1945–1954* (New York: Cambridge University Press, 1998), 69–118.

32. See the communications between Truman and Hoover before Hoover's trip: Truman to Hoover, 18 January 1947; Hoover to Truman, 19 January 1947; Hoover's notes from a meeting with Truman, 22 January 1947; Hoover's statement, 22 January 1947, all available at: http://www.trumanlibrary.org/hoover/europe.htm (accessed 2 June 2010). See also Leffler, *A Preponderance of Power*, esp. 116–21.

33. See "Hoover Weighs Bid to Study Germany," *New York Times*, 22 January 1947, and "Hoover Accepts Mission to Europe to Ease U.S. Taxpayers' Burden," *New York Times*, 23 January 1947. For background on Hoover's experience with nation-building, and his approach to what one scholar calls the "associative state," see Ellis W. Hawley, "Herbert Hoover, the Commerce Secretariat, and the Vision of an 'Associative State,' 1921–1928," *Journal of American History* 61 (June 1974): 116–40; George H. Nash, *The Life of Herbert Hoover: Master of Emergencies, 1917–1918* (New York: W. W. Norton, 1996); Kendrick A. Clements, *The Life of Herbert Hoover: Imperfect Visionary, 1918–1928* (New York: Palgrave Macmillan, 2010).

34. "Hoover in Deutschland," *Rhein-Neckar Zeitung*, 6 February 1947. See a similar article in the *Rhein-Neckar Zeitung*, 8 February 1947. See the Herbert-Hoover-Schule in Berlin, http://www.herbert-hoover-oberschule.cidsnet.de/index.htm, and the Herbert-Hoover-Schule in Stuttgart, http://www.stutt gart.de/item/show/305802/1/dept/108061? (both accessed 4 June 2010).

35. "Hoover in Stuttgart," *Rhein-Neckar Zeitung*, 13 February 1947.

36. On the "associative" approach to politics, see Hawley, "Herbert Hoover, the Commerce Secretariat, and the Vision of an 'Associative State,' 1921–1928"; Emily S. Rosenberg, *Spreading the American Dream: American Economic and Cultural Expansion, 1890–1945* (New York: Hill & Wang, 1982), 138–60; Frank Costigliola, *Awkward Dominion: American Political, Economic, and Cultural Relations with Europe, 1919–1933* (Ithaca: Cornell University Press, 1988).

37. "Hoover in Stuttgart," *Rhein-Neckar Zeitung*, 13 February 1947.

38. Hoover's first two reports are reprinted in Hoover, *An American Epic*, Vol. 4, 229–56. Hoover's third report, dated 18 March 1947, is available from the Harry S. Truman Presidential Library, Independence, Missouri, online document collection, at: http://www.trumanlibrary.org/hoover/internaltemplate .php?tldate=1947-03-18&groupid=5170&collectionid=hoover (accessed 4 June 2009). See also Jean Edward Smith, *Lucius D. Clay: An American Life* (New York: Henry Holt, 1990), 339–40.

39. "Mr. Hoover's Report," *New York Times*, 28 February 1947; H. B. Ripman, British Embassy in Washington to J. W. Nicholls, Supply and Relief De-

partment, 24 March 1947; Minute on Hoover Report, 11 April 1947, FO 371/65019, National Archives of the United Kingdom, Kew, London [hereafter NAUK]; Meeting of British and French Delegations, Quai d'Orsay, 11:AM, 28 February 1947, FO 371/65037, NAUK.

40. Hoover, *An American Epic*, Vol. 4, 242–43.

41. Hoover's third report, 18 March 1947, Truman Library.

42. Hoover, *An American Epic*, Vol. 4, 253, 246.

43. Herbert Hoover to George Marshall, 12 May 1947; Herbert Hoover to Robert Patterson, Secretary of War, 7 May 1947, Herbert Hoover Papers, Post-Presidential Individuals File—Marshall, George C., 1945–1960, Herbert Hoover Presidential Library, West Branch, Iowa [hereafter HPL].

44. Diary entry, Edgar Rickard, 1 March 1947, Papers of Edgar Rickard, available at: www.trumanlibrary.org; Dean Acheson to George Marshall, 20 March 1947, FRUS, 1947, Vol. 2, 394–95; "Mr. Hoover's Report," *New York Times*, 28 February 1947, 22; "Hoover Ties Relief to Reimbursement," *New York Times*, 1 March 1947, 5; "Hoover Bars Relief Post," *New York Times*, 13 March 1947, 54; "End German Drain on Us, Hoover Says," *New York Times*, 24 March 1947, 1; "Hoover Is Lauded for Food Survey," *New York Times*, 30 March 1947, 39.

45. For an excellent account of the U.S. government debates about the Hoover Report, and the declining support for a continuation of prior policies, see Mausbach, *Zwischen Morgenthau und Marshall*, 167–81.

46. See George Marshall to Herbert Hoover, 15 May 1947, Herbert Hoover Papers, Post-Presidential Individuals File—Marshall, George C., 1945–1960, HPL; Wilson D. Miscamble, *George F. Kennan and the Making of American Foreign Policy, 1947–1950* (Princeton: Princeton University Press, 1992), 37–57.

47. Undersecretary Dean Acheson, "The Requirements of Reconstruction," 8 May 1947, *Department of State Bulletin* (18 May 1947), 994; Miscamble, *George F. Kennan and the Making of American Foreign Policy*, 37–57; Beisner, *Dean Acheson*, 70–73.

48. Secretary of State George Marshall's speech at Harvard University, 5 June 1947, available at: http://www.marshallfoundation.org/documents/MarshallPlan.pdf (accessed 30 April 2009).

49. See Note 12, p. 309.

50. Forrest C. Pogue, *George C. Marshall: Statesman, 1945–1959* (New York: Viking, 1989), 215; Note of a Meeting on Tuesday, 24 June 1947, in the Chancellor of the Exchequer's Room, PREM 8/495, NAUK. Emphasis added. See also Aide Memoire for Foreign Secretary Ernest Bevin, 25 June 1947.

51. George F. Kennan, *Memoirs, 1925–1950* (Boston: Little, Brown, 1967), 343. See also Charles Kindleberger, *Marshall Plan Days* (London: Allen & Unwin, 1987).

52. For the strongest statement of this case, see Alan S. Milward, "Was the Marshall Plan Necessary?," *Diplomatic History* 13 (April 1989): 231–53; Milward, *The Reconstruction of Western Europe*. Milward offers an important corrective to the common overestimation of the Marshall Plan's effects. Milward, however, goes much too far in the other direction, diminishing the real and enduring effects of U.S. aid for postwar European economy, politics, and society.

53. This is the key point of Michael Hogan's foundational book, *The Marshall Plan*. See also, among others, Maier with Bischof, eds., *The Marshall Plan and Germany*.

54. On the efforts to fill the "dollar gap" and create open trading markets with Marshall Plan aid, see Committee of European Economic Cooperation, General Report, Final Draft III, Chapter V: "Economic Co-operation," Fall 1947; Aide Memoire for the Foreign Secretary, 25 June 1947; PREM 8/495, NAUK; European Recovery Programme, Record of Informal Discussion at British Embassy, 21 June 1948, FO 371/71826, NAUK; European Recovery Programme, September–October 1948, FO 371/71828, NAUK.

55. My analysis here draws on the seminal work by Charles Maier on the postwar "politics of productivity." See Charles S. Maier, *In Search of Stability: Explorations in Historical Political Economy* (New York: Cambridge University Press, 1987), esp. 121–52.

56. On the failure of international control over the Ruhr Valley after the First World War, see Walter McDougall, *France's Rhineland Diplomacy, 1914–1924: The Last Bid for a Balance of Power in Europe* (Princeton: Princeton

University Press, 1978); Zara Steiner, *The Lights That Failed: European International History, 1919–1933* (Oxford: Oxford University Press, 2005), esp. 182–255, 349–86.

57. See the Agreement for an International Authority for the Ruhr, signed in London, 28 April 1949, available at: http://www.ena.lu (accessed 8 June 2010). Article 14 of the treaty made it clear that West Germany would manage the Ruhr Valley on a day-to-day basis. The International Authority for the Ruhr would oversee the mix between West German consumption and the export of iron and coal. It would "ensure adequate access to supplies of these products by countries cooperating in the common economic good, taking into account the essential needs of Germany." The International Authority would assure against German hoarding or German military uses of the Ruhr resources. See also the Treaty Establishing the European Coal and Steel Community, signed 18 April 1951, available at: http://www.unizar.es/euro-constitucion/library/historic%20documents/Paris/TRAITES_1951_CECA.pdf (accessed 8 June 2010). The treaty came into force on 25 July 1952, creating the European Coal and Steel Community and ending the International Authority for the Ruhr. For excellent background on these issues, and the role of French negotiators in particular, see William I. Hitchcock, *France Restored: Cold War Diplomacy and the Quest for Leadership in Europe, 1944–1954* (Chapel Hill: University of North Carolina Press, 1998).

58. William Clayton's report on his 29 July 1947 dinner with Jean Monnet in Paris, Undersecretary of State for Economic Affairs William Clayton to Undersecretary of State Robert Lovett, 30 July 1947, FRUS, 1947, Vol. 2, 1012.

59. Memorandum of Conversation by the Undersecretary of State for Economic Affairs, William Clayton, 20 June 1947, FRUS, 1947, Vol. 2, 929.

60. French Foreign Minister Georges Bidault to Secretary of State George Marshall, 17 July 1947, FRUS, 1947, Vol. 2, 992. For an examination of how French leaders used similar arguments about "psychology" and perception to motivate American assistance in Indochina and other areas, see Mark Atwood Lawrence, *Assuming the Burden: Europe and the American Commitment to War in Vietnam* (Berkeley: University of California Press, 2005). The Paris Conference—including representatives from the United States, Great Britain, and

France—met in the summer of 1947 to discuss the future of the Ruhr Valley, postwar reparations, and interzonal cooperation in western Germany. The conference presumed the creation of a separate West German state.

61. For evidence that European federalism was encouraged—and debated—within the context of the Marshall Plan, see, among other documents, European Recovery Programme, Record of Informal Discussion at the Luxembourg Legation on 28 June 1948; Roger Makins, Foreign Office, Draft Memorandum, circa June 1948, FO 371/71826, NAUK.

62. See George Marshall's off-the-record reflections on the Marshall Plan, in similar terms: Report of Special Conference at the Shoreham Hotel, Washington DC, 5 March 1948, FO 371/71825, NAUK.

63. On postwar Japan and South Korea, see, among many other works, Dower, *Embracing Defeat*; Gregg Brazinsky, *Nation Building in South Korea: Koreans, Americans, and the Making of Democracy* (Chapel Hill: University of North Carolina Press, 2007).

64. See, for example, the collection of articles on "modernization" and foreign policy in *Diplomatic History* 33 (June 2009).

65. On the collapse of communist East Germany and the unification of the former two Germanys through the Federal Republic, see Charles S. Maier, *Dissolution: The Crisis of Communism and the End of East Germany* (Princeton: Princeton University Press, 1997), Mary E. Sarotte, *1989: The Struggle to Create Postwar Europe* (Princeton: Princeton University Press, 2009); Stephen Kotkin with Jan Gross, *Uncivil Society: 1989 and the Implosion of the Communist Establishment* (New York: Random House, 2009).

66. On the stability and prosperity of West Germany and Western Europe as a whole since 1945, and the remarkable turn away from militarism in this region, especially after 1989, see James J. Sheehan, *Where Have All the Soldiers Gone? The Transformation of Modern Europe* (Boston: Houghton Mifflin, 2008).

Chapter 5: Reconstruction After Communist Revolution

1. Minutes of the Pacific War Council, 21 July 1943, quoted in Mark Philip Bradley, *Imagining Vietnam and America: The Making of Postcolonial Vietnam, 1919–1950* (Chapel Hill: University of North Carolina Press, 2000), 76.

2. Ho Chi Minh's National Independence Day speech, 2 September 1945, quoted in David Marr, *Vietnam 1945: The Quest for Power* (Berkeley: University of California Press, 1995), 535.

3. On this point, see Warren F. Kimball, *The Juggler: Franklin Roosevelt as Wartime Statesman* (Princeton: Princeton University Press, 1991), esp. 7–19. For a poignant criticism of Roosevelt's indecision and arbitrariness, see George F. Kennan, *Memoirs, 1925–1950* (Boston: Little, Brown, 1967), esp. 172–73, 417–18.

4. See Kimball, *The Juggler*, 127–57, 185–200; Robert Dallek, *Franklin D. Roosevelt and American Foreign Policy, 1932–1945* (New York: Oxford University Press, 1979), esp. 323–28; Gary R. Hess, *The United States' Emergence as a Southeast Asian Power, 1940–1950* (New York: Columbia University Press, 1987), 47–82, 121–58.

5. See Kimball, *The Juggler*, 127–57.

6. On Roosevelt's and Churchill's strong differences over the future role of France, and the British prime minister's deep frustrations with his American counterpart, see Max Hastings, *Winston's War: Churchill, 1940–1945* (New York: Alfred A. Knopf, 2010), Chapter 15.

7. See Gary R. Hess, "Franklin Roosevelt and Indochina," *Journal of American History* 59 (September 1972): 353–68; Walter LaFeber, "Roosevelt, Churchill, and Indochina: 1942–1945," *American Historical Review* 80 (December 1975): 1277–95; Ronald H. Spector, *In the Ruins of Empire: The Japanese Surrender and the Battle for Postwar Asia* (New York: Random House, 2007), 93–116.

8. Quotation from Kimball, *The Juggler*, 143. See also Hastings, *Winston's War*, Chapter 15.

9. See Mark Atwood Lawrence, *Assuming the Burden: Europe and the American Commitment to War in Vietnam* (Berkeley: University of California Press, 2005), 45–58. On the connections between U.S. anticolonialism in Southeast Asia and American hopes for an Open Door to trade in the region, see Andrew J. Rotter, *The Path to Vietnam: Origins of the American Commitment to Southeast Asia* (Ithaca: Cornell University Press, 1987); LaFeber, "Roosevelt, Churchill, and Indochina," 1277–95.

10. Quotations from Lawrence, *Assuming the Burden*, 51.

11. A U.S. marine colonel allegedly claimed that Americans in Vietnam were "destroying the village in order to save it." See Robert D. Schulzinger, *A Time of War: The United States and Vietnam, 1941–1975* (New York: Oxford University Press, 1997), 262.

12. See Hess, "Franklin Roosevelt and Indochina," 353–68; Kimball, *The Juggler*, 83–125; William Roger Louis, *Imperialism at Bay: The United States and the Decolonization of the British Empire, 1941–45* (New York: Oxford University Press, 1978), 88–117; Lloyd C. Gardner, *Approaching Vietnam: From World War II Through Dienbienphu, 1941–1954* (New York: W. W. Norton, 1988), 21–53; Stein Tønnesson, "Franklin Roosevelt, Trusteeship, and Indochina: A Reassessment," in Mark Atwood Lawrence and Fredrik Logevall, eds., *The First Vietnam War: Colonial Conflict and Cold War Crisis* (Cambridge: Harvard University Press, 2007), 56–73.

13. Minutes of the Pacific War Council, 21 July 1943, quoted in Bradley, *Imagining Vietnam and America*, 76.

14. See Ronald Spector's excellent book about the strategic and political dilemmas caused by the Second World War in the Pacific, *In the Ruins of Empire*, esp. 264–76. See also Lawrence, *Assuming the Burden*, 45–58; Marc Gallichio, *The Cold War Begins in Asia: American East Asian Policy and the Fall of the Japanese Empire* (New York: Columbia University Press, 1988). For an analysis of the political dilemmas in the region that accompanied the collapse of British power, see Christopher Bayly and Tim Harper, *Forgotten Wars: Freedom and Revolution in Southeast Asia* (Cambridge: Belknap Press of Harvard University Press, 2007).

15. On the racist nature of American political judgments in Vietnam and the Philippines, see Bradley, *Imagining Vietnam and America*, 45–106; Paul A. Kramer, *The Blood of Government: Race, Empire, the United States, and the Philippines* (Chapel Hill: University of North Carolina Press, 2006), esp. 159–227.

16. On this point, see Jeremi Suri, *Power and Protest: Global Revolution and the Rise of Détente* (Cambridge: Harvard University Press, 2003), 131–63.

17. For an excellent account of the shifting Allied policies surrounding Indochina as a consequence of war pressures, see Christopher Thorne, "Indochina

and Anglo-American Relations, 1942–1945," *Pacific Historical Review* 45 (February 1976): 73–96.

18. Quotation from Lawrence, *Assuming the Burden*, 63.

19. See Lawrence, *Assuming the Burden*, 61–74; LaFeber, "Roosevelt, Churchill, and Indochina," 1277–95; Thorne, "Indochina and Anglo-American Relations," 73–96.

20. Douglas J. Macdonald, *Adventures in Chaos: American Intervention for Reform in the Third World* (Cambridge: Harvard University Press, 1992), 29–73, 249–53. See also Michael E. Latham, *Modernization as Ideology: American Social Science and "Nation-Building" in the Kennedy Era* (Chapel Hill: University of North Carolina Press, 2000), 69–108; D. Michael Shafer, *Deadly Paradigms: The Failure of U.S. Counterinsurgency Policy* (Princeton: Princeton University Press, 1988), 96–102.

21. On this point, see the detailed and insightful analysis in Stein Tønnesson, *The Vietnamese Revolution of 1945: Roosevelt, Ho Chi Minh, and de Gaulle in a World at War* (Oslo: International Peace Research Institute, 1991), esp. 156–237.

22. See Spector, *In the Ruins of Empire*; Bayly and Harper, *Forgotten Wars*.

23. William J. Duiker, *Ho Chi Minh: A Life* (New York: Hyperion, 2000), 254.

24. See ibid., esp. 229–306; Jean Lacouture, *Ho Chi Minh: A Political Biography*, trans. Peter Wiles (New York: Random House, 1968), esp. 3–84; George McT. Kahin, *Intervention: How America Became Involved in Vietnam* (New York: Alfred A. Knopf, 1986), esp. 13–15; Sophie Quinn-Judge, *Ho Chi Minh: The Missing Years* (Berkeley: University of California Press, 2003).

25. See Duiker, *Ho Chi Minh*, 286. Ho Chi Minh appealed to Vietnamese patriotism (*ai quoc*), which had broader and more populist associations in the local vernacular than elitist nationalism (*ai quan*). I thank Professor Robert Brigham for bringing this important Vietnamese distinction to my attention. E-mail from Robert Brigham, 5 November 2010.

26. Numerous scholars have analyzed the ideological, institutional, and circumstantial differences between Ho Chi Minh's and Franklin Roosevelt's approaches to nation-building. Ho was anticapitalist, he believed in a monopoly of power for the Communist Party, he accepted political terror

against opponents, and he emphasized the collective over the individual. My point here is to show that despite these significant differences, there were also points of overlap between Ho and Roosevelt. These points of overlap provided a possible opening for limited cooperation. The areas of agreement on nation-building between Ho Chi Minh and Franklin Roosevelt were probably greater than the areas of agreement between Roosevelt and the French leaders that the president consistently criticized. See, among many others, Marr, *Vietnam 1945*, 473–539; Duiker, *Ho Chi Minh*, 258–345; Bradley, *Imagining Vietnam and America*, 107–45; Marilyn B. Young, *The Vietnam Wars, 1945–1990* (New York: HarperCollins, 1991), 1–19.

27. Many of these issues are covered in Melvyn P. Leffler, *A Preponderance of Power: National Security, the Truman Administration, and the Cold War* (Stanford: Stanford University Press, 1992); James T. Sparrow, *Americanism and Entitlement: Authorizing Big Government in an Age of Total War* (New York: Oxford University Press, 2011).

28. Truman quoted in Arnold A. Offner, *Another Such Victory: President Truman and the Cold War, 1945–1953* (Stanford: Stanford University Press, 2002), 127. See also Leffler, *A Preponderance of Power*, 92–94.

29. See Lawrence, *Assuming the Burden*, 102–44; Leffler, *A Preponderance of Power*, 165–67, 258–59, 300–302. For an account that highlights Truman's indecision and his ultimate reliance on French occupation for stability in Vietnam, see Tønnesson, *The Vietnamese Revolution of 1945*, 255–80. On the divisions within the Truman administration over policy toward Indochina, see George C. Herring, "The Truman Administration and the Restoration of French Sovereignty in Indochina," *Diplomatic History* 1 (April 1977): 97–117.

30. Quotation from Marr, *Vietnam 1945*, 402. On the famine, the floods, and the insurrections of August 1945, see ibid., 402–514; Duiker, *Ho Chi Minh*, 307–16; Tønnesson, *The Vietnamese Revolution of 1945*, 292–95, 378–79.

31. See Tønnesson, *The Vietnamese Revolution of 1945*, 335–61, 379–407.

32. Quotations from Duiker, *Ho Chi Minh*, 303, 306.

33. On Ho Chi Minh's Leninist background and his time in Russia, see Duiker, *Ho Chi Minh*, esp. 46–104.

34. See ibid., 304–6; David Marr, "Creating Defence Capacity in Vietnam, 1945–1947," in Lawrence and Logevall, eds., *The First Vietnam War*, 74–104.

35. See Duiker, *Ho Chi Minh*, 307–20; Marr, *Vietnam 1945*, 511–14.

36. See Duiker, *Ho Chi Minh*, 324–25.

37. Quotation from Duiker, *Ho Chi Minh*, 344. See also Marr, *Vietnam 1945*, 516–39.

38. Quotation from Vu Ngu Chieu in Marr, *Vietnam 1945*, 537.

39. Quotation from Ho Chi Minh in Marr, *Vietnam 1945*, 535. See also Duiker, *Ho Chi Minh*, 321–24; Bradley, *Imagining Vietnam and America*, 107–9.

40. Quotation from Marr, *Vietnam 1945*, 532–33. The Fatherland Front officially replaced the Vietminh in 1955. Most observers—and later historians—continued to refer to it as the Vietminh. It functioned in very similar ways. I thank Professor Robert Brigham for elucidating this point. E-mail from Robert Brigham, 5 November 2010.

41. On James Madison's constitutional fiction, see Chapter 1.

42. See Duiker, *Ho Chi Minh*, 347. See also Greg Lockhart, *Nation in Arms: The Origins of the People's Army of Vietnam* (Sydney: Allen & Unwin, 1989).

43. See Duiker, *Ho Chi Minh*, 325.

44. On this point, see Leffler, *A Preponderance of Power*, 1–24, 506–11; John Lewis Gaddis, *Strategies of Containment: A Critical Appraisal of American National Security Policy During the Cold War*, rev. ed. (New York: Oxford University Press, 2005), 53–124.

45. On this point, see Herring, "The Truman Administration and the Restoration of French Sovereignty in Indochina," 97–117; Marr, *Vietnam 1945*, 541–52; Tønnesson, "Franklin Roosevelt, Trusteeship, and Indochina," in Lawrence and Logevall, eds., *The First Vietnam War*, 56–73.

46. Acheson quoted in Lawrence, *Assuming the Burden*, 101.

47. Secretary of State George Marshall to Jefferson Caffery (American ambassador to France), 3 February 1947, FRUS, 1947, Vol. 6: 68. See also Lawrence, *Assuming the Burden*, 102–89; Kathryn C. Statler, *Replacing France: The Origins of American Intervention in Vietnam* (Lexington: University Press of Kentucky, 2007); Leffler, *A Preponderance of Power*, 164–67, 258–59.

48. See Leffler, *A Preponderance of Power*, 374–83, 395–97; Gaddis, *Strategies of Containment*, 87–124; Marc J. Selverstone, *Constructing the Monolith: The United States, Great Britain, and International Communism, 1945–1950* (Cambridge: Harvard University Press, 2009).

49. The one clear exception to American anticommunist absolutism in the early Cold War was the relationship forged between the United States and communist Yugoslavia, especially after the public split between the Soviet Union and Yugoslavia in 1948. See Gaddis, *Strategies of Containment*, 64–69; Leffler, *A Preponderance of Power*, 417–18.

50. On this point, see Campbell Craig and Fredrik Logevall, *America's Cold War: The Politics of Insecurity* (Cambridge: Belknap Press of Harvard University Press, 2009), 59–138.

51. Walter Lippmann, *The Cold War: A Study in U.S. Foreign Policy* (New York: Harper & Row, 1947), 50. For more on Lippmann's critique and its implications for American foreign policy, see Ronald Steel, *Walter Lippmann and the American Century* (Boston: Little, Brown, 1980); Fredrik Logevall, "A Critique of Containment," *Diplomatic History* 28 (September 2004): 473–99; Craig and Logevall, *America's Cold War*, 82–86.

52. See Lawrence, *Assuming the Burden*, 233–75; Schulzinger, *A Time for War*, 45–50; Christopher E. Goscha, "Choosing Between the Two Vietnams: 1950 and Southeast Asian Shifts in the International System," in Christopher E. Goscha and Christian F. Ostermann, eds., *Connecting Histories: Decolonization and the Cold War in Southeast Asia, 1945–1962* (Stanford: Stanford University Press, 2009), 207–37.

53. See David L. Anderson, *Trapped by Success: The Eisenhower Administration and Vietnam, 1953–1961* (New York: Columbia University Press, 1991); George C. Herring and Richard H. Immerman, "Eisenhower, Dulles, and Dienbienphu: 'The Day We Didn't Go to War Revisited,'" *Journal of American History* 71 (September 1984): 343–63; Kathryn C. Statler, "Building a Colony: South Vietnam and the Eisenhower Administration, 1953–1961," in Kathryn C. Statler and Andrew L. Johns, eds., *The Eisenhower Administration, the Third World, and the Globalization of the Cold War* (Lanham, Md.: Rowman & Littlefield, 2006), 101–23; Robert K. Brigham, *Guerrilla Di-*

plomacy: The NLF's Foreign Relations and the Viet Nam War (Ithaca: Cornell University Press, 1999), esp. 1–18; Duiker, *Ho Chi Minh*, 434–514.

54. See Seth Jacobs, *America's Miracle Man in Vietnam: Ngo Dinh Diem, Religion, Race, and U.S. Intervention in Southeast Asia, 1950–1957* (Durham: Duke University Press, 2004); Seth Jacobs, *Cold War Mandarin: Ngo Dinh Diem and the Origins of America's War in Vietnam, 1950–1963* (Lanham, Md.: Rowman & Littlefield, 2006). A number of authors have shown that Diem acted with sincerity, energy, and often some insight about the needs of the South Vietnamese people. Although he surrounded himself with corrupt sycophants, he was a committed nationalist. These excellent and sophisticated accounts do not, however, negate the overwhelming evidence of Diem's poor leadership, incompetent management, and very limited public appeal in South Vietnam. See Philip E. Catton, *Diem's Final Failure: Prelude to America's War in Vietnam* (Lawrence: University Press of Kansas, 2002), esp. 25–98; Edward Miller, "Vision, Power, and Agency: The Ascent of Ngo Dinh Diem, 1945–54," *Journal of Southeast Asian Studies* 35 (October 2004): 433–58; Edward Miller, "The Diplomacy of Personalism: Civilization, Culture, and the Cold War in the Foreign Policy of Ngo Dinh Diem," in Goscha and Ostermann, eds., *Connecting Histories*, 376–402; Mathew Masur, "Exhibiting Signs of Resistance: South Vietnam's Struggle for Legitimacy, 1954–1960," *Diplomatic History* 33 (April 2009): 293–313.

55. See Miller, "The Diplomacy of Personalism," 376–402.

56. Collins quoted in Jacobs, *America's Miracle Man in Vietnam*, 204.

57. See Kahin, *Intervention*, 148–53.

58. See James Carter, *Inventing Vietnam: The United States and State Building, 1954–1968* (New York: Cambridge University Press, 2008), 46–112. On the problems of inflation in South Vietnam in the 1960s, see J. E. Cable, "Vietnam: The Economic Situation," 10 November 1965, and accompanying British Foreign Office Minute, 9 December 1965, FO 371/180600, NAUK, Kew, London.

59. Collins quoted in Jacobs, *America's Miracle Man in Vietnam*, 203. See also ibid., 172–216; Carter, *Inventing Vietnam*, 46–112.

60. On this point, see Carter, *Inventing Vietnam*, 1–19.

61. The literature on the Vietnam War in the 1960s, and President Johnson's policies in particular, is enormous. For a start, see Fredrik Logevall, *Choosing War: The Lost Chance for Peace and the Escalation of War in Vietnam* (Berkeley: University of California Press, 1999); Mark Atwood Lawrence, *The Vietnam War: A Concise International History* (New York: Oxford University Press, 2008); Mark Philip Bradley, *Vietnam at War* (New York: Oxford University Press, 2009); Gareth Porter, *Perils of Dominance: Imbalance of Power and the Road to War in Vietnam* (Berkeley: University of California Press, 2005); David Kaiser, *American Tragedy: Kennedy, Johnson, and the Origins of the Vietnam War* (Cambridge: Belknap Press of Harvard University Press, 2000); Lloyd C. Gardner, *Pay Any Price: Lyndon Johnson and the Wars for Vietnam* (Chicago: Ivan Dee, 1995).

62. On Lyndon Johnson's deep personal commitment to economic development and political assistance for the most needy, and the tragic misapplication of these ideals in Vietnam, see Randall B. Woods, *LBJ: Architect of American Ambition* (New York: Free Press, 2006); Robert Dallek, *Lone Star Rising: Lyndon Johnson and His Times, 1908–1960* (New York: Oxford University Press, 1991); Suri, *Power and Protest*, 131–63; Robert Komer Oral History, Interview 1, Robert Komer Oral History 30 January 1970, p. 55, Lyndon Baines Johnson Presidential Library, Austin, Texas.

63. The literature on Nixon's and Kissinger's policies in Vietnam is also enormous. For a start, see Lien-Hang T. Nguyen, "Waging War on All Fronts: Nixon, Kissinger, and the Vietnam War," and Robert D. Schulzinger, "The End of the Vietnam War, 1973–1976," in Fredrik Logevall and Andrew Preston, eds., *Nixon in the World: American Foreign Relations, 1969–1977* (New York: Oxford University Press, 2008), 185–223; Jeffrey Kimball, *Nixon's Vietnam War* (Lawrence: University Press of Kansas, 1998); Jussi Hanhimäki, *Flawed Architect: Henry Kissinger and American Foreign Policy* (New York: Oxford University Press, 2004); Melvin Small, *The Presidency of Richard Nixon* (Lawrence: University Press of Kansas, 1999); Larry Berman, *No Peace, No Honor: Nixon, Kissinger, and Betrayal in Vietnam* (New York: Free Press, 2001).

64. On this point, see Jeremi Suri, *Henry Kissinger and the American Century* (Cambridge: Harvard University Press, 2007), esp. 197–248.

65. On Ronald Reagan's foreign policy, and the lingering influences of the Vietnam War, see Melvyn P. Leffler, *For the Soul of Mankind: The United States, the Soviet Union, and the Cold War* (New York: Hill & Wang, 2007), 338–450; John Lewis Gaddis, *The Cold War: A New History* (New York: Penguin, 2005), 195–236; Gaddis, *Strategies of Containment*, 342–79.

66. See Robert D. Kaplan's enormously influential article, "The Coming Anarchy," *Atlantic Magazine* (February 1994), available at: http://www.theatlantic.com/magazine/archive/1994/02/the-coming-anarchy/4670 (accessed 9 September 2010).

Chapter 6: Reconstruction After September 11

1. President George W. Bush's Second Inaugural Address, 20 January 2005, available at: http://www.msnbc.msn.com/id/6848112 (accessed 1 October 2010).

2. Speech by President Barack Obama, United States Military Academy at West Point, New York, 1 December 2009, available at: http://www.whitehouse.gov/the-press-office/remarks-president-address-nation-way-forward-afghanistan-and-pakistan (accessed 13 September 2010).

3. Quotation from Thomas Barfield, *Afghanistan: A Cultural and Political History* (Princeton: Princeton University Press, 2010), 66. See the classic essay: H. J. Mackinder, "The Geographical Pivot of History," *The Geographical Journal* 23 (April 1904): 421–37. See also John Darwin, *After Tamerlane: The Rise and Fall of Global Empires, 1400–2000* (New York: Bloomsbury, 2008), esp. 4–45.

4. See the excellent overview of this long history in Willem Vogelsang, *The Afghans* (Malden, Mass.: Wiley-Blackwell, 2008).

5. Ibid.; Darwin, *After Tamerlane*, 50–155.

6. On this point, see Barfield, *Afghanistan*, esp. 56–65.

7. See the classic and still valuable account written at the time by George Nathaniel Curzon, *Russia in Central Asia in 1889 and the Anglo-Russian Question* (London: Longman, 1889). Curzon based his account on his knowledge of policy documents and his personal travels in the region.

8. See Patrick Macrory, *Retreat from Kabul: The Catastrophic British Defeat in Afghanistan, 1842* (Guilford, Conn.: Lyons, 2002; originally published, 1966); Brian Robson, *Crisis on the Frontier: The Third Afghan War and the Campaign in Waziristan, 1919–20* (Stroud, Gloucestershire: Spellmount, 2007); Barfield, *Afghanistan*, 110–63.

9. See Peter Hopkirk, *The Great Game: The Struggle for Empire in Central Asia* (New York: Kodansha, 1990).

10. See ibid.; Karl E. Meyer and Shareen Blair Brysac, *Tournament of Shadows: The Great Game and the Race for Empire in Central Asia* (New York: Basic Books, 1999); Jennifer Siegel, *Endgame: Britain, Russia, and the Final Struggle for Central Asia* (London: I. B. Tauris, 2002); Darwin, *After Tamerlane*, 298–364.

11. See Ahmed Rashid, *Taliban: The Power of Militant Islam in Afghanistan and Beyond*, 2nd ed. (London: I. B. Tauris, 2008); Robert D. Crews and Amin Tarzi, eds., *The Taliban and the Crisis of Afghanistan* (Cambridge: Harvard University Press, 2008).

12. See Peter Bergen's suggestive book about al Qaeda: *Holy War, Inc.: Inside the Secret World of Osama Bin Laden* (New York: Free Press, 2002). See also Peter L. Bergen, *The Longest War: The Enduring Conflict between America and al-Qaeda* (New York: Free Press, 2011).

13. Maureen Dowd, "A Grave Silence," *New York Times* (Late Edition, East Coast), 12 September 2001, A2.

14. Recounting a series of false alarms about terrorist attacks after 11 September 2001—including air and biological threats to the White House—President George W. Bush describes the horror: "We believed more attacks were coming, but we didn't know when, where, or from whom." George W. Bush, *Decision Points* (New York: Crown, 2010 Kindle edition), locations 3132–40.

15. For an analysis of how fear has driven misguided and counterproductive American responses to terrorism, see John Mueller, *Overblown: How Politicians and the Terrorism Industry Inflate National Security Threats, and Why We Believe Them* (New York: Free Press, 2006).

16. Military and cultural historians agree on the powerful connection between public fear and military aggression in American history. See, for example,

Richard Slotkin, *Regeneration Through Violence: The Mythology of the American Frontier, 1600–1860* (Norman: University of Oklahoma Press, 1973); Russell Weigley, *The American Way of War: A History of United States Military Strategy and Policy* (New York: Macmillan, 1973).

17. On this point, see John W. Dower, *Cultures of War: Pearl Harbor, Hiroshima, 9–11, Iraq* (New York: W. W. Norton, 2010); Michael Sherry, *In the Shadow of War: The United States Since the 1930s* (New Haven: Yale University Press, 1995); Robert A. Divine, *Perpetual War for Perpetual Peace* (College Station: Texas A&M University Press, 2000).

18. On this point, see Emily S. Rosenberg, *A Date Which Will Live: Pearl Harbor in American Memory* (Durham: Duke University Press, 2003).

19. President Bush recounts his anguish, anger, and fear in the aftermath of the terrorist attacks. He also describes his determination to rally Americans and respond with full force against the perpetrators and supporters of terrorism, broadly defined. See Bush, *Decision Points*, Chapters 5–6.

20. President George W. Bush's Televised Address to the Nation, 11 September 2001, available at: http://articles.cnn.com/2001-09-11/us/bush.speech .text_1_attacks-deadly-terrorist-acts-despicable-acts?_s=PM:US. A video of the speech is available at: http://www.youtube.com/watch?v=YMiqEUBux3o (both accessed 22 September 2010).

21. Transcript of President George W. Bush's Address to a Joint Session of Congress, 20 September 2001 available at: http://articles.cnn.com/2001-09-20/ us/gen.bush.transcript_1_joint-session-national-anthem-citizens?_s=PM:US (accessed 22 September 2010).

22. President Bush's Address to a Joint Session of Congress, 20 September 2001.

23. President Bush's Televised Address to the Nation, 11 September 2001.

24. President Bush's Address to a Joint Session of Congress, 20 September 2001.

25. President George W. Bush's Commencement Address at the United States Military Academy at West Point, New York, 1 June 2002. The text is available at: http://www.nytimes.com/2002/06/01/international/02PTEX-WEB .html (accessed 24 September 2010).

26. Ibid.

27. Ibid.

28. For examples of newfound attention to development issues and nation-building within the U.S. foreign policy community, see James Dobbins, John G. McGinn, Keith Crane, Seth G. Jones, Rollie Lal, Andrew Rathmell, Rachel Swanger, and Anga Timilsina, *America's Role in Nation-Building: From Germany to Iraq* (Santa Monica, Calif.: RAND Corporation, 2003); Francis Fukuyama, "Nation-Building 101," *Atlantic Monthly* (January/February 2004); Esther Pan, "United Nations: Nation-Building," Council on Foreign Relations Backgrounder, 2 October 2003, available at: http://www.cfr.org/publication/7755/united_nations.html (accessed 26 September 2010).

29. For an excellent overview of initial American military deployments in Afghanistan, see http://www.globalsecurity.org/military/ops/enduring-freedom_deploy.htm (accessed 25 September 2010).

30. This description comes from what remains one of the most insightful analyses of American military operations in Afghanistan in 2001–2002: Stephen Biddle, "Afghanistan and the Future of Warfare: Implications for Army and Defense Policy," U.S. Army War College Strategic Studies Institute (November 2002). This paper is available at: http://www.strategicstudies-institute.army.mil/pubs/display.cfm?pubID=109 (accessed 26 September 2010). See also Doug Stanton, *Horse Soldiers: The Extraordinary Story of a Band of U.S. Soldiers Who Rode to Victory in Afghanistan* (New York: Scribner, 2009).

31. See Biddle, "Afghanistan and the Future of Warfare," esp. 43–49. The term "face of battle" comes from John Keegan's seminal book, *The Face of Battle: A Study of Agincourt, Waterloo, and the Somme* (New York: Viking, 1976).

32. President George W. Bush's Speech to the Nation, 7 October 2001, available at: http://www.pbs.org/newshour/terrorism/combating/bush_10-7.html (accessed 25 September 2010). See also http://www.globalsecurity.org/military/ops/enduring-freedom-ops-air.htm (accessed 24 September 2010).

33. For a provocative account of the idealism that underpinned American war efforts after 11 September 2001, see Fred Kaplan, *Daydream Believers: How a Few Grand Ideas Wrecked American Power* (Hoboken: John Wiley, 2008). On the influence of the Vietnam War experience for the key policymakers in the

Bush White House, see James Mann, *Rise of the Vulcans: The History of Bush's War Cabinet* (New York: Viking, 2004).

34. President George W. Bush's Speech to the Nation, 7 October 2001. See also http://www.globalsecurity.org/military/ops/enduring-freedom-ops-air.htm (accessed 24 September 2010).

35. See Seth G. Jones, *In the Graveyard of Empires: America's War in Afghanistan* (New York: W. W. Norton, 2009), 86–108; http://www.globalsecurity.org/military/ops/enduring-freedom-ops-aciv.htm; http://www.globalsecurity.org/military/ops/enduring-freedom-ops-aloss.htm (accessed 24 September 2010).

36. See M. Ismail Khan and Danish Karokhel, "Northern Alliance Troops Enter Kabul," *Dawn* (14 November 2001), available at: http://www.dawn.com/2001/11/14/top2.htm (accessed 27 September 2010); James Meek, "Freedom, Joy—and Fear," *The Guardian* (14 November 2001), available at: http://www.guardian.co.uk/world/2001/nov/14/afghanistan.terrorism12 (accessed 27 September 2010); Keith Richburg, " 'Second Life' in Afghan Capital: Kabul Awakens to Find Taliban Gone, Harsh Rules Lifted," *Washington Post* (14 November 2001).

37. See Barfield, *Afghanistan*, 280–82.

38. Barfield writes of a "united people in a failed state," *Afghanistan*, 277–82. See also Barfield's discussion of the positive distinction many Afghan citizens drew between the American intervention and prior Soviet and British invasions. Based on interviews, Barfield reports that Afghan citizens looked to the United States for stability and reconstruction after civil war—for nation-building. See Barfield, *Afghanistan*, 275–77. See also Jones, *In the Graveyard of Empires*, 109–50.

39. Barnett Rubin argues that the influx of foreign aid in Afghanistan produced a "rentier state" dominated by figures who lived off external capital and under-invested in domestic production. Recipients of foreign aid had an incentive to hoard that money for their personal uses, not the needs of the country. See Barnett Rubin, *The Fragmentation of Afghanistan: State Formation and Collapse in the International System* (New Haven: Yale University Press, 1995). Rubin is surely correct, but foreign aid also had a contrary effect: it allowed central leaders to offer rival groups increased resources if they continued to

work with the national government. The distribution of foreign aid among different groups encouraged basic cooperation. This process broke down in the late 1970s because of poor central leadership and the Soviet invasion. See Barfield, *Afghanistan*, 195–225. For an analysis and critique of foreign-sponsored modernization efforts in Afghanistan during the Cold War, see Nick Cullather, "Damming Afghanistan: Modernization in a Buffer State," *Journal of American History* 89 (September 2002): 512–37. See also Nick Cullather, *The Hungry World: America's Cold War Battle against Poverty in Asia* (Cambridge, Mass.: Harvard University Press, 2010), esp. 108–33.

40. Louis Dupree, an American archaeologist and ethnographer by training, spent more than twenty years studying, lecturing, and traveling in Afghanistan. He was employed by the American Universities Field Staff—a consortium of higher education institutions in the United States—to provide firsthand accounts of life in Afghanistan for academic audiences. This is how "area studies" for regions like Central Asia began at American universities. Dupree's writings in the 1960s and 1970s capture the sense of hope among citizens and observers of Afghanistan. Quotations from Louis Dupree, "Afghanistan 1977: Does Trade Plus Aid Guarantee Development," American Universities Field Staff Report, South Asia Series, Vol. 21, No. 3 (Afghanistan), August 1977. For a report on youth culture in Afghanistan, see Louis Dupree, "It Wasn't Woodstock, But . . . : The First International Rock Festival in Kabul," American Universities Field Staff Report, South Asia Series, Vol. 20, No. 2 (Afghanistan), May 1976. These and numerous other reports from Dupree are available in Memorial Library, University of Wisconsin–Madison. See also Louis Dupree, *Afghanistan* (Princeton: Princeton University Press, 1973), esp. 559–666; Ralph Magnus, "The Constitution of 1964: A Decade of Political Experimentation," in Louis Dupree and Linette Albert eds., *Afghanistan in the 1970s* (New York: Praeger, 1974), 50–75; Robert S. McNamara, "Head of World Bank Sees Many Gains, More Needs Across a Continent," *New York Times*, 17 January 1969, C65; Drew Middleton, "Drive to Modernize Politics in Afghanistan Is Making Progress," *New York Times*, 25 May 1967, 6; Sydney Schanberg, "Reforms Are Slowly Taking Shape in Afghanistan Despite Conservative New Parliament," *New York Times*, 3 November 1969, 26.

41. See Dupree, *Afghanistan*, 559–658.

42. James F. Dobbins, *After the Taliban: Nation-Building in Afghanistan* (Washington, D.C.: Potomac, 2008), 77–78.

43. The final document at the Bonn conference was formally titled the "Agreement on Provisional Arrangements in Afghanistan Pending the Reestablishment of Permanent Government Institutions." See the full text at: http://www.un.org/News/dh/latest/afghan/afghan-agree.htm (accessed 29 September 2010).

44. Ibid.; Dobbins, *After the Taliban*, 77–116.

45. For background on Hamid Karzai and traditional Pashtun political authority in Afghanistan, see Ahmed Rashid, *Descent into Chaos: The U.S. and the Disaster in Pakistan, Afghanistan, and Central Asia* (New York: Penguin, 2008), 3–23; Barfield, *Afghanistan*, 288–94.

46. Quotation from Dobbins, *After the Taliban*, 161. King Zahir Shah was born on 15 October 1914. He was eighty-seven at the time of the Bonn conference.

47. On this point, see Rashid, *Descent into Chaos*, 61–83; Jones, *In the Graveyard of Empires*, 86–108.

48. Donald Rumsfeld, "Transforming the Military," *Foreign Affairs* 81 (May/June 2002), 20–32. Rumsfeld's arguments drew on an emerging post–Cold War fascination with the "small wars" in American history, and their role in the growth of American power. Rumsfeld and others in the Pentagon came to see the "big wars" (the Civil War, the Second World War, and others) as exceptions to the more standard experience of deploying flexible and limited American power, across a broad terrain, for maximum political effect. See, for example, Max Boot, *The Savage Wars of Peace: Small Wars and the Rise of American Power* (New York: Basic Books, 2002).

49. Rumsfeld, "Transforming the Military."

50. For an excellent account of the political agenda behind the Bush administration's domestic and foreign policies, see Julian E. Zelizer, *Arsenal of Democracy: The Politics of National Security from World War II to the War on Terrorism* (New York: Basic Books, 2010), 431–503. See also Kaplan, *Daydream Believers*; Mann, *Rise of the Vulcans*.

51. See Condoleezza Rice, "Promoting the National Interest," *Foreign Affairs* 79

(January/February 2000); Bob Woodward, *Bush at War* (New York: Simon & Schuster, 2002), 220–41.

52. Rumsfeld quoted in Jones, *In the Graveyard of Empires*, 117.

53. For an essay that powerfully articulates the neoconservative attack on Europe's alleged military cowardice, see Robert Kagan, *Of Paradise and Power: America and Europe in the New World Order* (New York: Alfred A. Knopf, 2002). For a historical account of Europe's evolving aversion to military force in the late twentieth century, see James J. Sheehan, *Where Have All the Soldiers Gone? The Transformation of Modern Europe* (New York: Houghton Mifflin, 2008).

54. Data from Jones, *In the Graveyard of Empires*, 119–20. See also Rashid, *Descent into Chaos*, 171–218.

55. On the Soviet invasion of Afghanistan in 1979, and its role in undermining national unity and state institutions, see Mohammed Kakar, *Afghanistan: The Soviet Invasion and the Afghan Response, 1979–1982* (Berkeley: University of California Press, 1997); Odd Arne Westad, *The Global Cold War: Third World Interventions and the Making of Our Times* (Cambridge: Cambridge University Press, 2005), 299–330; Barfield, *Afghanistan*, 233–54.

56. Data from Jones, *In the Graveyard of Empires*, 120–23.

57. On this point, see the bitter conclusion in Rashid, *Descent into Chaos*, 402–18. For an articulation of this argument, applied to the international system as well as Afghanistan, see G. John Ikenberry, "Liberal Order Building," in Melvyn P. Leffler and Jeffrey W. Legro, eds., *To Lead the World: American Strategy After the Bush Doctrine* (New York: Oxford University Press, 2008), 85–108.

58. Quotations from President George W. Bush's Second Inaugural Address, 20 January 2005, available at: http://www.msnbc.msn.com/id/6848112 (accessed 1 October 2010).

59. See Richard N. Haass, *War of Necessity, War of Choice: A Memoir of Two Iraq Wars* (New York: Simon & Schuster, 2009), 202–66; Jones, *In the Graveyard of Empires*, 124–29; Kaplan, *Daydream Believers*, esp. 113–48.

60. Quotations from President George W. Bush's Second Inaugural Address, 20 January 2005.

61. See Charles Tripp, *A History of Iraq*, 3rd ed. (Cambridge: Cambridge University Press, 2007), 277–322.

62. Ibid., 278.

63. For a compelling account of how well-trained American soldiers and civilians were unprepared for the challenges of Iraq, see George Packer, *The Assassin's Gate: America in Iraq* (New York: Farrar, Straus and Giroux, 2005). For more devastating accounts of poor American planning and disorganized execution of policy, see Thomas E. Ricks, *Fiasco: The American Military Adventure in Iraq* (New York: Penguin, 2006); Larry Diamond, *Squandered Victory: The American Occupation and the Bungled Effort to Bring Democracy to Iraq* (New York: Henry Holt, 2005); Rajiv Chandrasekaran, *Imperial Life in the Emerald City: Inside Iraq's Green Zone* (New York: Alfred A. Knopf, 2006).

64. See Tripp, *A History of Iraq*, 278–92.

65. See Ricks, *Fiasco*, esp. 158–67. In his memoir, Bremer argues that his orders to purge former Ba'th Party members and disband the military and security services followed instructions from Washington. He also emphasizes his efforts at cooperation with reform-minded Iraqis. See Ambassador L. Paul Bremer III, with Malcolm McConnell, *My Year in Iraq: The Struggle to Build a Future of Hope* (New York: Threshold, 2006).

66. See Ricks, *Fiasco*, 321–412.

67. David Kilcullen explains how foreign interventions, with insufficient security and inadequate partners on the ground, encourage local groups to join insurgencies for self-preservation—and sometimes profit. Kilcullen, *The Accidental Guerrilla: Fighting Small Wars in the Midst of a Big One* (New York: Oxford University Press, 2009), esp. 1–38.

68. This paragraph draws on my more extended reflections about the difficulties of policymaking, especially as a superpower, in Jeremi Suri, *Henry Kissinger and the American Century* (Cambridge: Belknap Press of Harvard University Press, 2007).

69. See Thomas E. Ricks, *The Gamble: General David Petraeus and the American Military Adventure in Iraq, 2006–2008* (New York: Penguin, 2009), esp. 106–227.

70. General David Petraeus, "Multi-National Force-Iraq Commander's Counterinsurgency Guidance," 21 June 2008, reprinted in Ricks, *The Gamble*,

369–71. For background on Petraeus's thinking about counterinsurgency and nation-building, see the field manual that he co-authored before assuming command in Iraq: U.S. Army and Marine Corps, *Counterinsurgency Field Manual* (Chicago: University of Chicago Press, 2007). See also John A. Nagl, *Learning to Eat Soup with a Knife: Counterinsurgency Lessons from Malaya and Vietnam* (Westport, Conn.: Praeger, 2002).

71. See Ricks, *The Gamble*, 294–325; Kilcullen, *The Accidental Guerrilla*, 115–85. For an excellent collection of statistics on security, economy, and society in Iraq, updated every two weeks, see the "Iraq Index," compiled by Michael O'Hanlon and the Saban Center for Middle East Policy at the Brookings Institution: http://usliberals.about.com/gi/o.htm?zi=1/XJ&zTi=1&sdn=us liberals&cdn=newsissues&tm=85&gps=431_386_1276_852&f=00&tt=2 &bt=0&bts=0&zu=http%3A//www.brookings.edu/iraqindex (accessed 4 October 2010).

72. On the role of Pakistani support to the Taliban, see Matt Waldman, "The Sun in the Sky: The Relationship Between Pakistan's ISI and Afghan Insurgents," Discussion Paper 18, Crisis States Research Center, London School of Economics and Political Science (June 2010), available at: http://www.crisistates .com/download/dp/DP%2018.pdf (accessed 4 October 2010). See also Rashid, *Descent into Chaos*, 265–401; Jones, *In the Graveyard of Empires*, 163–312.

73. Quotation from Jones, *In the Graveyard of Empires*, 201.

74. Kilcullen, *The Accidental Guerrilla*, 39–114. On the Vietnam comparison, see Robert K. Brigham, *Iraq, Vietnam, and the Limits of American Power* (New York: PublicAffairs, 2006).

75. Bob Woodward describes the political pressures that motivated President Obama to increase American military commitments in Afghanistan, despite contrary personal preferences. See Bob Woodward, *Obama's Wars* (New York: Simon & Schuster, 2010).

76. For the data on foreign troops in Afghanistan, see the "Afghanistan Index," updated every week, compiled by Ian S. Livingston, Heather L. Messera, and Michael O'Hanlon at the Brookings Institution: http://usliberals.about .com/gi/o.htm?zi=1/XJ&zTi=1&sdn=usliberals&cdn=newsissues&tm=85& gps=431_386_1276_852&f=00&tt=2&bt=0&bts=0&zu=http%3A//www

.brookings.edu/iraqindex (accessed 5 October 2010). On 23 June 2010 President Obama nominated Petraeus to replace General Stanley A. McChrystal as commander of American forces in Afghanistan. McChrystal resigned following insubordinate public remarks about civilian leaders in Washington.

77. See the data on civilian personnel in the "Afghanistan Index."

78. Speech by President Barack Obama, United States Military Academy at West Point, New York, 1 December 2009, available at: http://www.whitehouse .gov/the-press-office/remarks-president-address-nation-way-forward-afghani stan-and-pakistan (accessed 13 September 2010).

79. Despite his skepticism about American activities, Rory Stewart's compelling account of contemporary Afghanistan captures this vision of the country as an orderly mosaic of diverse peoples, with some common rules and institutions. See Rory Stewart, *The Places in Between* (New York: Mariner, 2006).

80. The data on increased violence and unimproved living conditions in Afghanistan is documented in detail in the "Afghanistan Index."

81. Speech by President Barack Obama, United States Military Academy at West Point, New York, 1 December 2009.

Conclusion: The Future of Nation-Building

1. Edmund Burke, "Remarks on the Policy of the Allies with Respect to France," October 1793, reprinted in *The Works of the Right Honourable Edmund Burke*, Vol. 3 (London: George Bell and Sons, 1887), 414. Emphasis in original.

2. On the economic origins of American expansion see, among many others, William Appleman Williams, *The Tragedy of American Diplomacy*, 50th anniversary edition (New York: W. W. Norton, 2009); Walter LaFeber, *The New Empire: An Interpretation of American Expansion* (Ithaca: Cornell University Press, 1998 edition); Thomas J. McCormick, *China Market: America's Quest for Informal Empire, 1893–1901* (Chicago: Ivan Dee, 1990 edition); Andrew J. Bacevich, *American Empire: The Realities and Consequences of U.S. Diplomacy* (Cambridge: Harvard University Press, 2002).

3. For some of the classic and still most valuable scholarship on federalism and nation-states, see Carl J. Friedrich, *Constitutional Government and Democracy: Theory and Practice in Europe and America*, rev. ed. (Boston: Ginn, 1950;

originally published 1937); Carl J. Friedrich, *Trends of Federalism in Theory and Practice* (New York: Praeger, 1968). See also Jeremi Suri, *Henry Kissinger and the American Century* (Cambridge: Belknap Press of Harvard University Press, 2007), 138–96. Some of the inspiration for federalism in the United States and Western Europe came from Immanuel Kant's famous 1795 essay, "Perpetual Peace: A Philosophical Sketch," available at: http://www.mtholy oke.edu/acad/intrel/kant/kant1.htm (accessed 15 January 2010).

4. See Jack N. Rakove, *Original Meanings: Politics and Ideas in the Making of the Constitution* (New York: Alfred A. Knopf, 1996), 161–202.

5. Thomas Friedman's popular writings frequently discount the barriers to communication and cooperation in the contemporary world. Friedman does, however, give extensive attention to the vital role played by powerful nation-states in charting the course of globalization. See Thomas Friedman, *The World Is Flat: A Brief History of the Twenty-first Century* (New York: Farrar, Straus and Giroux, 2005). See also Fareed Zakaria, *The Post-American World* (New York: W. W. Norton, 2008).

6. Burke, "Remarks on the Policy of the Allies with Respect to France," 414.

7. This is an argument echoed in Richard N. Haass, *The Opportunity: America's Moment to Alter History's Course* (New York: PublicAffairs, 2005). On the dangers of excessive zeal and self-confidence, see Peter Beinart, *The Icarus Syndrome: A History of American Hubris* (New York: HarperCollins, 2010).

8. On this point, see Andrew J. Bacevich, *Washington Rules: America's Path to Permanent War* (New York: Metropolitan, 2010); Beinart, *The Icarus Syndrome.*

9. Clausewitz used the term "friction" to describe the uncertainty, unpredictability and nonlinearity of war. See Carl von Clausewitz, *On War*, ed. and trans., Michael Howard and Peter Paret (Princeton: Princeton University Press, 1976), 117–21, 133–47. See also Alan Beyerchen, "Clausewitz, Nonlinearity and the Unpredictability of War," *International Security* 17 (Winter 1992): 59–90.

10. On American public awareness of uncertainty and unpredictability during the Cold War, see, among others, Melvyn P. Leffler, *For the Soul of Mankind: The United States, the Soviet Union, and the Cold War* (New York: Hill & Wang, 2007); John Lewis Gaddis, *The Cold War: A New History* (New York: Penguin, 2005).

Acknowledgments

I began this book teaching my students. One of my greatest professional joys is my daily contact with eager undergraduates and sleep-deprived graduate students. They keep me on my toes. They push me to think in new ways. Most of all, they challenge me to see new connections between fields of study, time periods, parts of the world, and contemporary events. The analysis in this book emerged from many years of lecturing, listening, reading, and talking with my students. They made this book possible.

The events of the last decade made this book necessary. I began my career as a professor at the University of Wisconsin–Madison teaching about the late eighteenth century in the days before the 11 September 2001 attacks. After a week of disorientation and some soul-searching around campus, teaching and research resumed their normal routines. This was even true for a young scholar of American foreign policy, like me. I continued to write lectures, articles, and books as my mentors had done in prior years. That's what historians do—we study the past. That's what historians do—we contribute to an evolving body of knowledge.

As much as I treasure traditional scholarship, it was not enough for me after the destruction of the World Trade Center. Saturated by controversies that hinge on how we understand the past, I was not comfortable leaving the application of history to others. Confronted by difficult questions about the nature of our society and its role in the world, I was not satisfied to separate study of the past from policymaking in the present. Historians and policymakers must work together more closely. This book is my effort to make that happen, at least in some small way.

Acknowledgments

I have elucidated this ambition in countless lectures during my travels in the last decade. Many students, scholars, businesspeople, policymakers, soldiers, veterans, and other citizens have contributed to my thinking. I thank them for their help. Many friends have guided and encouraged me. I thank them for their support. My sparring partner, James Kurtz, deserves special praise. As he did with my last book, he slogged through every page of this manuscript in draft. We discussed his reactions over many a sudsy beverage. Kurtz and I did not always agree, but our debates sharpened my analysis. The same is true for my frequent conversations with Harral Burris, Daniel Checki, Andrew Seaborg, and David Schiff. A good book should inspire bantering among friends.

A number of fine young scholars contributed directly to my research. They helped to find key sources and organize my thoughts. They broadened my thinking. They enabled me to burrow deep into specific questions. I want to thank Paul Axel, Kelly Creech, Mario Glanzmann, Nick Gonzales, Marisa Kovacs, Eric O'Connor, Brittany Taylor, Vanessa Walker, and Debbie Sharnak. Debbie was particularly heroic as my research assistant during the last eighteen months of this project. She made it possible for me to explore new topics and complete all of the book details, especially the maps. She kept me on track. Tanya Buckingham and the University of Wisconsin cartographic laboratory worked closely with Debbie, often late at night and on weekends.

Numerous institutions supported this project. They provided a mix of funding, access to research materials, and, most important, stimulating space for intellectual engagement with diverse thinkers. I owe a debt of gratitude to the Department of History, the European Union Center of Excellence (EUCE), and the Grand Strategy Program at the University of Wisconsin–Madison; the Heidelberg Center for American Studies; the Legatum Institute; the Norwegian Nobel Institute; the Tobin Project; the University of Wisconsin Center for World Affairs and the Global Economy (WAGE); the Wisconsin Historical Society; and the Wisconsin Veterans Museum.

I want to single out the University of Wisconsin and the Madison com-

340

munity as a whole. I have grown immeasurably as a scholar and a citizen thanks to this nourishing environment. It is much more than a university or a capital city. I have experienced Madison as a remarkable hothouse (or cold igloo, in winter) of serious and open public engagement, with a contagious enthusiasm for discussion. Madison is a community of talkers—face-to-face talkers—in the best sense of the term. Every day, my neighbors make me better. Every day, I am reminded that my work connects closely to local challenges and opportunities. As I have said before, the Wisconsin Idea is alive and well. I am honored to be a small part of it.

The writing and publishing of this book reflects three guiding hands that I greatly value. Andrew Wylie and Scott Moyers, my agents, helped me to turn a good scholarly idea into a project for a broad readership. Hilary Redmon, my editor, made certain that my arguments and my prose met the highest standards. Hilary also made sure that my book received wide public notice. I thank Andrew, Scott, and Hilary for believing in this book. It is much better because of them. At Free Press, Sydney Tanigawa, Al Madocs, and Fred Chase handled the crucial production details. I want to thank them too.

My final and most important words of gratitude go to my family—Alison, Natalie, and Zachary. I love being a historian, a writer, and a teacher, but that all comes second to my role as a father and a husband. I thank them for reminding me of that. I thank them for making my life so full. Nation-building really begins at home.

Index

Page numbers that are *italicized* indicate illustrations and captions

Index

Index

About the Author

Jeremi Suri holds the Mack Brown Distinguished Chair for Global Leadership, History, and Public Policy at the University of Texas at Austin. For the past decade he was the E. Gordon Fox Professor of History, the director of the European Union Center of Excellence, and the director of the Grand Strategy Program at the University of Wisconsin–Madison. He is the author of four previous books on contemporary politics and foreign policy: *Henry Kissinger and the American Century; Power and Protest; The Global Revolutions of 1968;* and *American Foreign Relations Since 1898.* Professor Suri's research and teaching have received numerous prizes. In 2007 *Smithsonian Magazine* named Professor Suri one of America's "Top Young Innovators" in the Arts and Sciences. His writings appear widely in newspapers and magazines around the world. Professor Suri is also a frequent public lecturer and guest on radio and television programs. He blogs at: http://globalbrief.ca. See Professor Suri's professional Web page at: http://jeremisuri.net.